中英文版高速铁路运营管理系列教材
Chinese-English High Speed Railway Operation Management Coursebook Series

铁路信号与通信设备

RAILWAY SIGNAL AND COMMUNICATION EQUIPMENT

主　编　李云飞　张世涛
副主编　雷　钧　易赛岚　李精忠　徐　昕　陈　珺　汪海燕
翻　译　王艳苹

云南出版集团
云南人民出版社

图书在版编目（CIP）数据

铁路信号与通信设备 / 李云飞, 张世涛主编; 王艳苹翻译. -- 昆明：云南人民出版社, 2020.12
中英文版高速铁路运营管理系列教材
ISBN 978-7-222-19580-6

Ⅰ. ①铁… Ⅱ. ①李… ②张… ③王… Ⅲ. ①铁路信号—信号设备—高等职业教育—教材—汉、英②铁路通信—通信设备—高等职业教育—教材—汉、英 Ⅳ. ①U284.7 ②U285

中国版本图书馆CIP数据核字(2020)第251520号

出 品 人：	赵石定
责任编辑：	冯 琰
封面设计：	张益珲
责任校对：	胡元青
责任印制：	马文杰

铁路信号与通信设备
TIELU XINHAO YU TONGXIN SHEBEI

主　编：李云飞　张世涛
副主编：雷　钧　易赛岚　李精忠
　　　　徐　昕　陈　珺　汪海燕
翻　译：王艳苹

出　版	云南出版集团　云南人民出版社
发　行	云南人民出版社
社　址	昆明市环城西路609号
邮　编	650034
网　址	www.ynpph.com.cn
E-mail	ynrms@sina.com
开　本	787mm×1092mm　1/16
印　张	18.75
字　数	342千
版　次	2020年12月第1版第1次印刷
印　刷	云南金伦云印实业股份有限公司
书　号	ISBN 978-7-222-19580-6
定　价	52.00元

云南人民出版社微信公众号

如需购买图书、反馈意见，请与我社联系
总编室：0871-64109126　发行部：0871-64108507　审校部：0871-64164626　印制部：0871-64191534

版权所有　侵权必究　印装差错　负责调换

前　言
Preface

《铁路信号与通信设备》采用中英文对照排版模式，为中外读者深入解读铁路信号与通信系统相关设备知识。教材本着促进职业教育科学化、标准化、规范化的原则，运用创新的教学方法，设置了项目、任务、模块等教学单元，具有非常强的操作性、指导性和实用性。教材每个项目包括学前准备、课堂学习、课堂练习、课后拓展4个模块，学中做、做中学，能充分调动教师教学能动性，丰富教师课堂教学内容形式，激发学生学习主动性。

本教材主要包括以下内容：信号显示设备、联锁设备、区间闭塞设备、列车运行控制系统（CTCS）、列车调度指挥系统（TDCS）和分散自律调度集中系统（CTC）、驼峰信号设备及铁路通信设备。

学生学完本课程应熟悉铁路信号设备的基本组成，掌握有关信号设备的操作，在运输生产中合理运用各项设备，保证铁路行车安全，提高运输效率。

学习本教材时，应主动或在教师带

Railway Signal and Communication Equipment is English-Chinese typesetting for domestic and overseas readers to deeply understand railway signals and communication system related equipment. The coursebook is compiled with innovative teaching method and has the teaching units of project, task, module and so on, and is based on the principle of scientific, standard and normalized vocational education. The coursebook is highly operational, instructive and practical. Each project in the coursebook includes four modules of Preparation before Class, In-class Learning, In-class exercise and After-class Activity. The mode of "practice during learning and learning through practice" will highly motivate teachers, enrich teaching content and forms and greatly inspire students.

The coursebook includes the following content: signal display equipment, interlocking equipment, section block equipment, China train control system(CTCS), train operation dispatching and command system (TDCS) and decentralized autonomous dispatching and command system (CTC), hump signal equipment and railway communication equipment.

On learning the course, students shall get familiar with the basic composition of

领下多去铁路现场了解信号设备的运用知识，提高自身综合素质。

本教材由云南交通职业技术学院李云飞、张世涛主编并统稿，负责编写的老师有雷钧、易赛岚、李精忠、徐昕、陈珺、汪海燕等，王艳苹老师主要负责英文翻译。在本教材编写过程中，参考了许多专家的研究成果和有关文献资料，在此谨向各位专家、作者表示衷心的感谢。

由于编者水平有限，书中难免有疏漏之处，敬请广大读者谅解。真诚期待读者和同行多提宝贵意见。

编 者

2020 年 12 月

railway signal equipment, and master the operation of relevant signal equipment to use the equipment properly during transportation to ensure the safety of railway traffic and improve transportation efficiency.

Students shall go to the railway site to learn about the application of signal equipment with or without the guidance of teachers in learning the course book, to improve themselves.

The coursebook was chiefly compiled and edited by Li Yunfei and Zhang Shitao of Yunnan Jiaotong College, Lei Jun, Yi Sailan, Li Jingzhong, Xu Xin, Chen Jun and Wang Haiyan took part in the compilation of the coursebook, and Wang Yanping was in charge of the translation. In the process of compilation, research and documents of many experts were also referred to, and we wish to express our heartfelt thanks to the experts and authors.

Due to the limited knowledge of the editors, there may be inevitable omissions in the book, we expect the understanding of readers and sincerely look forward to the valuable suggestions from readers and peers.

Editor

December 2020

目　　录

项目一　信号显示设备
Project 1　Signal Display Equipment

任务一　铁路信号认识 ··· 1

Task 1　Understanding Railway Signal ··· 1

任务二　信号机的设置和结构 ··· 9

Task 2　Setting and Structure of Signal Machine ··· 9

任务三　固定信号设备运用 ··· 19

Task 3　Utilization of Fixed Signal Equipment ·· 19

任务四　信号表示器 ·· 30

Task 4　Signal Indicator ·· 30

项目二　联锁设备
Project 2　Interlocking Equipment

任务一　继电器 ·· 43

Task 1　Relay ·· 43

任务二　轨道电路及计轴设备 ··· 53

Task 2　Track Circuit and Axle Counter Equipment ···································· 53

任务三　转辙机、应答器 ··· 62

Task 3　Point Switch，Transponder ·· 62

任务四　联锁及联锁图表 ·· 74

Task 4　Interlocking and Interlocking Diagram ··· 74

任务五　6502 电气集中联锁设备 ·· 85

Task 5　6502 Electric Interlocking Equipment ··· 85

任务六　计算机联锁 ·· 94

Task 6　Computer Interlocking ·· 94

项目三　区间闭塞设备

Project 3　Section Block Equipment

任务一　认识闭塞 ·· 104

Task 1　Understand Block ·· 104

任务二　半自动闭塞设备运用 ·· 111

Task 2　Application of Semi-automatic Block Equipment ······························ 111

任务三　自动闭塞设备运用 ··· 121

Task 3　Automatic Block Equipment Application ··· 121

任务四　移动闭塞设备识别 ··· 128

Task 4　Mobile Block Equipment Recognition ··· 128

项目四　列车运行控制系统（CTCS）

Project 4　China Train Control System（CTCS）

任务一　机车信号认知 ··· 134

Task 1　Understand Locomotive Signal ··· 134

任务二　列车运行控制系统（CTCS）认知 ·· 141

Task 2　Understand China Train Control System（CTCS） ·························· 141

任务三　列车运行监控记录装置和列车超速防护系统……………………………152

Task 3　Train Operation Supervision Record Device and Train Over-speed Protection System ……………………………………………………………152

任务四　CTCS-2 级列车运行控制系统运用………………………………………164

Task 4　Application of CTCS-2 …………………………………………………164

任务五　CTCS-3 级列车运行控制系统运用………………………………………170

Task 5　Application of CTCS-3 …………………………………………………170

项目五　列车调度指挥系统（TDCS）和分散自律调度集中系统（CTC）

Project 5　Train Operation Dispatching and Command System（TDCS）and Decentralized Autonomous Dispatching and Command System（CTC）

任务一　铁路列车调度指挥系统（TDCS）……………………………………………177

Task 1　Railway Train Operation Dispatching and Command System（TDCS）……177

任务二　分散自律调度集中系统（CTC）………………………………………………200

Task 2　Centralized Traffic Control（CTC）……………………………………………200

任务三　行车凭证和调度命令的发送…………………………………………………219

Task 3　Train Operation Certificate and Dispatching Order Sending ………………219

项目六　驼峰信号设备

Project 6　Hump Signal Equipment

任务一　驼峰概述………………………………………………………………………230

Task 1　Hump Overview …………………………………………………………………230

任务二　驼峰基本信号设备认知………………………………………………………239

Task 2　Understanding Hump Basic Signal Equipment …………………………………239

| 任务三　驼峰道岔自动集中操纵 | 251 |

Task 3　Hump Turnout Automatic Centralized Control ······ 251

任务四　自动化驼峰设备认知 ······ 259

Task 4　Understanding Automatic Hump Signal ······ 259

项目七　铁路通信设备

Project 7　Railway Communication Equipment

任务一　铁路通信概述 ······ 269

Task 1　Railway Communication Overview ······ 269

任务二　铁路专用通信设备运用 ······ 276

Task 2　Railway Specialized Communication Equipment Application ······ 276

任务三　铁路综合数字移动通信系统（GSM-R）运用 ······ 284

Task 3　Global System for Mobile Communications-Railway（GSM-R）Application ······ 284

参考文献 ······ 291

Reference ······ 291

项目一 信号显示设备

Project 1　Signal Display Equipment

任务一　铁路信号认识

Task 1　Understanding Railway Signal

模块一　学前准备

拍摄或查找道路上的信号标志或铁路线路信号标志的照片，比较二者有何不同之处。

Module 1　Preparation before Class

Take pictures or search pictures of road signal signs and railway signal signs, and compare the differences between the two types.

课前学习笔记
Study Notes before Class

模块二　课堂学习

知识点一：铁路信号的种类

1. 什么是铁路信号

铁路信号是向有关行车人员显示的指示列车运行及调车作业的命令。常见的信号设备有信号机、表示器、手信号灯旗等。

Module 2　In-class Learning

Key Point 1：Types of Railway Signals

1. What is Railway Signal

Railway signal is the order displaying train operating and dispatching to relevant train operation employees. Common signal equipment are signal machine, indicator, hand signal and flag, and so on.

图 1-1　铁路信号机

Figure 1-1　Railway Signal Machine

图 1-2　铁路信号表示器

Figure 1-2　Railway Signal Indicator

图 1-3　手信号（信号旗）

Figure 1-3　Hand Signal（Signal Flag）

图 1-4　手信号（信号灯）

Figure 1-4　Hand Signal（Signal Light）

2. 铁路信号的种类

铁路信号的分类如图 1-5 所示。

2. Types of Railway Signals

Types of railway signal are as shown in Figure 1-5.

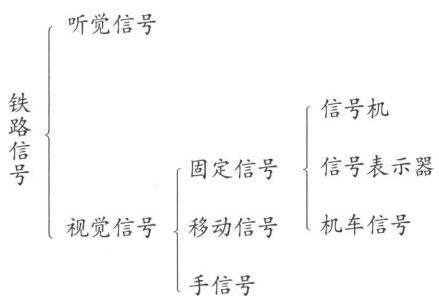

铁路信号：railway signals　听觉信号：audio signal　视觉信号：visual signal
固定信号：fixed signal　信号机：signal machine　信号表示器：signal indicator
机车信号：cab signal　移动信号：mobile signal　手信号：hand signal

图 1-5　铁路信号的分类

Figure 1-5　Types of Railway Signals

听觉信号是用声音的强度、频率和时间的长短来表达信号的含义。

视觉信号是用颜色、形状、位置、显示的数目和灯光的状态来表达信号的含义，如图 1-1 至图 1-4。

知识点二：铁路信号对颜色的规定

铁路信号颜色是用来指示列车运行速度的，信号显示系统一般由基本颜色和辅助颜色组成。

各种颜色的含义如图 1-6 所示。

Visual signal indicates the meaning of signals through the intensity and frequency of voice and length of time.

Visual signal indicates meaning of signals through color, shape, position, number of displayed signals and status of light, as shown from Figure1-1 to Figure1-4.

Key Point 2：Rules of Colors in Railway Signals

Color of railway signals is to indicate train speed, and signal display system usually consists of basic colors and sub colors.

Meanings of the colors are shown in Figure 1-6.

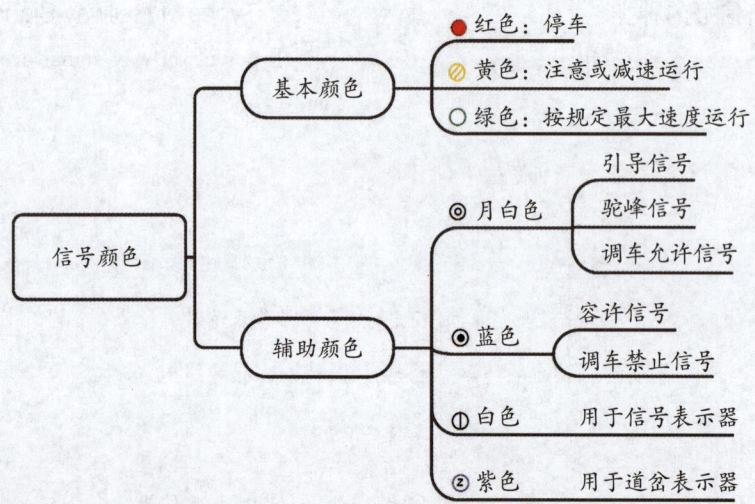

信号颜色：signal colors　基本颜色：basic colors　红色：red　停车：stop　黄色：yellow
注意或减速运行：caution or slow down　绿色：green
按规定最大速度运行：run at the maximum speed stipulated　辅助颜色：sub colors
月白色：pale green　引导信号：guiding signal　驼峰信号：hump signal
调车允许信号：dispatching permission signal　蓝色：blue　容许信号：permission signal
调车禁止信号：dispatching prohibition signal　白色：white　用于信号表示器：used in signal indicator
紫色：purple　用于道岔表示器：used in turnout indicator

图 1-6　信号颜色含义及对应的图形符号
Figure 1-6　Meanings of Signal Colors and the Corresponding Graphic Symbols

学习笔记
Study Notes

模块三 课堂练习

练习1：小组组员分别介绍自己拍摄或搜集到的铁路信号标志的照片，并讨论这些信号标志属于哪种铁路信号的哪种类型。

练习2：讨论图1-7所示的信号机的图形符号分别采用了哪几种颜色的灯光设计。

Module 3 In-class Exercises

Exercise 1：Group members introduce the collected photos of railway signal signs and discuss the types of colors and railway signals.

Exercise 2：Look at the graphic symbols in Figure 1-7 and discuss the colors used in the light designs.

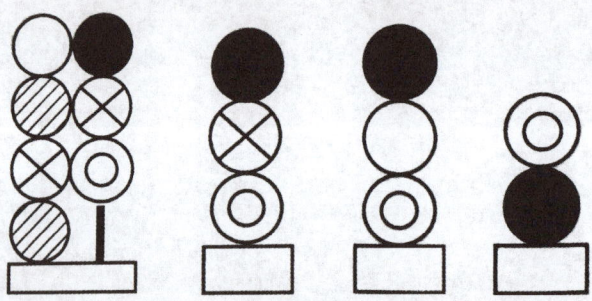

图1-7 各种信号机图形符号

Figure 1-7 Various Types of Signal Machine Graphic Symbols

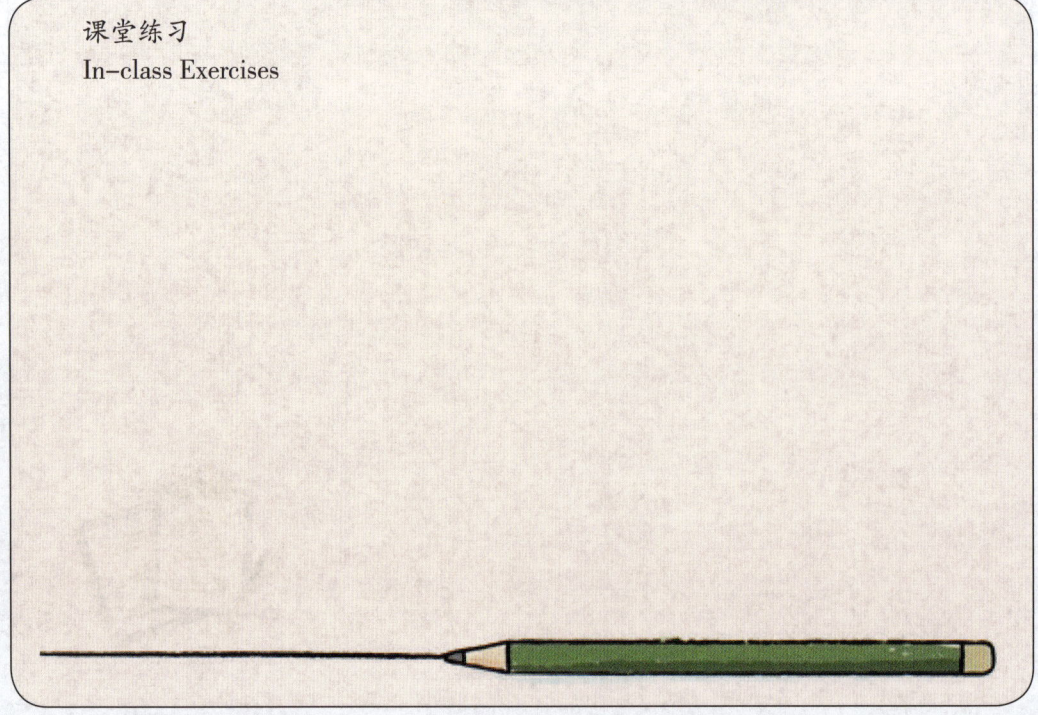

课堂练习
In-class Exercises

学习笔记
Study Notes

模块三 课堂练习

练习1：小组组员分别介绍自己拍摄或搜集到的铁路信号标志的照片，并讨论这些信号标志属于哪种铁路信号的哪种类型。

练习2：讨论图1-7所示的信号机的图形符号分别采用了哪几种颜色的灯光设计。

Module 3 In-class Exercises

Exercise 1：Group members introduce the collected photos of railway signal signs and discuss the types of colors and railway signals.

Exercise 2：Look at the graphic symbols in Figure 1-7 and discuss the colors used in the light designs.

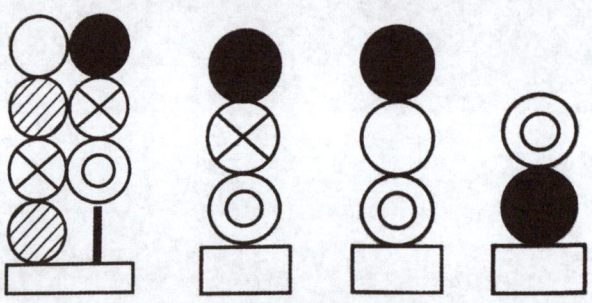

图1-7 各种信号机图形符号

Figure 1-7 Various Types of Signal Machine Graphic Symbols

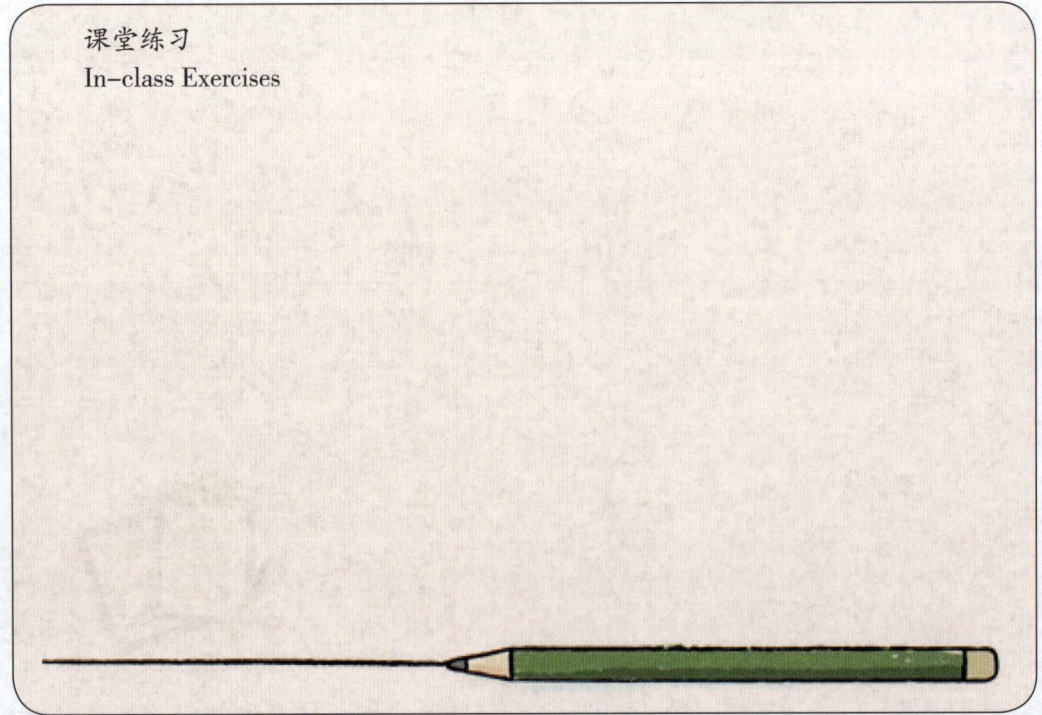

课堂练习
In-class Exercises

| 模块四　课后拓展 | Module 4　After-class Activity |

查阅相关资料，了解以下信号机图形符号表示的含义，将表 1-1 补充完整。

Search information to understand the meanings of the following graphic symbols, and fill in Chart 1-1.

表 1-1　信号机图形符号的含义

Chart 1-1　Meanings of the Graphic Symbols of the Signal Machine

图形符号 graphic symbols	对应的含义 corresponding meanings
 ⊗	
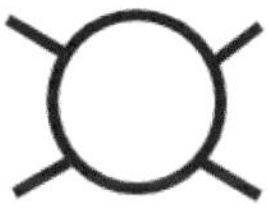 ⨂ (four-legged)	
 ⨂ (four-legged double)	
 ⊢○○⊣	
 ⌐⌐	
 ⊢○○○○⊣	

课后拓展

After-class Activity

任务二 信号机的设置和结构

Task 2　Setting and Structure of Signal Machine

模块一　学前准备

Module 1　Preparation before Class

拍摄或搜集铁路线路上的各种信号设备的图片，不少于5张，并将其粘贴于下方笔记区域。

Take photos or collect pictures of the signal equipment on railways. Collect at least 5 pictures and stick them in the following area.

课前学习笔记
Study Notes before Class

模块二　课堂学习

知识点一：信号装置的分类

信号装置一般分为固定信号机和信号表示器两类，信号装置的分类如图1-8所示。

Module 2　In-class Learning

Key Point 1：Types of Signal Equipment

Signal equipment is generally divided into fixed signal machine and signal indicator. The classification is shown in Figure 1-8.

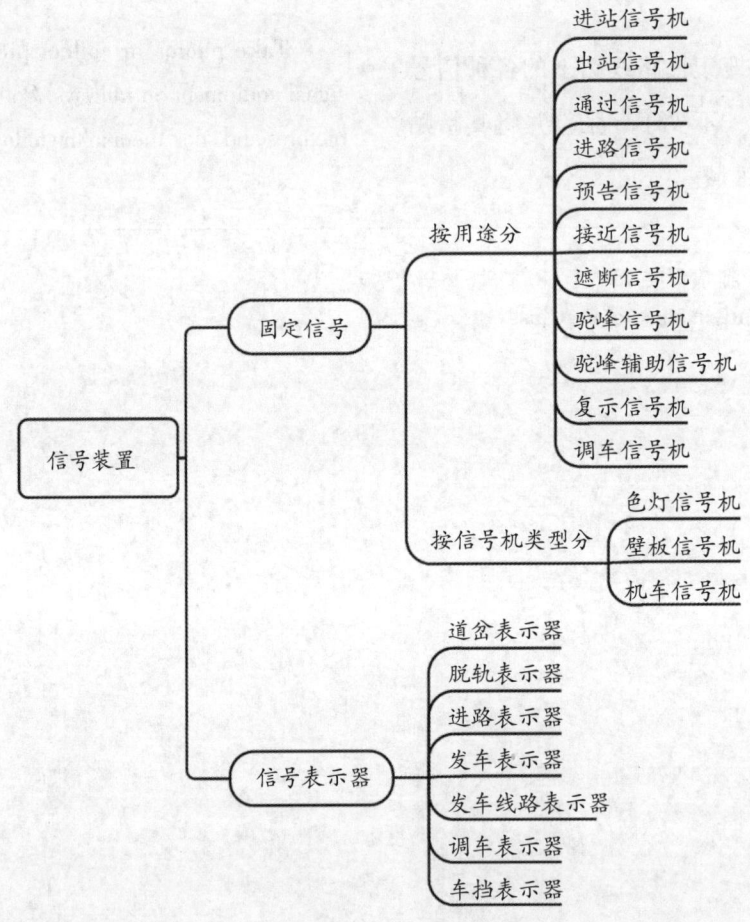

信号装置：signal equipment　　固定信号：fixed signal　　按用途分：classification on usage
进站信号机：arrival signal machine　　出站信号机：exit signal machine
通过信号机：passage signal machine　　进路信号机：route signal machine
预告信号机：forecast signal machine　　接近信号机：approaching signal machine
遮断信号机：obstruction signal machine　　驼峰信号机：hump signal machine
驼峰辅助信号机：hump auxiliary signal machine　　复示信号机：repeating signal machine
调车信号机：dispatching signal machine　　按信号机类型分：classification on types
色灯信号机：color light signal　　壁板信号机：board signal machine

机车信号机：locomotive signal machine 信号表示器：signal indicator
道岔表示器：turnout indicator 脱轨表示器：derail indicator 进路表示器：route indicator
发车表示器：departure indicator 发车线路表示器：departure route indicator
调车表示器：dispatching indicator 车挡表示器：buffer stop indicator

图 1-8 信号装置的分类

Figure 1-8 Classification of Signal Equipment

知识点二：信号机的设置

1. 信号机设置的原则

（1）地面固定信号机应设置于线路的左侧。

采用左侧行车制的地面固定信号机，机车司机座位统一设在驾驶室左侧，为便于瞭望信号，规定固定信号机应设置在行车线路的左侧。如果两线路之间不足以装设信号机，可采用信号桥或信号托架，装设在信号桥或信号托架上的信号机，可设置于线路左侧，也可设于所属线路的中心线上方，如图1-9所示。

Key Point 2：Setting of Signal Machine

1.Principle of Signal Machine Setting

（1）Ground signal machine shall be set on the left of the circuit.

Ground fixed signal machine under the left side driving system: driver's seat is in the left of the driving cab, fixed signal machine is on the left side of the route for signal observing. If the space between two routes is not enough for installation, signal bridge or bracket can be set on the left or above the center line of the route for signal machine installation. See Figure 1-9.

（a）信号托架

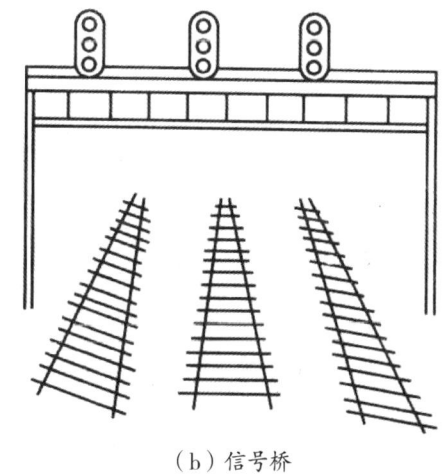
（b）信号桥

图 1-9 信号托架与信号桥

Figure 1-9 Signal Bracket and Signal Bridge

· 11 ·

（2）任何信号机不得侵入铁路建筑限界。

（3）信号机的设置地点应避免影响行车安全和运输效率。

（2）No signal machine shall be set to intrude into railway building boundary.

（3）Installation place of signal machine shall not affect the safety and efficiency of train operation.

2. 信号机的显示状态

信号机的显示状态一般有稳定灯光、稳定灯光组合、闪光信号，以此来表示特定的行车命令。信号机的状态有关闭与允许两个状态。如图1-10所示。

2. Display Status of Signal Machine

General display status of signal machine consists of stable light, stable light group and flash signal showing specific train operation order. Status of signal machine are turning off and permission. See Figure 1-10.

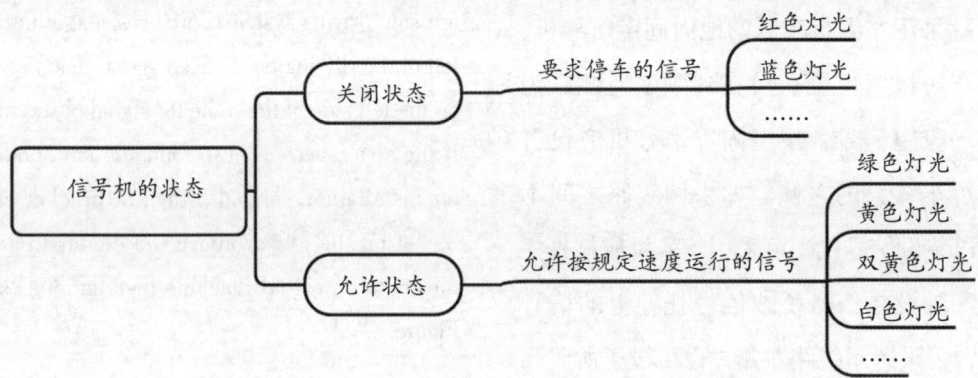

信号机的状态：status of signal machine 关闭状态：turning off 要求停车的信号：stop signal
红色灯光：red light 蓝色灯光：blue light 允许状态：permission
允许按规定速度运行的信号：signal permitting running at stipulated speed 绿色灯光：green light
黄色灯光：yellow light 双黄色灯光：dual yellow light 白色灯光：white light

图1-10 信号机的状态

Figure 1-10 Status of Signal Machine

知识点三：信号机的结构

1. 透镜式色灯信号机

透镜式色灯信号机根据机柱的不同，分为高柱和矮柱两种，如图 1-11 和 1-12 所示。以高柱信号机为例，介绍透镜式色灯信号机的结构。

Key Point 3：Structure of Signal Machine

1. Lenticular Color Light Signal Machine

Lenticular color light signal machines are divided into high-pillar type and short-pillar type based on the differences of the pillars, see Figure 1-11 and 1-12. Take high-pillar signal machine as an example. Structure of lenticular color signal machine is introduced.

图 1-11 高柱信号机

Figure 1-11　High-pillar Signal Machine

图 1-12 矮柱信号机

Figure 1-12　Short-pillar Signal Machine

高柱透镜式信号机结构由机柱、机构、梯子等部分组成。如图1-13所示。

High-pillar lenticular signal machine consists of pillar, mechanism, stairs and so on. See Figure 1-13.

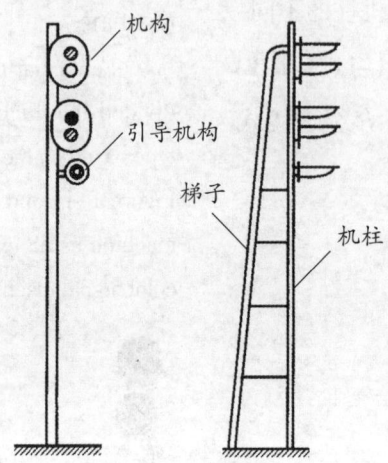

机构：machanism　引导机构：guiding mechanism　梯子：stairs　机柱：pillar

图1-13　高柱透镜式色灯信号机

Figure 1-13　High-pillar Lenticular Color Light Signal Machine

透镜式色灯信号机机构的每个灯位由透镜组、灯泡、灯座、遮檐组成。如图1-14所示。

Lenticular signal machine consists of lens group, bulbs, lamp holder and covering brim. See Figure 1-14.

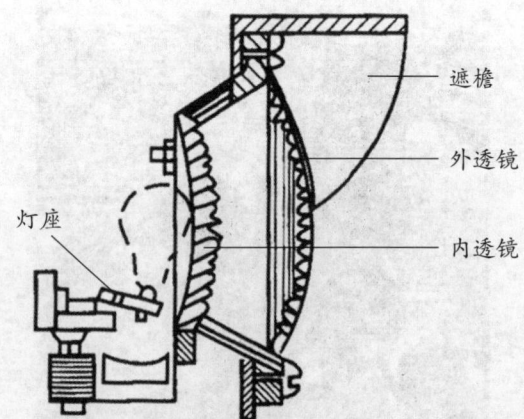

灯座：lamp holder　遮檐：covering brim　外透镜：outer lens　内透镜：inner lens

图1-14　透镜式色灯信号机机构

Figure 1-14　Lenticular Color Light Signal Machine Structure

2. 组合式信号机

组合式信号机的每个机构只有一个灯室，在使用时，根据信号显示要求可以分别组装成单显示、二显示、三显示机构，故称为组合式信号机。组合式信号机结构如图 1-15 所示。

2. Combined Signal Machine

There is only one lamp house in each mechanism of the combined signal machine, and it can be combined into singular, double or triple mechanism based on signal display requirement, therefore, it is called combined signal machine. The structure is shown in Figure 1-15.

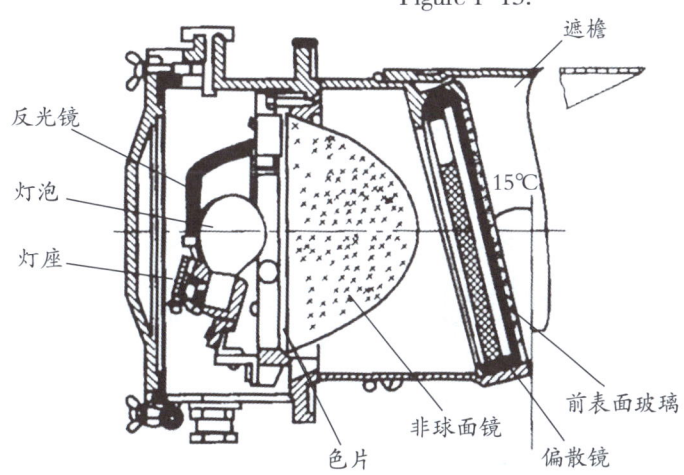

反光镜：retro-reflector　灯泡：bulb　灯座：lamp holder　色片：color chip　遮檐：covering brim
非球面镜：aspherical mirror　前表面玻璃：front surface glass　偏散镜：dispersion mirror

图 1-15　组合式信号机结构

Figure 1-15　Structure of Combined Signal Machine

3. LED 信号机

LED 信号机发光盘是采用发光二极管制成的铁路信号灯光源，一般由铝合金机构、发光盘、点灯装置、报警单元组成。发光盘的结构如图 1-16 所示。

3. LED Signal Machine

LED signal machine is the railway signal light source made of diodes. It usually consists of aluminium alloy mechanism, luminosity panel, lighting device, alarm unit. The structure is shown in Figure 1-16.

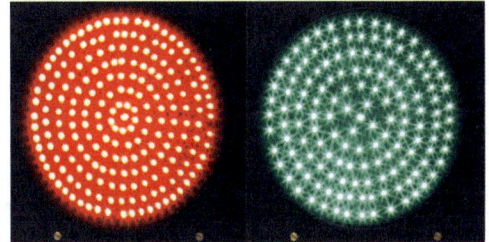

图 1-16　LED 信号机的发光盘

Figure 1-16　Luminosity Pannel of the Signal Machine

学习笔记
Study Notes

模块三 课堂练习

练习1：小组组员相互分享自己拍摄或者搜集到的信号机图片，说说这些信号机分别属于哪种类型的信号机。

练习2：讨论透镜式信号机、组合式信号机、LED信号机分别有哪些优点和缺点。

Module 3 In-class Learning

Exercise 1: Group members share the pictures of signal machines, and talk about the types of the signal machines.

Exercise 2: Discuss the advantages and disadvantages of lenticular signal machine, combined signal machine and LED signal machine.

课堂练习
In-class Exercises

模块四 课后拓展

查阅铁路技规等相关规程和标准，了解线路上信号机在设置位置上的具体要求，并将关于各种信号机显示距离的规定写到下方空白处。

Module 4 After–class Activity

Search information on regulations and standards of railway technical specifications to understand the specific requirements of signal machine positions. Write the display distances of signal machines in the following form.

任务三 固定信号设备运用

Task 3　Utilization of Fixed Signal Equipment

模块一　学前准备

Module 1　Preparation before Class

在任务二中,我们初步学习了固定信号的种类。请你搜集不同类型的固定信号机的图片,注意其灯光的组合和显示,不少于5张,并将图片粘贴于下方区域。

Types of fixed signal are introduced in the previous task. Collect at least five pictures of fixed signal machine, and pay attention to the light combination and display. Stick the pictures in the following form.

课前学习笔记
Study Notes before Class

模块二　课堂学习

Module 2　In-class Learning

知识点一：固定信号设备的用途

Key Point 1：Usage of Fixed Signal Equipment

固定信号机的位置分布及用途见图1-17 所示。

Position deploy and usage of fixed signal machine is shown in Figure 1-17.

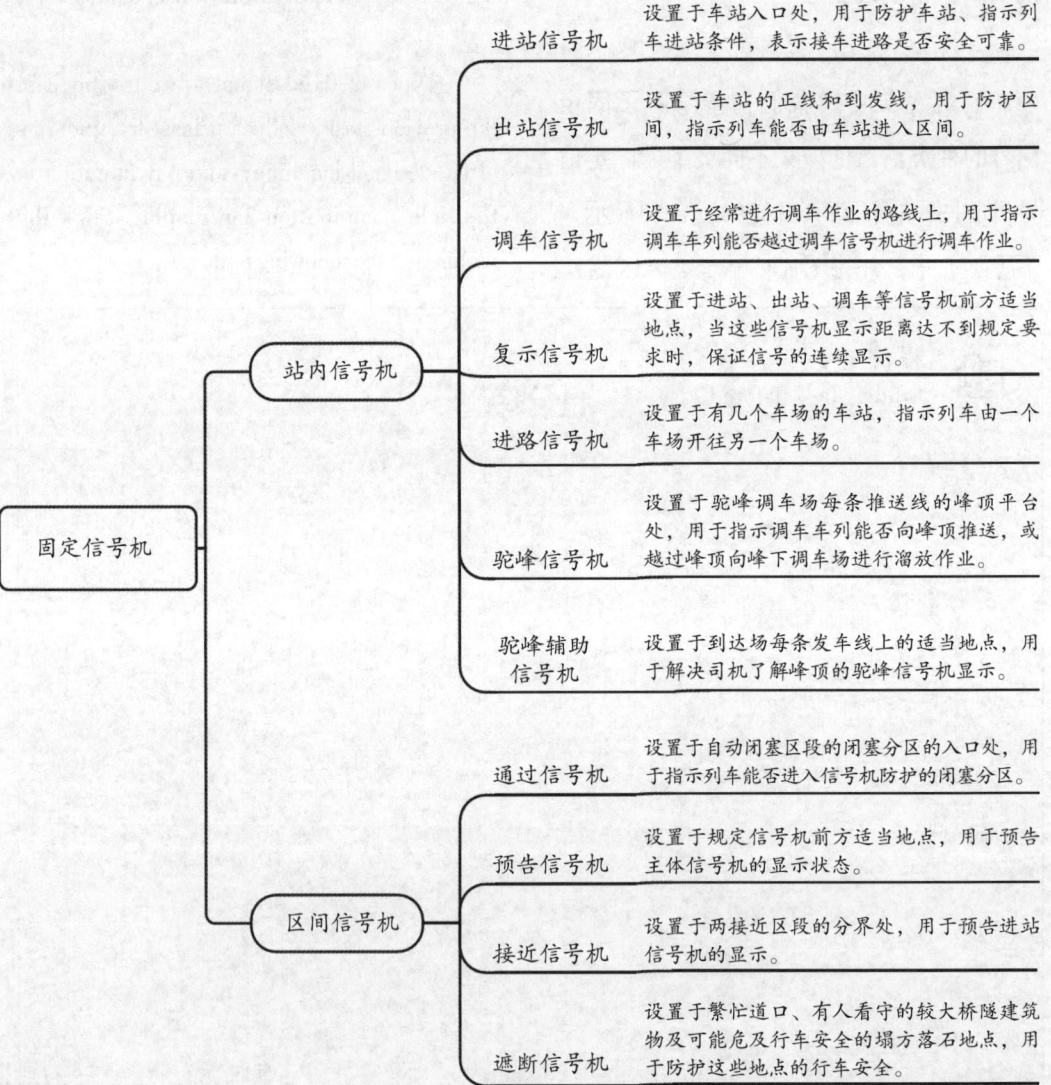

固定信号机：fixed signal machine　站内信号机：in-station signal machine
进站信号机：设置于车站入口处，用于防护车站、指示列车进站条件，表示接车进路是否安全可靠。 Arrival signal machine: set at the entrance of the station for station protection, guiding trains arriving condition and showing the safety and reliability of the receiving route.
出站信号机：设置于车站的正线和到发线，用于防护区间，指示列车能否由车站进入区间。Departure signal machine: set at the main track and arrival and departure route for section protection, indicating if trains can enter the section through the station.
调车信号机：设置于经常进行调车作业的路线上，用于指示调车车列能否越过调车信号机进行调车作业。 Dispatching signal machine: set on routes with frequent dispatching orders, indicating if trains can be dispatched through dispatching signal.
复示信号机：设置于进站、出站、调车等信号机前方适当地点，当这些信号机显示距离达不到规定要求时，保证信号的连续显示。Repeating signal machine: set the proper position in front of arrival, departure and dispatching signal machine, ensuring the continuous display of the signals in case the display distance of the machines is not enough.
进路信号机：设置于有几个车场的车站，指示列车由一个车场开往另一个车场。Route signal machine: set in station with several parking lots, indicating trains run from one parking lot to another lot.
驼峰信号机：设置于驼峰调车场每条推送线的峰顶平台处，用于指示调车车列能否向峰顶推送，或越过峰顶向峰下调车场进行溜放作业。Hump signal machine: set at the summit platform of each pushing track of the hump dispatching lot, indicating if trains can be pushed to the summit, or be rolled to sub-summit dispatching lot over the summit.
驼峰辅助信号机：设置于到达场每条发车线上的适当地点，用于解决司机了解峰顶的驼峰信号机显示。Hump auxiliary signal machine: set at the proper location of each departure route, for driver's understanding of the hump signal at the summit.
区间信号机：section signal machine
通过信号机：设置于自动闭塞区段的闭塞分区的入口处，用于指示列车能否进入信号机防护的闭塞分区。Passing signal machine: set at the entrance of the block section of the automatic block section, indicating if trains can enter the block section protected by the signal machine.
预告信号机：设置于规定信号机前方适当地点，用于主体进站信号机的显示状态。 Forecast signal machine: set at a proper location in front of the designated signal machine, forecasting the display status of the main signal machine.
接近信号机：设置于两接近区段的分界处，用于预告进站信号机的显示状态。 Approaching signal machine: set at the boundary of the neighbouring sections, forecasting display status of the main signal machine.
遮断信号机：设置于繁忙道口、有人看守的较大桥隧建筑物及可能危及行车安全的塌方落石地点，用于防护这些地点的行车安全。 Obstruction signal machine: set at the busy railroad crossing, watched bridges, tunnels and buildings, and landslide locations to ensure train running safety.

图 1-17　固定信号机的位置分布及用途

Figure 1-17　Position Deploy and Usage of Fixed Signal Machine

知识点二：固定信号设备定位显示的规定

在任务二中，我们学过，信号机有开放和关闭两种状态。而信号机经常保持的显示状态称为定位显示。不同的信号机定位显示是不同的，一般应考虑保证行车安全、提高运输效率及信号显示的自动化等因素。具体情况见图1-18所示。

Key Point 2: Positioning Display Rules of Fixed Signal Machines

We have learned the power on and turning off status of signal machines in Task 2 and the frequent display status of the signal machine is called positioning display. Positioning display of the signal machine vary. Factors of train running safety, transportation efficiency and automatic signal display shall be taken into consideration. See Figure 1-18 for more details.

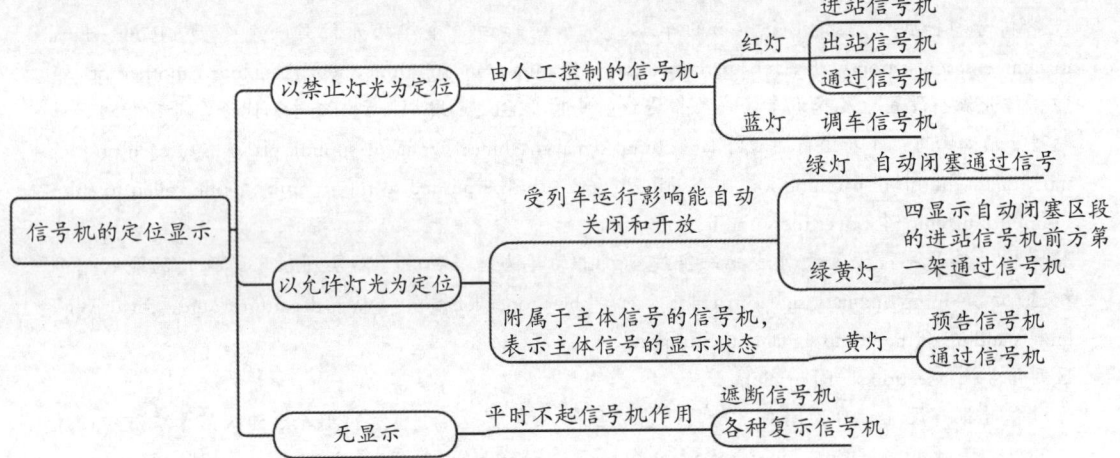

信号机的定位显示：positioning display of signal machine　　以禁止灯光为定位：positioning with prohibition light
由人工控制的信号机：manually controlled signal machine　　红灯：red light
进站信号机：arrival signal machine　　出站信号机：departure signal machine　　通过信号机：passing signal machine
蓝灯：blue light　　调车信号机：dispatching signal machine　　以允许灯光为定位：positioning with permission light
受列车运行影响能自动关闭和开放：automatic turning off and power on affected by train running
绿灯：green light　　自动闭塞通过信号：automatic block of passing signal　　绿黄灯：green and yellow light
四显示自动闭塞区段的进站信号机前方第一架通过信号机：the first passing signal machine in front of the arrival signal machine at the automatic block section with quadruple display
附属于主体信号的信号机，表示主体信号的显示状态：auxiliary signal machine of the main signal, indicating display status of the main signal
黄灯：yellow light　　预告信号机：forecast signal machine　　通过信号机：passing signal machine
无显示：no display　　平时不起信号机作用：normally not functioning as signal machine
遮断信号机：obstruction signal machine　　各种复示信号机：various kinds of repeating signal machines

图1-18　固定信号机的定位显示

Figure 1-18　Positioning Display of Fixed Signal Machine

学习笔记
Study Notes

模块三　课堂练习

Module 3　In-class Exercises

以小组为单位，结合你所搜集到的各种固定信号的图片，讨论固定信号机显示不同灯光的意义。将相应的显示意义填入相应的表格中。

Discuss the meanings of various lights of the fixed signal machines of the collected pictures of the fixed signals in groups. Fill the corresponding meanings in the following form.

表 1-2　进站信号机（三显示自动闭塞）的灯光配列及主要显示

Chart 1-2　Light Arrangement and Major Display of Arrival Signal Machine
（Triple Display Automatic Block）

信号机 signal machine	灯光显示 light display	显示的意义 meanings
	 〇	
	 ⌀	
	 ⌀⌀	
	 ⌀⌀	
	 ●	
	 〇⌀	
	 ●◉	

表 1-3　出站信号机（三显示自动闭塞）的灯光配列及主要显示

Chart 1-3　Light Arrangement and Major Display of Departure Signal Machine
（Triple Display Automatic Block）

信号机 signal machine	灯光显示 light display	显示的意义 meanings
	 〇	
	 ⌀	
	 ●	
	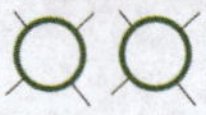 〇〇	

表 1–4 调车信号机的灯光配列及主要显示
Chart 1–4 Light Arrangement and Major Display of Dispatching Signal Machine

信号机 signal machine	灯光显示 light display	显示的意义 meanings
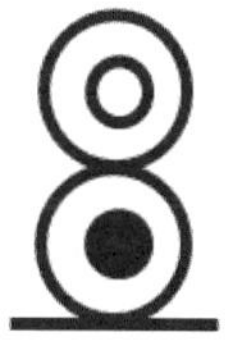	 ⊙	
	 ◎	
	 ⊙	

表 1–5 复示信号机（进站）的灯光配列及主要显示
Chart 1–5 Light Arrangement and Major Display of Repeating Signal Machine（Arrival）

信号机 signal machine	灯光显示 light display	显示的意义 meanings
	 ◎ ◎	
	 ◎　◎	
	无显示 no display	

表 1–6 复示信号机（出站）的灯光配列及主要显示
Chart 1–6 Light Arrangement and Major Display of Repeating Signal Machine（Departure）

信号机 signal machine	灯光显示 light display	显示的意义 meanings
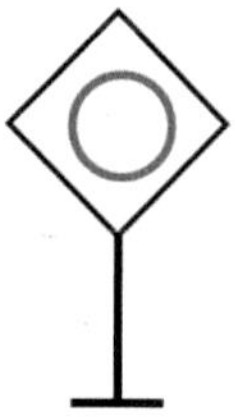	 ○	
	无显示 no display	

表 1-7 进路信号机（发车）的灯光配列及主要显示
Chart 1-7 Light Arrangement and Major Display of Route Signal Machine (Departure)

信号机 signal machine	灯光显示 light display	显示的意义 meanings
	○（绿）	
	⊘（黄）	
	○（绿）	
	⊘（黄）	
	●（红）	
	◉	

表 1-8 通过信号机（三显示自动闭塞）的灯光配列及主要显示
Chart 1-8 Light Arrangement and Major Display of Passing Signal Machine (Triple Display Automatic Block)

信号机 signal machine	灯光显示 light display	显示的意义 meanings
	○（绿）	
	⊘（黄）	
	●（红）	
	●（红）	
	◉	

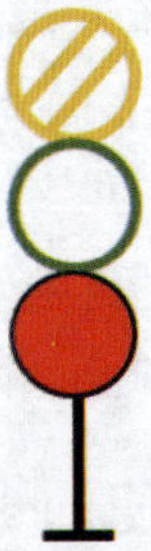

表 1-9 预告信号机的灯光配列及主要显示
Chart 1-9 Light Arrangement and Major Display of Forecast Signal Machine

信号机 signal machine	灯光显示 light display	显示的意义 meanings
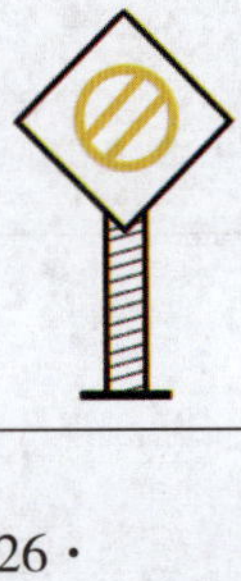	 ⊘（黄）	
	无显示 no display	

表 1–10　接近信号机的灯光配列及主要显示
Chart 1–10　Light Arrangement and Major Display of Approaching Signal Machine

信号机 signal machine	灯光显示 light display	显示的意义 meanings
	绿色灯光	
	绿色灯光	
	黄色灯光	
	黄色灯光	

表 1–11　遮断信号机的灯光配列及主要显示
Chart 1–11　Light Arrangement and Major Display of Obstruction Signal Machine

信号机 signal machine	灯光显示 light display	显示的意义 meanings
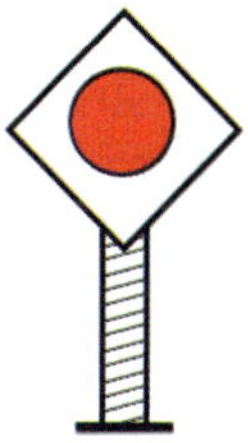	 红色灯光	
	无显示 no display	

课堂练习
In-class Exercises

模块四　课后拓展

图 1-19 所示为铁路线路上某个中间站。请试着对该站应该设置的各种固定信号机进行标注，并注明该信号机的编号。

Module 4　After-class Activity

Figure 1-19 is a medium station on railway. Try to mark the fixed signal machines set on the station and write down the number of the signal machine.

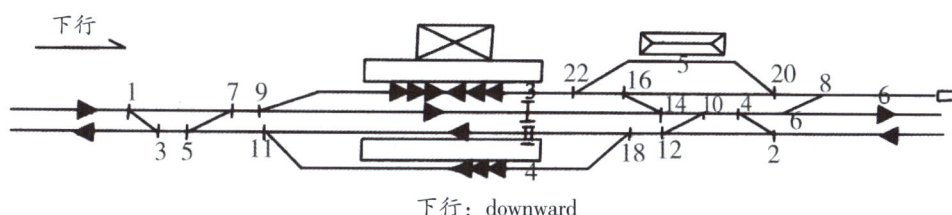

下行：downward

图 1-19　中间站

Figure 1-19　Medium Station

课后拓展

After-class Activity

任务四 信号表示器

Task 4　Signal Indicator

模块一　学前准备

搜集铁路线路上的各种信号表示器的图片，不少于5张，并将其粘贴于下方笔记区域。

Module 1　Preparation before Class

Collect at least 5 pictures of signal indicators on railway and stick them in the following form.

课前学习笔记
Study Notes before Class

模块二 课堂学习

Module 2　In-class Learning

知识点一：什么是信号表示器

Key Point 1：What is Signal Indicator

信号表示器是对行车人员传达行车或调车意图、对信号进行某些补充说明所用的设备，本身没有防护意义。常见的信号表示器如图1-20所示。

Signal indicator is the equipment to transmit train operation or dispatching order to operators or supplement some signals, and it does not bear protection meaning. Common indicators are shown in Figure 1-20.

道岔表示器：turnout indicator　　进路表示器：route indicator

图1-20　信号表示器示例

Figure 1-20　Examples of Signal Indicator

知识点二：信号表示器的种类

Key Point 2：Types of Signal Indicators

1. 进路表示器

1. Route Indicator

进路表示器的用途、设置位置、显示的含义如图1-21所示。

Usage, position and meaning of route indicator is shown in Figure 1-21.

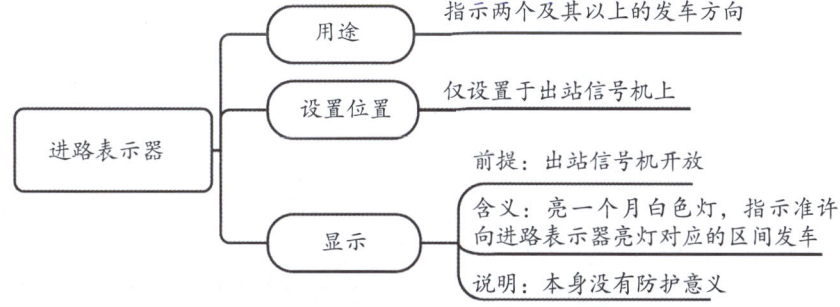

进路表示器：route indicator　　用途：usage

指示两个及其以上的发车方向：indicating two and more departure directions　　设置位置：position

仅设置于出站信号机上：only set on departure signal machine　显示：display
前提：prerequisite　出站信号机开放：departure signal machine is open
含义：meaning　亮一个月白色灯，指示准许向进路表示器亮灯对应的区间发车：a pale green light is on, indicating train departures towards the corresponding section of the route indicator
说明：note　本身没有防护意义：no protection meaning

图 1-21　进路表示器的运用

Figure 1-21　Application of Route Indicator

进路表示器不能单独构成信号命令，只有在出站信号机开放后，才能用月白色灯光表示开往方向。如图 1-22 和图 1-23 所示。

Route indicator doesn't form signal order by itself, pale green light indicates the heading direction when departure signal machine is open. See Figure 1-22 and 1-23.

图 1-22　进路表示器亮灯状态

Figure 1-22　Route Indicate Light on Status

图 1-23　进路表示器灭灯状态

Figure 1-23　Route Indicator Light off Status

2．线路表示器

线路表示器是在某些特定场合指示某线路上的列车出发的设备，但本身不能单独构成信号，须在线群出站信号机①开放后才能显示，如图 1-24 所示。其用途、设置位置、显示的含义见图 1-25。

2. Track Indicator

Track indicator is the equipment indicating train departure on certain routes under certain circumstances. It can not form independent signal and display only after track set departure signal machine① is open. It is shown in Figure 1-24. The usage, position and meanings are shown in Figure 1-25.

---

① 线群出站信号机：在调车场内的编组兼发车线上，原则上应分别设置出站信号机，但在发车次数较少的情况下，可以在编组线群的外方，设置有线群共用的出站信号机，叫作线群出站信号机。

① Track set departure signal machine: In principle, departure signal machine should be set on marshalling and dispatching lines respectively in the shunting yard. But in cases of less frequent train dispatching, departure signal machine shared by track set can be set outside the marshalling track set, and it is called track set departure signal machine.

图 1-24 线路表示器

Figure 1-24　Track Indicator

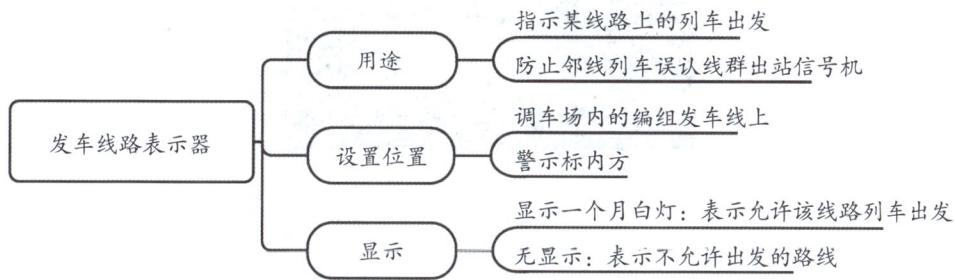

发车线路表示器：departure track indicator　用途：usage
指示某线路上的列车出发：indicating train departure on certain track
防止邻线列车误认线群出站信号机：prevent the train on the neighbouring track from misunderstanding track set departure signal machine
设置位置：position　调车场内的编组发车线上：on the group departure track of the dispatching lot
警示标内方：warning parties inside the signs　显示：display
显示一个月白灯：a pale green light　表示允许该线路列车出发：train departure permission of the route
无显示：no display　表示不允许出发的路线：route not permitted for departure

图 1-25　线路表示器的运用

Figure 1-25　Utilization of Track Indicator

3. 发车表示器

当车站设置于弯道上或车站客流量较大时，司机辨认发车信号有困难时，可根据需要在列车停车位置前恰当地点装设一个发车表示器，便于司机瞭望。图1-26为某站的发车表示器。

3. Departure Indicator

In case the station is on a curve road or the passenger flow volume is large, and it is difficult for driver to recognize departure signal, a departure indicator can be installed in a proper position in front of the stop for driver's observation. In Figure 1-26 is a departure indicator in a station.

图1-26 发车表示器

Figure 1-26 Departure Indicator

发车表示器的用途、设置位置、显示的含义见图1-27。

Usage, position and meaning of departure indicator are shown in Figure 1-27.

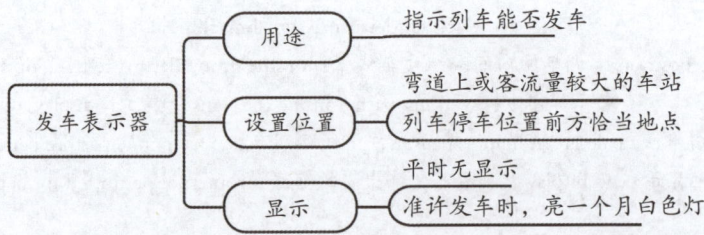

发车表示器: departure indicator 用途: usage 指示列车能否发车: indicating if trains can depart
设置位置: position 弯道上或客流量较大的车站: on the curve road or stations with large passenger flow volume
列车停车位置前方恰当地点: proper location in front of the train stop
显示: display 平时无显示: no display usually
准许发车时，亮一个月白色灯: a pale green light is on for departure permission

图1-27 发车表示器的运用

Figure 1-27 Utilization of Departure Indicator

4．调车表示器

调车表示器是调车机车司机瞭望调车人员手信号有困难时，用以代替调车人员手信号的设备，一般设置于受地形地物影响的繁忙编组场。图 1-28 所示为调车表示器。

4. Shunting indicator

Shunting indicator is the equipment used to replace the hand signal of the shunter if it is difficult for the shunting train driver to watch the hand signal of the shunter. It is usually set in the busy marshaling lot influenced by landform or surface features. See Figure 1-28.

图 1-28　调车表示器

Figure 1-28　Shunting Indicator

调车表示器的用途、设置位置、显示的含义见图 1-29。

Usage，position and meanings of the shunting indicator is shown in Figure 1-29.

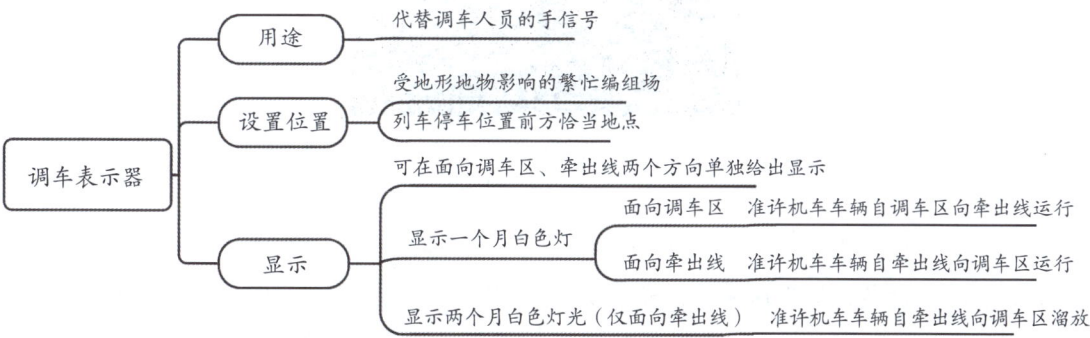

调车表示器：shunting indicator　用途：usage　代替调车人员的手信号：replace hand signal of the shunter
设置位置：position　受地形地物影响的繁忙编组场：busy marshaling lot influenced by landform or surface features

列车停车位置前方恰当地点：proper location in front of the train stop　显示：display
可在面向调车区、牵出线两个方向单独给出显示：independent display facing shunting area and shunting track
显示一个月白色灯：a pale green light
面向调车区：facing shunting area　准许机车车辆自调车区向牵出线运行：permitting trains running from shunting area to shunting track
面向牵出线：facing shunting track　准许机车车辆自牵出线向调车区运行：permitting trains running from shunting track to shunting area
显示两个月白色灯光（仅面向牵出线）：two pale green lights (only facing shunting track)
准许机车车辆自牵出线向调车区溜放：permitting train sliding from shunting track to shunting area

图 1-29　调车表示器的运用
Figure 1-29　Utilization of Shunting Indicator

5. 道岔表示器

道岔表示器是用于反映道岔开通位置的信号设备，设置于道岔旁边。在非集中联锁的车站，为便于行车人员确认道岔开通的方向，必须设置道岔表示器，如图 1-30 所示。

5. Turnout Indicator

Turnout indicator is the signal equipment reflecting turnout opening position which is set beside the turnout. It must be set in non-centralized interlocking stations for train operators to confirm turnout opening direction. It is shown in Figure 1-30.

图 1-30　道岔表示器
Figure 1-30　Turnout Indicator

道岔表示器可以用灯光颜色和中央画有黑线的黄色鱼尾形牌来表示道岔开通的位置是定位还是反位。显示方式如图 1-31 所示。

Light color and fish tail board with black line in the center is used in turnout indicator to indicating the fixed or anti-position of the turnout opening. Displaying ways are shown in Figure 1-31.

昼间：道岔开通直向　　　　　　　　　　　昼间：道岔开通侧向

daytime: straight direction of turnout opening　　　daytime: slide direction of turnout opening

夜间：道岔开通直向　　　　　　　　　　　夜间：道岔开通侧向

night: straight direction of turnout opening　　　night: slide direction of turnout opening

图 1-31　道岔表示器的显示方式

Figure 1-31　Displaying Ways of Turnout Indicator

图 1-32 所示为道岔表示器显示的含义。　　　　　Meanings of turnout is shown in Figure 1-32.

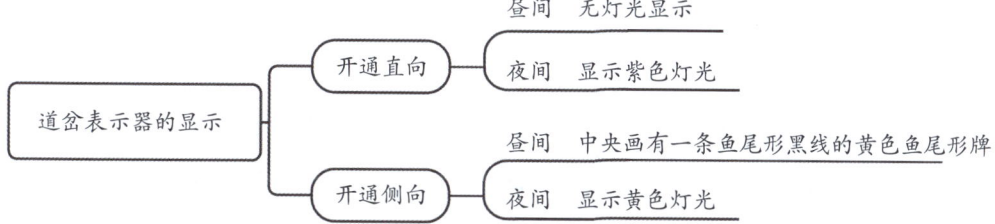

道岔表示器的显示：display of turnout indicator　开通直向：straight direction　昼间：daytime
无灯光显示：no light　夜间：night　显示紫色灯光：purple light　开通侧向：slide direction
中央画有一条鱼尾形黑线的黄色鱼尾形牌：yellow fish tail board with a black fish tail line in the center
显示黄色灯光：yellow light

图 1-32　道岔表示器显示的含义

Figure 1-32　Meanings of Turnout Indicator Display

·37·

6．脱轨表示器

脱轨表示器设置在联锁集中站以外的车站线路上，用来表示线路的开通或遮断状态。如图1-33所示。

6. Derail Indicator

Derail indicator is set on station tracks outside centralized interlocking stations to indicate opening or obstructing status of the track. See Figure 1-33.

图1-33 脱轨表示器

Figure 1-33 Derail Indicator

脱轨表示器的显示方式如图1-34所示。

Display ways of the derail indicator are shown in Figure 1-34.

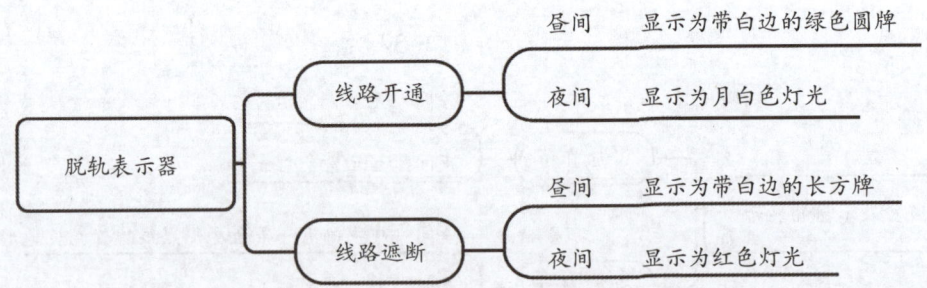

脱轨表示器：derail indicator　线路开通：open track
昼间：daytime　显示为带白边的绿色圆牌：round green board with white edge
夜间：night　显示为月白色灯光：pale green light　线路遮断：obstructed track
显示为带白边的长方牌：rectangular board with white edge　显示为红色灯光：red light

图1-34 脱轨表示器的显示方式

Figure 1-34 Display Ways of Derail Indicator

学习笔记

Study Notes

模块三　课堂练习

练习 1：小组共享各组员所搜集的信号机图片，并讨论其属于哪一种信号机。

练习 2：小组讨论，信号表示器与信号机的区别在什么地方。

练习 3：图 1-35 为道岔表示器的四个显示状态。请说明此图中的道岔表示器分别表示道岔开通的什么位置。

Module 3　In-class Exercises

Exercise 1：Group members shared the collected pictures of the signal machines and discuss the types.

Exercise 2：Group members discuss, differences between signal indicators and signal machines.

Exercise 3：There are the four status of turnout indicators in Figure 1-35. Explain what the turnout open positions of the indicators.

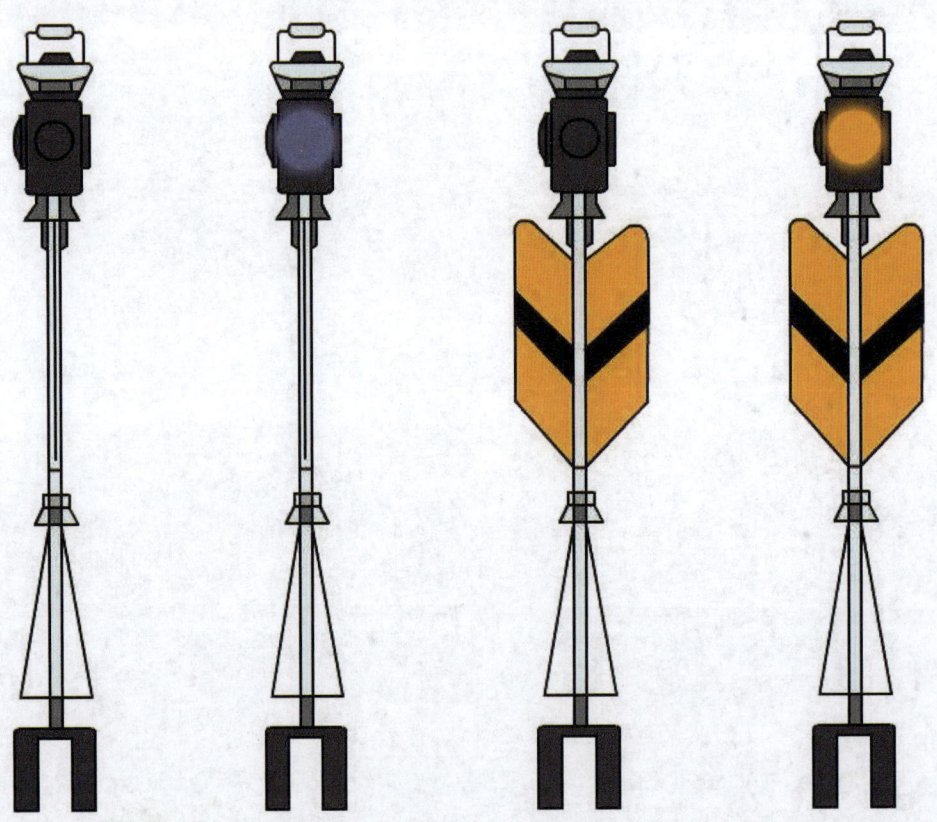

图 1-35　道岔表示器的显示状态
Figure 1-35　Display Status of Turnout Indicator

课堂练习
In-class Exercises

模块四　课后拓展

除任务三中学习的固定信号机与本任务中学习的信号表示器以外，铁路上往往还需要对不同用途的信号机给出的显示附加某些特殊的含义，这就需要用到一些信号标志。例如，前面说过的，信号机显示红色灯光，表示绝对的停车信号，而自动闭塞区间的通过信号机给出的红色灯光，是一种容许的停车信号。

请查询相关资料，了解包括容许信号在内的信号标志的作用和显示，并将相应的内容记录在下方。

Module 4　After-class Activity

Apart from the fixed signal machine in Task 3 and the signal indicator learned in this task, special meanings shall be added to the signal machine display with various functions. Therefore, some signal signs are needed. For example, as mentioned above, red light of signal machine means absolute stop, and red light of passing signal machine in automatic block section means permissive stop.

Consult relevant information to understand the signal signs function and display, including permissive signals. Write down the content in the following form.

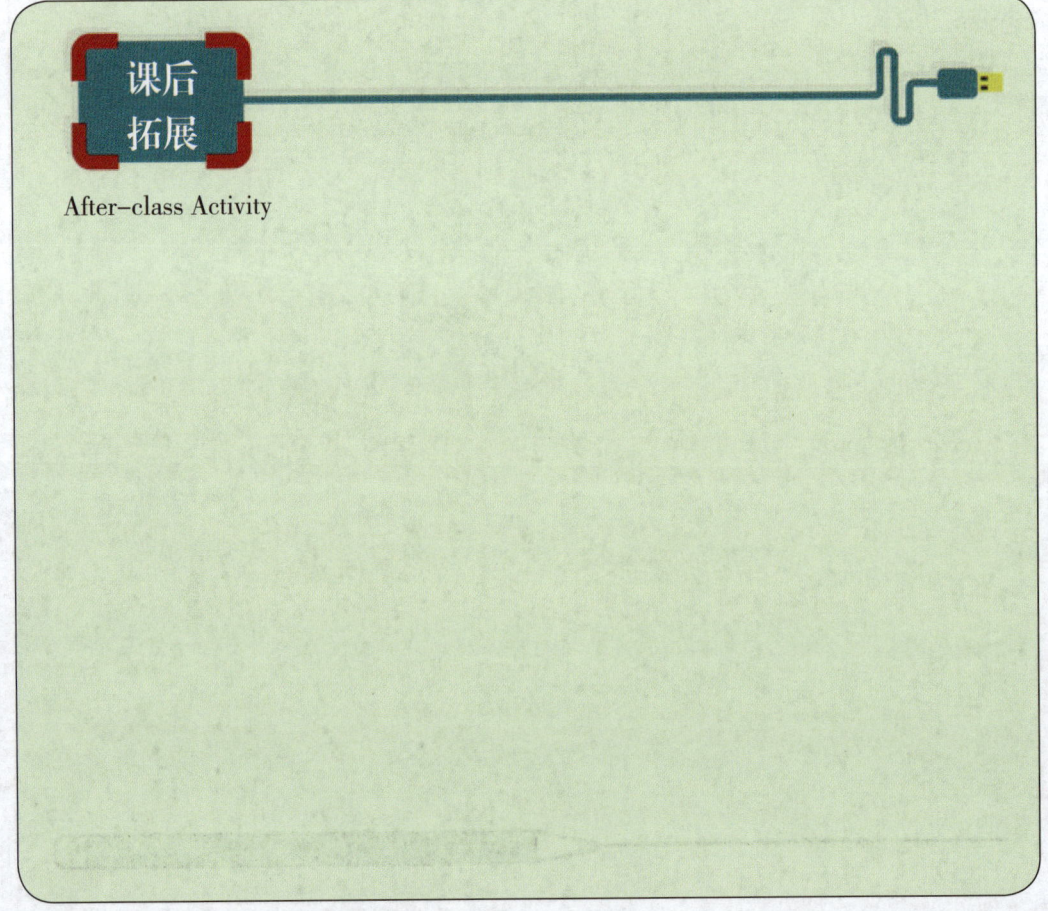

After-class Activity

项目二 联锁设备

Project 2　Interlocking Equipment

任务一　继电器

Task 1　Relay

模块一　学前准备

Module 1　Preparation before Class

到图书馆或者网络上搜集直流无极继电器、有极继电器、偏极继电器、整流式继电器及交流二元继电器的相关图片。

Consult books in the library or search on the Internet for pictures of direct current neutral relay, polarized relay, polar-biased relay, rectifier relay, and alternating current two element relay.

课前学习笔记
Study Notes before Class

模块二　课堂学习

知识点一：继电器结构

如图 2-1 所示为直流无极继电器。它是一种电磁开关，能以较小的电信号控制执行电路中的大功率设备，是实现控制和远程控制的重要设备。

图 2-2 为直流无极继电器的结构示意图，由接点系统和电磁系统两大部分组成。

Module 2　In-class Exercises

Key Point 1：Structure of Relay

In Figure 2-1 is direct current DC for short neutral relay. It is the electro-magnetic switch to control high-power equipment in the execution circuit with small electrical signal. It is a significant equipment for control and remote control.

Figure 2-2 is the structure of DC neutral relay, consisting of contact system and electro-magnetic system.

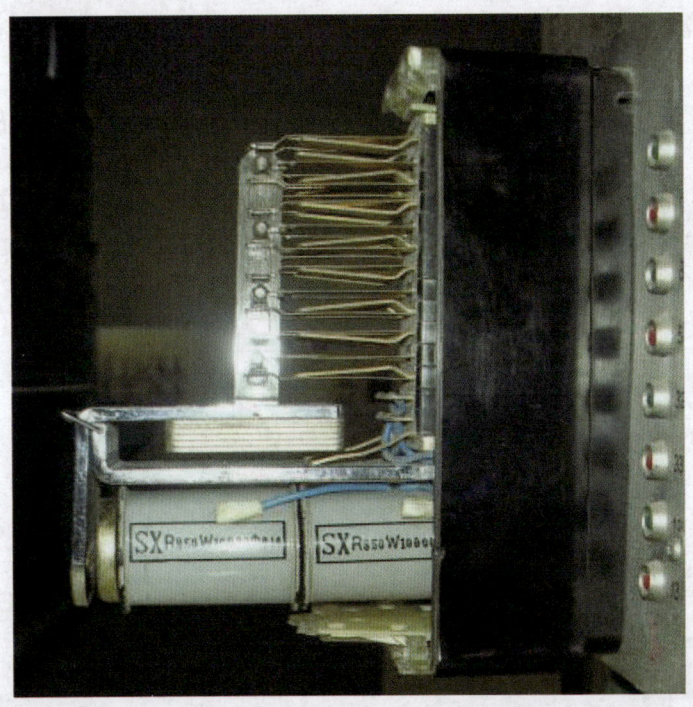

电磁系统由线圈、固定的铁芯、轭铁以及可动的衔铁构成。Electro-magnetic system consists of coil, fixed iron core, yoke and movable armature.

接点系统由动接点、静接点构成。Contact system consists of movable and stable contacts.

图 2-1　直流无极继电器外形

Figure 2-1　Appearance of DC Neutral Relay

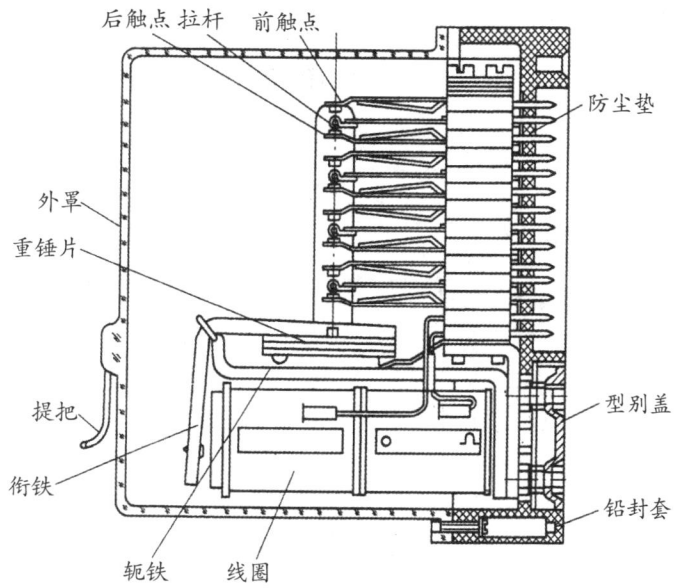

后触点：back contact　拉杆：pull rod　前触点：front contact　外罩：exterior cover
防尘垫：dust-proof mat　重锤片：counter weight piece　提把：bale handle　衔铁：Armature
型别盖：model cover　轭铁：yoke　线圈：coil　铅封套：lead sealing

图 2-2　直流无极继电器的结构示意图
Figure 2-2　Structure of DC Neutral Relay

知识点二：继电器工作原理

1. 励磁状态（吸起状态）

线圈通电→产生磁通（衔铁、铁芯）→产生吸引力→克服衔铁阻力→衔铁吸向铁芯→衔铁带动动接点动作→前接点闭合、后接点断开。

2. 失磁状态（落下状态）

电流减少→吸引力下降→衔铁依靠重力落下→动接点与前接点断开，后接点闭合。如图 2-3 所示。

Key Point 2: Operating Principle of Relay

1. Excitation Status (Energized Status)

Coil energized → magnetic flow (yoke, iron core) → magnetic attraction force → overcome yoke resistance → attract yoke to iron core → yoke drives movable contact → front contact closed and back contact open.

2. Loss of Excitation (Drop Status)

Electric flow reduced → attraction reduced → yoke dropped due to gravity → movable and front contact disconnected, back contact closed. See Figure 2-3.

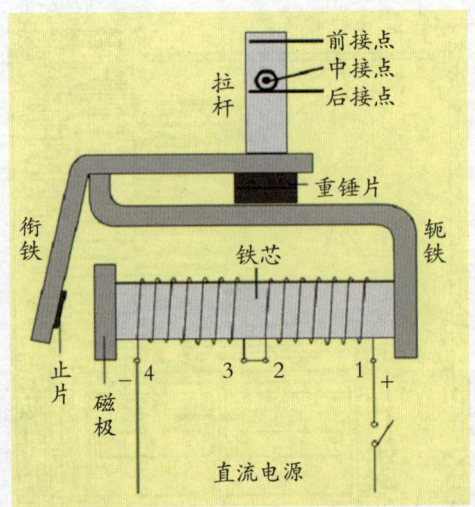

拉杆：pull rod　前接点：front contact　中接点：middle contact　后接点：back contact
重锤片：counter weight piece　衔铁：armature　铁芯：iron core　轭铁：yoke　止片：stop piece
磁极：magnetic pole　直流电源：direct current

图 2-3　继电器工作原理

Figure 2-3　Working Principle of Relay

知识点三：继电器的作用	Key Point 3: Function of Relay
（1）表示功能，如图 2-4 所示。	（1）Indicating function, as illustrated in Figure 2-4.
（2）驱动功能。	（2）Driving function.
（3）实现逻辑电路。	（3）Realizing logical circuit.

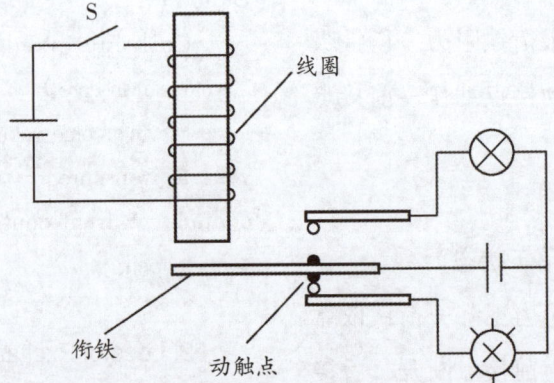

线圈：coil　衔铁：armature　动触点：movable contact

图 2-4　继电器控制信号灯转换灯光

Figure 2-4　Relay Controlling Signal Light to Switch the Lamp

知识点四：铁路主要信号继电器

1. 有极继电器（如图2-5所示）

（1）有定位和反位两种稳定状态。

（2）通入规定极性电流吸起，断电保持；通入反极性电流打落，断电保持。

Key Point 4：Major Signal Relay

1. Polarized Relay (See Figure 2-5)

（1）Two stable status: positioning and anti-position.

（2）Picking up with regulated electric flow, maintain status in case of outage; knocking off with reversed polarity electric flow, maintain the status in case of outage.

图2-5 有极继电器外形图

Figure 2-5 Appearance of Polarized Relay

2. 偏极继电器（如图2-6所示）

（1）为满足信号电路中鉴别电流极性的需要而设计。

（2）只有通入规定方向电流，才吸起。电流方向相反时，衔铁不动作。它不同于有极继电器，只有一种稳态，即衔铁靠电磁力吸起，断电后落下，落下是稳态。

2. Polar-biased Relay (See Figure 2-6)

（1）It is designed to identify the electricity polarity in signal circuit.

（2）Armature picks up when charged with electric flow of regulated direction. Armature doesn't work if the direction of electric flow is reversed. Unlike polarized relay, there is only one stable status. Armature is picked up by electromagnetic power and drops in case of outage, and drop is the stable status.

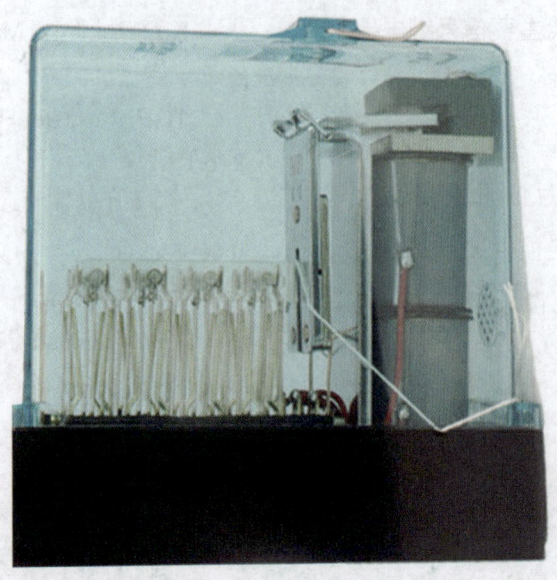

图 2-6 偏极继电器外形图

Figure 2-6 Appearance of Polar-biased Relay

3. 整流式继电器

整流式继电器应用于交流电路中，其电磁系统、接点系统、动作原理与直流无极继电器基本相同，只是在直流无极继电器的基础上增加整流电路，一般采用四个二极管组成桥式整流电路，如图 2-7 所示，将交流电源整流后输入继电器线圈。

3. Rectifier Relay

Rectifier relay is used in alternating current circuit. Its electromagnetic system, contact system and operating principle are basically the same as DC neutral relay. Only the rectifier circuit is added, and the bridge-type rectifier circuit consists of four diodes. As illustrated in Figure 2-7, alternating current is transmitted into relay coil after rectifying.

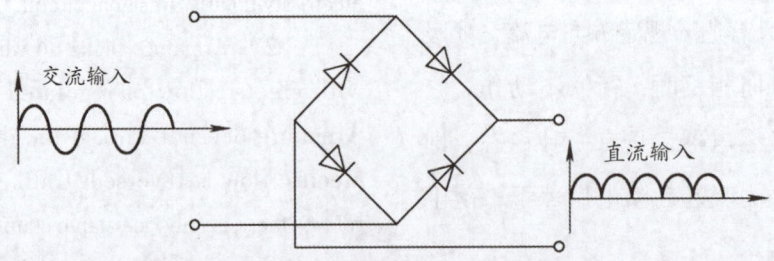

交流输入：AC input   直流输入：DC input

图 2-7 整流式继电器桥式整流电路

Figure 2-7 Bridge Type Rectifier Circuit of Rectifier Relay

4. 交流二元继电器

（1）交流二元继电器中的二元指有两个互相独立又互相作用的交变电磁系统。如图 2-8 所示。

（2）根据频率不同，交流二元继电器分为 25 Hz 和 50 Hz 两种。

4. Alternating Current Two Element Relay

（1） Two element means there are two independent and interacting alternating electromagnetic systems in the relay. See Figure 2-8.

（2） Alternating current two element relay is divided into 25Hz and 50Hz types based on the differences of the frequency.

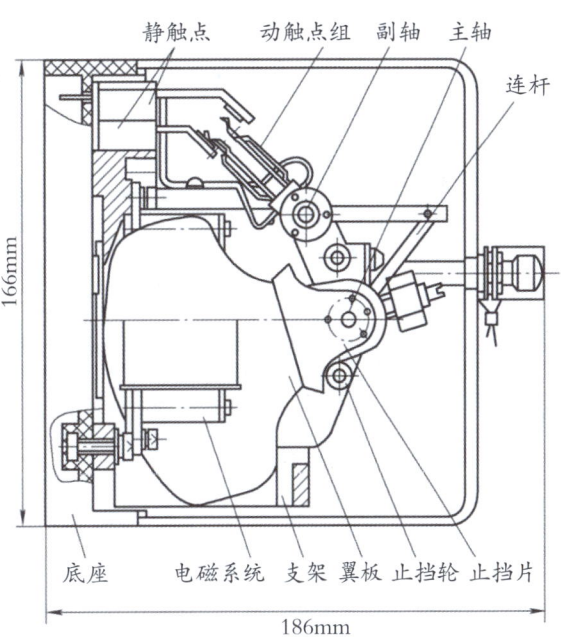

静触点：stable contact　动触点组：movable contact group　副轴：sub shaft　主轴：main shaft
连杆：connecting rod　底座：foundation　电磁系统：electromagnetic system　支架：support
翼板：flange　止挡轮：stop wheel　止挡片：stop piece

图 2-8　交流二元继电器外形及结构

Figure 2-8　Appearance and Structure of AC Two Element Relay

学习笔记

Study Notes

模块三　课堂练习

练习1：根据"学前准备"搜集到的图片，认识和区分不同继电器，并讨论继电器名称中有关字母的含义。

练习2：根据图2-9所示电路，讨论调车信号机工作原理。

Module 3　In-class Exercises

Exercise 1：Understand and differentiate different types of relays based on the pictures collected in "Preparation before Class". Discuss the meanings of the letters in the relay.

Exercise 2：Discuss the operating principle of the shunting signal machine based on the circuit in Figure 2-9.

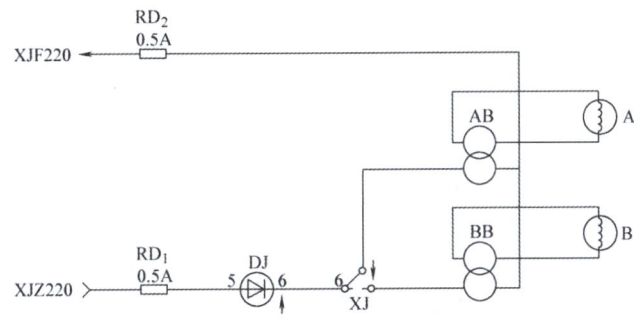

图 2-9　调车信号机控制电路

Figure 2-9　Controlling Circuit in Shunting Signal Machine

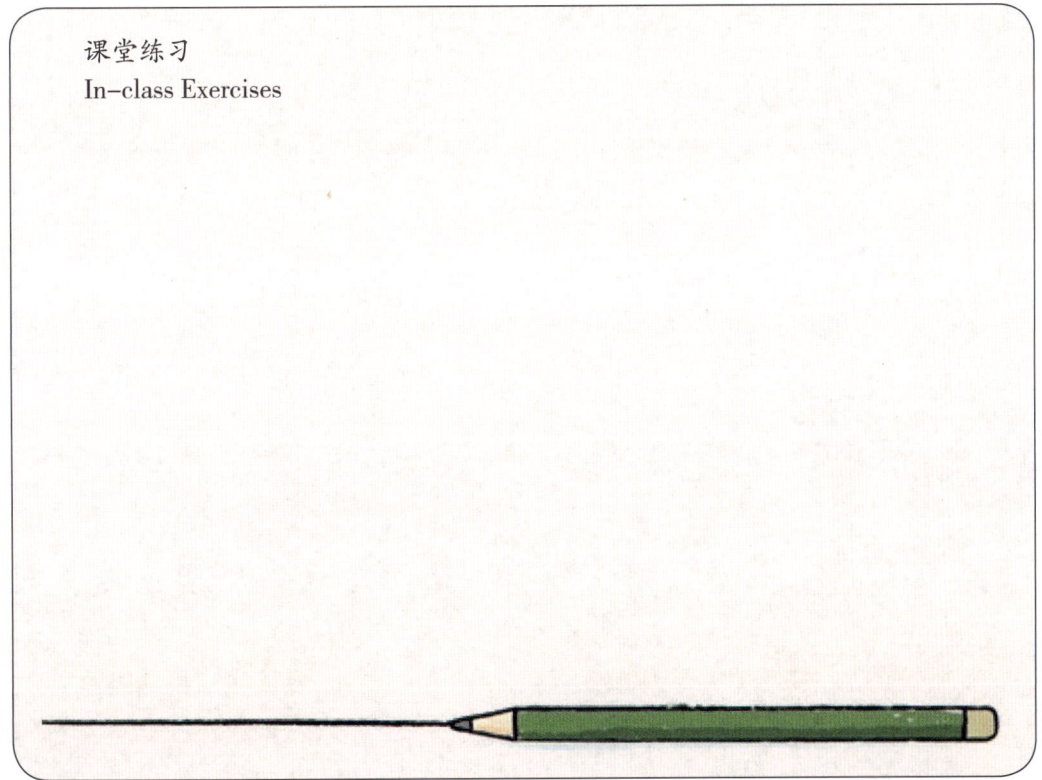

课堂练习
In-class Exercises

模块四　课后拓展

Module 4　After-class Activity

参观所在学校信号实训中心继电器实训室，认识继电器。

Visit relay training room on campus and get to know relay.

任务二 轨道电路及计轴设备

Task 2 Track Circuit and Axle Counter Equipment

模块一 学前准备

Module 1 Preparation before Class

借助图书馆和网络资源思考问题：如何判断区间是否有列车？

Consult information in the library and on the Internet, and think about the following question. How to judge if there is train in the section?

 课前学习笔记
Study Notes before Class

模块二 课堂学习

知识点一：轨道电路

1. 轨道电路的结构

如图 2-10 所示，轨道电路由钢轨、钢轨绝缘、轨端接续线、送电端（轨道电源）、受电端（轨道继电器）等组成。

Module 2　In-class Learning

Key Point 1：Track Circuit

1. Structure of Track Circuit

As shown in Figure 2-10, it consists of steel track, steel track insulation, track match line, sending end (rail power source), receiving end (rail relay) and so on.

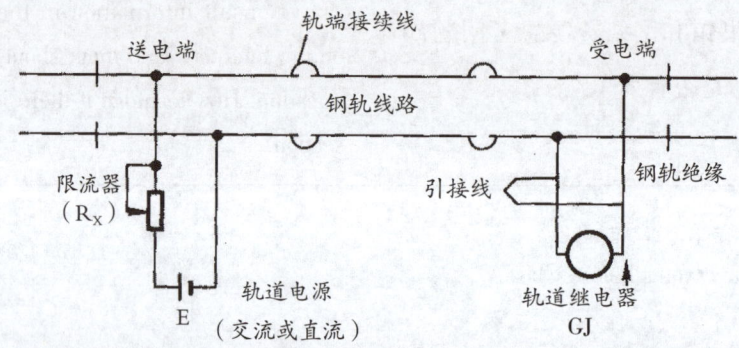

限流器：current limiter　送电端：feed end　轨道电源（交流或直流）：rail power source (AC or DC)
轨端接续线：track match line　钢轨线路：steel track circuit　引接线：lead wire
受电端：receiving end　轨道继电器：rail relay　钢轨绝缘：steel track insulation

图 2-10　轨道电路的结构
Figure 2-10　Structure of Track Circuit

2. 轨道电路的工作原理

（1）空闲（调整状态） 如图 2-11 所示。

2. Operating Principle of Track Circuit

（1） Idle (adjusting state). See Figure 2-11.

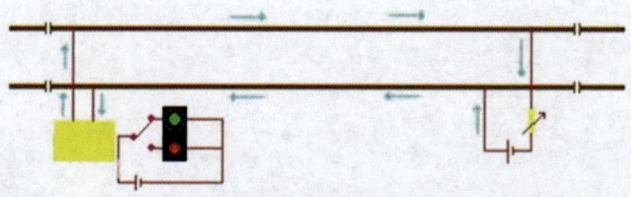

图 2-11　空闲检测
Figure 2-11　Idle Test

（2）占用（分路状态） 如图 2-12 所示。

（2） Occupation (shunting state). See Figure 2-12.

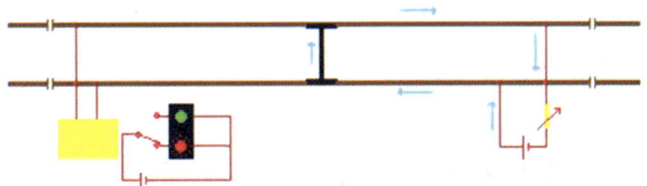

图 2-12 占用检测

Figure 2-12 Occupation Test

（3）故障（断轨状态）。

3. 轨道电路的作用

（1）监督列车对轨道区段的占用情况，检测列车所占用的轨道区段。

（2）传递行车信息（向列车传输速度或距离信息）。

知识点二：计轴设备

1. 计轴设备概述

计轴设备是利用轨道传感器、计数器来记录和比较驶入和驶出轨道区段的轴数，以此确定轨道区段的占用或空闲的设备。如图 2-13 所示。

（3）Error (broken rail).

3. Function of Track Circuit

（1）Supervising train occupation status of rail section and testing the occupied rail section.

（2）Transmitting train running information (transmitting speed or distance information to trains).

Key Point 2：Axle Counter Equipment

1. Axle Counter Equipment Overview

Axle counter equipment records and compares axle numbers arriving and departing the rail section with rail sensors and counters. See Figure 2-13.

图 2-13 计轴设备

Figure 2-13 Axle Counter Equipment

2. 设备组成

（1）轨道传感器，如图2-14所示。

2. Components of the Equipment

（1）Rail sensor, as shown in Figure 2-14.

图 2-14　轮轴传感器
Figure 2-14　Axle Sensor

（2）电子单元EAK，如图2-15所示。

（2）Electronic unit EAK, as shown in Figure 2-15.

图 2-15　EAK
Figure 2-15　EAK

（3）计轴评估器，如图 2-16 所示。

(3) Axle evaluator, as in Figure 2–16.

图 2-16　计轴评估器 ACE

Figure 2–16　Axle Evaluator ACE

3. 基本工作原理

如图 2-17 所示，依据该轨道区段驶入点和驶出点所记录轴数的比较结果，确定该区段的占用或空闲状态，输出控制信息使该区段的轨道继电器吸起。

3. Basic Operating Principle

As shown in Figure 2–17, occupation or vacancy status of the section is confirmed based on the comparison of the axle counting results recorded at the arriving and departure points, and control information is transmitted to draw up the rail relay in the section.

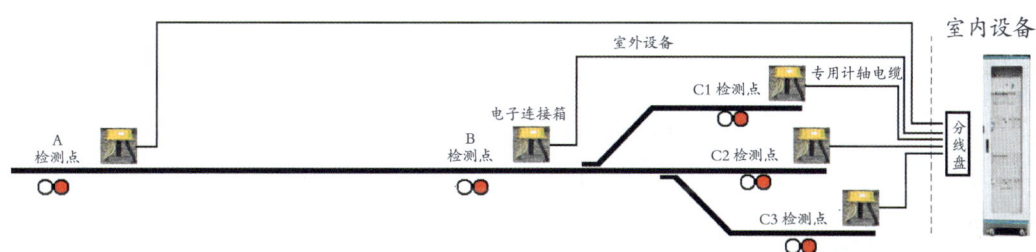

检测点：test point　电子连接箱：electronic connection box　室外设备：outdoor equipment
专用计轴电缆：specialized axle counting cable　室内设备：indoor equipment　分线盘：noseplate

图 2-17　计轴设备基本工作原理

Figure 2–17　Basic Operating Principle of Axle Counting Equipment

学习笔记
Study Notes

模块三 课堂练习

从轨道电路和计轴设备的结构组成、功能及作用原理等方面进行讨论，总结两者的优、缺点。

Module 3　In-class Exercises

Discuss the structures, functions and operating principles of track circuit and axle counter equipment. Summarize the advantages and disadvantages of them.

课堂练习
In-class Exercises

模块四　课后拓展

1. 参观所在学校信号实训中心轨道电路实训室，认识轨道电路的组成。（目标要求：掌握轨道电路各组成部分的作用和轨道电路的工作原理。）

2. 到学校信号实训中心完成计轴设备的安装连接。

（1）目标。

① 了解系统组成及各部分的作用。

② 能根据外观区分不同的单元，掌握其原理。

（2）设备。

钻孔工具包、常用安装工具、导线、焊接工具等。

（3）实施步骤。

① 以 4~5 人为一组。

② 室外计轴磁头的定位及安装。

③ 室外电子单元EAK各组件的连接。

④ EAK 接入室内 ACE。

Module 4　After-class Activity

1. Visit track circuit training room in the signal training center on campus and get to know the components of the rail circuit.（Aim: understand the function of the components and functions of the rail circuit.）

2. Finish the installation and connection of axle counter equipment in the training center.

（1）Aim.

① Understand the components and their functions.

② Differentiate the units according to the appearances and understand the principle.

（2）Equipment.

Drilling tool kit, common installation tool, lead wire and welding tool.

（3）Steps.

① In groups of 4~5 students.

② Position and install outdoor axle counter magnetic rod.

③ Connect outdoor electronic units EAK parts.

④ Connect EAK with indoor ACE.

课后拓展

After-class Activity

任务三 转辙机、应答器

Task 3　Point Switch, Transponder

模块一　学前准备

Module 1　Preparation before Class

借助图书馆和网络资源思考如下问题：道岔如何搬动？如何确认道岔是否已经搬动到位？

Consult information in the library or on the Internet, think the following questions: How to move the turnout? How to ensure the turnout is moved in place?

课前学习笔记
Study Notes before Class

模块二　课堂学习

知识点一：转辙机

1. 转辙机的作用

（1）根据操作要求，将道岔转换至定位或反位。如图 2-18 所示。

Module 2　In-class Learning

Key Point 1：Point Switch

1. Function of Point Switch

（1）Change the turnout to normal or reverse position as required. See Figure 2-18.

图 2-18　转辙机搬动道岔至定位

Figure 2-18　Point Switch Moves the Turnout to Normal Position

（2）道岔转换至规定位置且密贴后，自动实行机械锁闭，防止外力改变道岔位置。如图 2-19 所示。

（2）When the turnout is switched to the stipulated position and closed tightly, it is locked mechanically and automatically to prevent position moved by external force. See Figure 2-19.

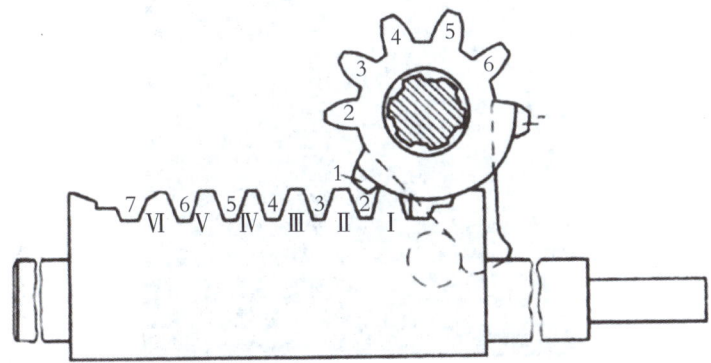

图 2-19　定位锁闭状态

Figure 2-19　Normal Locking Status

（3）当道岔尖轨与基本轨密贴后，正确反映道岔位置，并给出相应表示。如图 2-20 所示。

(3) When turnout switch rail is closed tightly with stock rails, it indicates position of turnout correctly and displays correspondingly. See Figure 2-10.

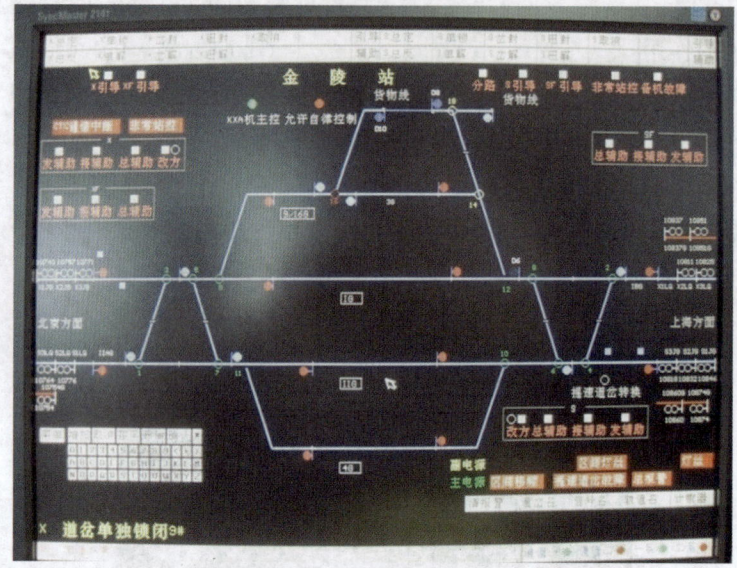

图 2-20　正确反映道岔位置

Figure 2-20　Indicating Position of Turnout Correctly

（4）发生挤岔及道岔长时间处于"四开"位置（两侧尖轨与基本轨均不密贴）时，及时发出报警。如图 2-21 所示。

(4) In case of switch split or long time "cross-open" (switch points at the both sides are not closed with stock rails), alarm sounds immediately. See Figure 2-21.

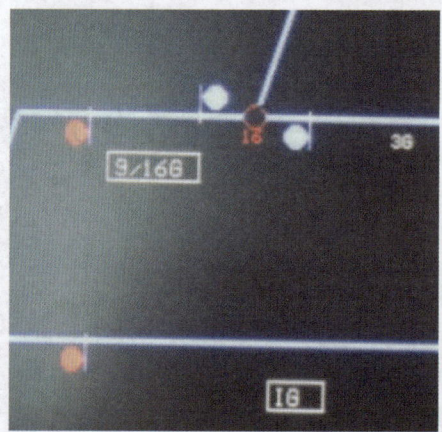

图 2-21　道岔被挤岔

Figure 2-21　Turnout Split

2. 转辙机的结构

（1）ZD6 系列电动转辙机，如图 2-22、图 2-23 所示。

2. Structure of Point Switch

（1）ZD6 series electric point switch, as shown in Figure 2-22 and Figure 2-23.

图 2-22 ZD6 系列电动转辙机外形图

Figure 2-22 Appearance of ZD6 Series Point Switch

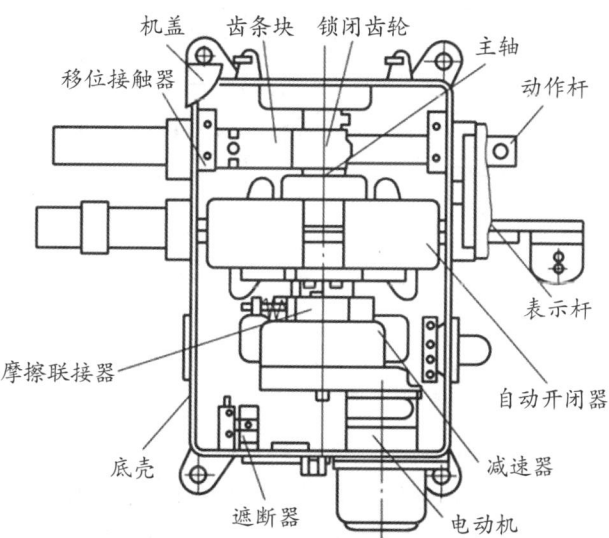

机盖：cover　齿条块：rack piece　锁闭齿轮：locking gear　主轴：principle axis
移位接触器：shifting contactor　动作杆：operation rod　表示杆：display rod
摩擦联接器：friction connector　底壳：bottom shell　遮断器：breaker　自动开闭器：automatic switch
减速器：reducer　电动机：electro motor

图 2-23 ZD6 系列电动转辙机结构图

Figure 2-23 Structure of ZD6 Series Electric Point Switch

（2）S700K 型电动转辙机，如图 2-24、图 2-25 所示。

(2) S700K electric point switch, as shown in Figures 2-24, Figures 2-25.

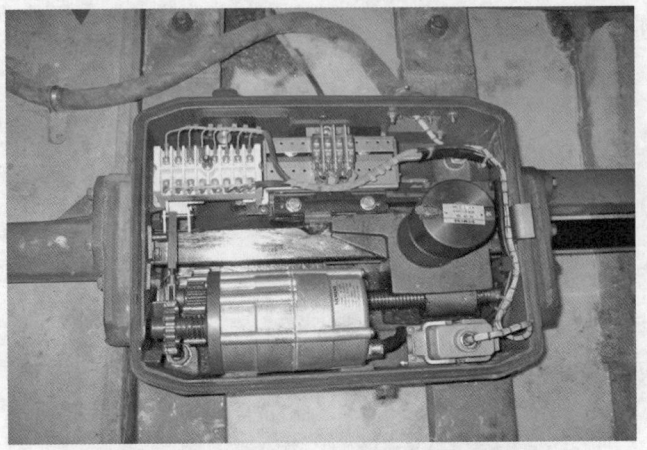

图 2-24　S700K 型电动转辙机外形图
Figure 2-24　Appearance of S700K Electric Point Switch

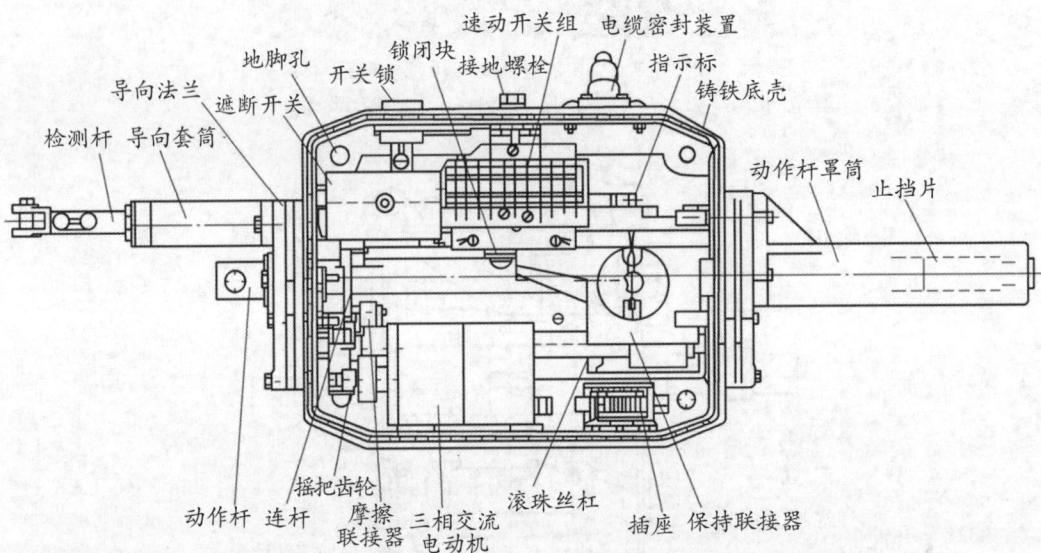

检测杆：testing rod　　导向套筒：pilot sleeve　　导向法兰：pilot flange　　遮断开关：interruption switch
地脚孔：anchor hole　　开关锁：switch lock　　锁闭块：locking piece　　接地螺栓：ground connection bolt
速动开关组：quick-action switch group　　电缆密封装置：cable sealing device　　指示标：indicating mark
铸铁底壳：iron cast bottom shell　　动作杆罩筒：operating rod cover　　止挡片：stop piece
动作杆：operating rod　　连杆：connecting rod　　摇把齿轮：crank gear　　摩擦联接器：friction connector
三相交流电动机：three-phase AC electro motor　　滚珠丝杠：ball screw　　插座：plug
保持联接器：holding mode connector

图 2-25　S700K 型电动转辙机结构图
Figure 2-25　Structure of S700K Electric Point Switch

·66·

S700K 型电动转辙机由外壳、动力传动机构、检测和锁闭机构、安全装置、配线接口五大部分组成。

知识点二：应答器

应答器（Balise）：一种用于地面向列车信息传输的点式设备，分为固定（无源）应答器和可变（有源）应答器。主要用途是向列控车载设备提供可靠的地面固定信息和可变信息。

应答器是一种能向车载子系统发送报文信息的传输设备，既可以传送固定信息，也可连接轨旁单元传送可变信息。如图 2-26 所示。

S700K electric point switch consists of shell, power transmission mechanism, testing and locking mechanism, safety device and wiring port.

Key Point 2：Transponder

Transponder（Balise）：It is the intermittent equipment for information transmission from ground to train, and there are stable（passive）transponder and variable（active）transponder. The main usage is to provide reliable ground stable and variable information to train control on board equipment.

Transponder is the transmission equipment to send information message to on board sub system. It can transmit stable information and connect units by the track to send variable information. See Figure 2-26.

图 2-26　地面应答器与列车之间进行信息传递

Figure 2-26　Information Transmission between Ground Transponder and Train

1. 无源应答器

无源应答器（组），用于发送固定不变的数据，用于提供线路固定参数，如线路坡度、线路允许速度、轨道电路参数、链接信息、列控等级切换等。如图 2-27 所示。

1. Passive Transponder

Passive transponder (group) is used to send stable data and provide track stable parameters, such as track slope, track speed limit, connection information, train control grade switch and so on. See Figure 2-27.

图 2-27　无源应答器组

Figure 2-27　Passive Transponder Group

2. 有源应答器

有源应答器，用于传输可变信息，必须通过专用的应答器电缆与 LEU 设备连接，根据 LEU 设备所发送的报文，可以变化地向列车传送应答器报文信息。它与 LEU（地面电子单元）连接，用于发送来自 LEU 的报文；在既有线提速区段，有源应答器设置在车站进站端和出站端，主要发送进路信息和临时限速信息。如图 2-28 所示。

2. Active Transponder

Active transponder is used for variable information transmission, it must be connected with LEU equipment by special transponder cable and send transponder information message to trains according to the information message sent by LEU equipment. It is connected with LEU to send information message from LEU; in the existing accelerating sections, it is installed in the arrival point and departure point to send information and temporary speed limit information. See Figure 2-28.

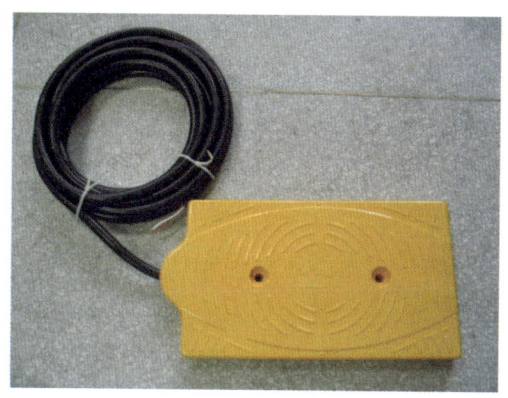

图 2-28 有源应答器组

Figure 2-28 Active Transponder Group

3. 设置

无源应答器（也称固定应答器）设于闭塞分区入口和车站进、出站端处，用于向列控车载设备传输闭塞分区长度、线路速度、线路坡度、列车定位等信息。有源应答器（也称可变应答器）设置于车站进、出站端，当列车通过应答器时，应答器向列车提供接车进路参数、临时限速等信息。如图 2-29 所示。

3. Setting

Passive transponder (also referred to as stable transponder) is set at the entrance of block section, entrance and exit of stations to send block section length, route speed, route slope, train positioning information and so on to train control on board equipment. Active transponder (also referred to as variable transponder) is set at the entrance and exit of the station; when the train passes the transponder, it provides route parameter, temporary speed limit and other information to the train. See Figure 2-29.

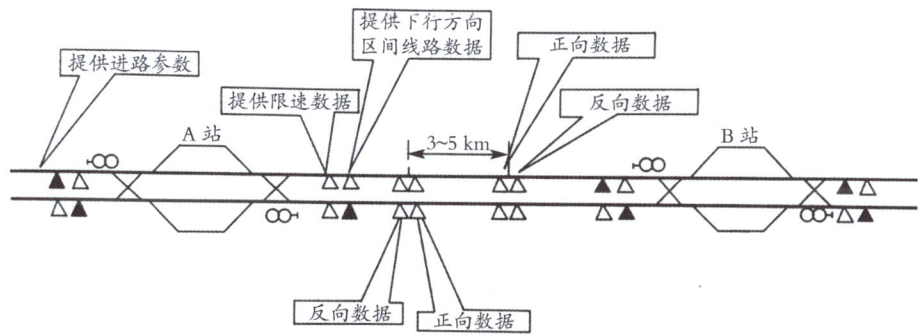

提供进路参数: provide route parameter　提供限速数据: provide speed limit data
提供下行方向区间线路数据: provide down direction section route data
正向数据: forward data　反向数据: reverse data

图 2-29 应答器布置示意图

Figure 2-29 Transponder Set Diagram

学习笔记

Study Notes

模块三 课堂练习

认识转辙机基本结构和作用。

1. 目标

（1）掌握转辙机的作用。

（2）了解转辙机内部结构，了解各部件的作用。

2. 设备

（1）ZD6 型和 S700K 型转辙机。

（2）由转辙机牵引的道岔。

（3）转辙机组件：电动机、减速器、摩擦联接器、移位接触器、齿条块、挤切销、锁闭齿轮等。

3. 实施步骤

（1）打开转辙机机盖，观察转辙机内部组成。

（2）观察转撤机各部件，了解转辙机各部件作用。

（3）操纵转辙机动作，观察转辙机牵引尖轨转换的过程。

Module 3　In-class Exercises

Understand the basic structure and function of point switch.

1. Aim

（1）Understand the function of point switch.

（2）Understand the internal structure of point switch and functions of the parts.

2. Equipment

（1）ZD6 and S700K point switch.

（2）Turnout tracted by point switch.

（3）Components of point switch: electromotor, decelerator, friction connector, shift contactor, rack piece, cutting bolt, locking gear and so on.

3. Steps

（1）Open the cover of point switch to observe its interior.

（2）Observe the internal parts and understand their functions.

（3）Operate the point switch and observe the procedure of its traction of point rail transform.

课堂练习
In-class Exercises

模块四　课后拓展

Module 4　After-class Activity

练习手摇道岔,掌握转辙机的作用。

Practice hand turnout and command the function of point switch.

任务四　联锁及联锁图表

Task 4　Interlocking and Interlocking Diagram

模块一　学前准备

Module 1　Preparation before Class

请分析以下案例发生的根本原因。

2012 年 5 月 21 日 12:27，××站实习车站值班员在排列 6406 次列车上行 4G 接车进路时，漏按压上行坡道延续进路终端按钮；在继续排列 T283 次 IG 接车进路时，致使 4G 接车延续进路开通下行 IG 正线。值班员发现错误后及时取消了上行进站信号，但由于对坡道延续进路解锁方法和程序不熟悉，致使进路长时间不能解锁，经电务人员处理，下行于 12:48、上行于 13:56 恢复正常接车。影响客车 2 列、货车 1 列，构成一般 D 类事故。

Analyze the causes of the following case.

At 12:27 on May 21, 2012, station attendant intern at ×× station missed forward slope continuity route terminal when arranging train 6406 uplink 4G receiving route; it led to the 4G receiving continuity route opened down link IG main track when arranging train T283 IG receiving route, the attendant canceled uplink arrival signal when discovering the mistake, but the route couldn't be unlocked for a long time as the attendant was not familiar with unlocking method and procedure. With the settlement of electric service worker, normal route receiving of down link recovered at 12:48 and up link recovered at 13:56. Two passenger trains and one freight train were affected, and it was grade D accident.

课前学习笔记
Study Notes before Class

模块二 课堂学习

知识点一：进路

1. 进路的基本概念

进路是车站范围内列车或调车机车车辆运行的径路。进路分为列车进路和调车进路。进站、出发及通过列车经过的进路，称为列车进路。调车机车车辆为完成调车作业所经过的进路，称为调车进路。

进路的范围是由防护该进路的信号机起至同一方向限制列车或调车机车车辆运行的信号机（警冲标、站界标或车挡表示器）为止的一段线路，如图2-30所示。

Module 2 In-class Learning

Key Point 1：Route

1. Basic Concept of Route

Route is the tracks of trains or shunting trains within the station area. It is divided into train route and shunting train route. Routes passed by arrival, departure and passing trains are called train routes. Routes passed by shunting trains are called shunting routes.

Route range starts from the signal machine protecting the route to the signal machine (warning board, station boundary mark or bumper post indicator) at the same direction limiting trains or shunting trains, see Figure 2-30.

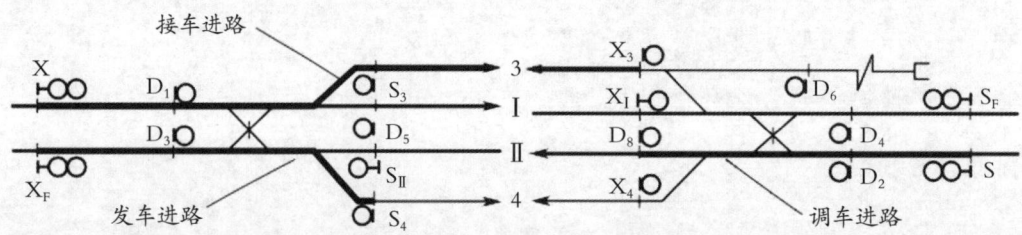

接车进路：receiving route   发车进路：departure route   调车进路：shunting route

图 2-30　进路的范围

Figure 2-30　Route Range

2. 敌对进路

用道岔位置不能间接控制的两条不允许同时建立的进路称敌对进路。进路如果同时建立会造成列车或调车车列冲突的危险。

把如图2-31所示的进路列入表2-1

2. Conflicting Routes

Two routes can't be indirectly controlled by turnout positions or not permitted for simultaneously built are called conflicting routes. Simultaneously building of the routes will lead to trains or shunting trains conflicts.

As shown in Figure 2-31, route is

中，则进路 2、进路 5 互为敌对进路；进路 3、进路 5 互为敌对进路。

listed in Chart 2-1, route 2 and route 5 are conflicting; route 3 and route 5 are conflicting.

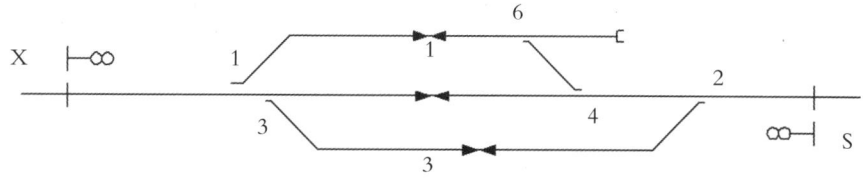

图 2-31 进路举例

Figure 2-31 Route Example

表 2-1 进路举例

Chart 2-1 Route Example

进路号 route number	进路名称 route name
1	1 道下行接车进路 Track 1 down link receiving route
2	2 道下行接车进路 Track 2 sown link receiving route
3	3 道下行接车进路 Track 3 down link receiving route
4	3 道上行接车进路 Track 3 up link receiving route
5	2 道上行接车进路 Track 2 up link receiving route
6	1 道上行接车进路 Track 1 up link receiving route

知识点二：联锁

1. 联锁的基本概念

为了保证行车安全，通过技术方法使道岔、进路和信号机三者之间按一定的程序、一定的条件建立起既联系而又制约的关系，这种关系称为联锁。

2. 联锁关系举例

如图 2-32 所示的车站，办理下行 Ⅱ 道通过时，有关道岔、进路和信号机之间的联锁关系如下：

（1）进路上的 4、2 号道岔，必须置于 Ⅱ 道开通位置。同时，进站信号机 S 必须置于关闭状态，才能开放 Ⅱ 道下行出站信号机 $X_Ⅱ$。

（2）出站信号机 $X_Ⅱ$ 开放后，4、2 号道岔和敌对信号机 S 被锁闭。

（3）出站信号机 $X_Ⅱ$ 开放后，1、3 号道岔置于 Ⅱ 道开通位置，且信号机 S 在关闭状态时，才能开放下行进站信号机 X 的正线通过信号。

（4）下行进站信号机 X 显示正线通过信号后，1、3、2、4 号道岔和敌对信号机 $S_Ⅱ$，以及 S 被锁闭。

（5）下行进站信号机 X 开放后，预告信号机 YX 才能开放。

Key Point 2：Interlocking

1. Basic Concept of Interlocking

The connected and restricting relation among the turnout, route and signal machine built on certain procedures and conditions to ensure the safety of train running is called interlocking.

2. Examples of Interlocking

As the station shown in Figure 2-32, in downlink track two passing, the interlocking relation of turnout, route and signal machine is as follows.

（1）Turnout 4 and 2 on the route shall be open for track 2. At the same time, arrival signal machine S shall be turned off before opening down link departure signal machine X2 on track 2.

（2）When departure signal machine X2 is open, turnout 4 and 2, and the conflicting signal machine S are locked.

（3）When departure signal machine X2 is open, turnout 1 and 3 is open on track 2 and signal machine S is closed, passing signal on the main track off the down link arrival signal machine X.

（4）When down link signal machine X indicates main track passing signal, number 1-4 turnouts, the conflicting signal machine S2 and S are locked.

（5）Forecast signal machine YX is opened after down link arrival signal machine X is opened.

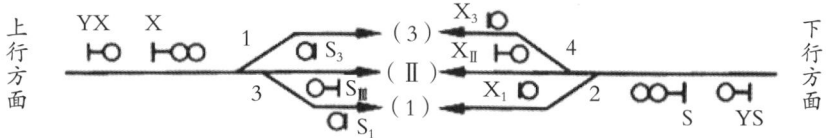

上行方面：up link direction 下行方面：down link direction

图 2-32 联锁示意图

Figure 2-32 Interlocking Diagram

3. 联锁设备

为完成联锁关系而装设的信号设备称为联锁设备。目前，我国铁路上采用的联锁设备主要有电锁器联锁、电气集中联锁和计算机联锁三种类型。

知识点三：联锁图表

一个车站的信号设备通常用平面图表示，称为车站信号设备平面布置图，如图 2-33 所示。依据车站信号设备平面布置图编制道岔、进路以及信号机之间的联锁关系，通常列在一个表里，称为联锁表（见表 2-2）。车站信号设备平面布置图和联锁表总称为联锁图表。

3. Interlocking Equipment

Signal equipment installed for interlock connection is called interlocking equipment. At present, interlocking equipment used in railways in China is mainly interlocking by electric locks, electric interlocking and computer interlocking.

Key Point 3: Interlocking Diagram

Plans are usually used to indicate signal equipment in stations, and they are called station signal equipment arrangement plans as shown in Figure 2-33. Interlocking relations among turnouts, routes and signal machines based on the station signal equipment arrangement plans are usually listed in a diagram, and it is called interlocking chart (Chart 2-2). Station signal equipment arrangement plan and general interlocking list are called interlocking diagram.

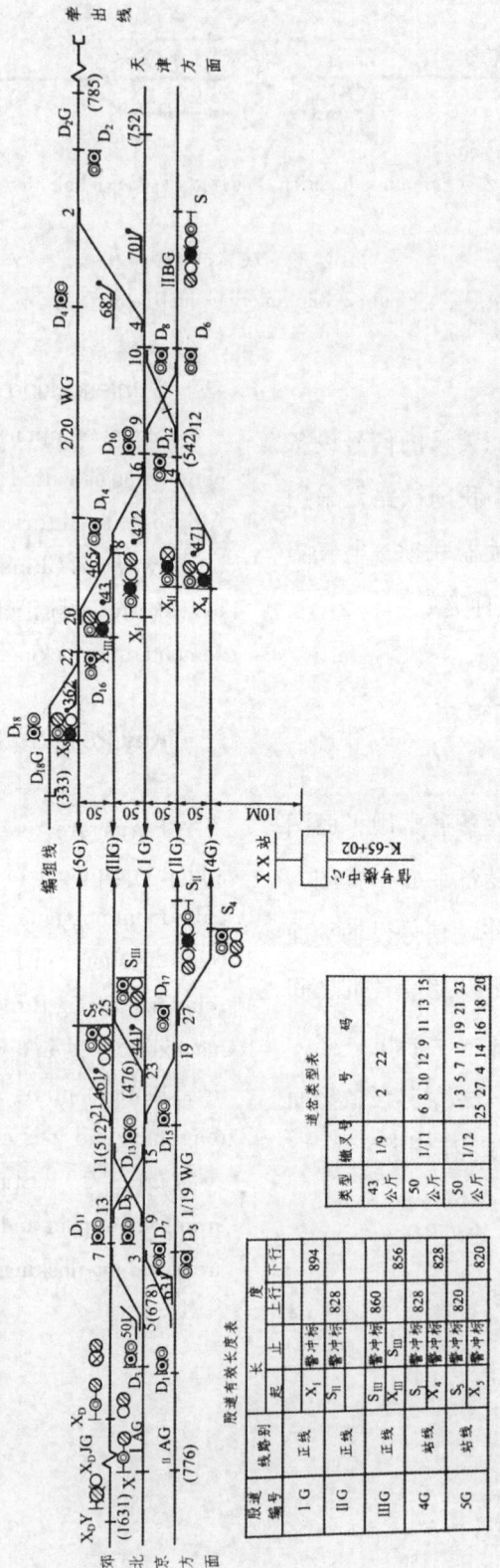

图 2-33 车站信号设备平面布置图

Figure 2-33 Station Signal Equipment Arrangement Plan

表 2-2 联锁表（列车进路部分）
Chart 2-2 Interlocking Chart

方向		进路	进路方式	排列进路按下按钮	确定运行方向道岔	信号机名称	信号机显示	表示器	道岔	敌对信号	轨道区段	迎面进路 列车	迎面进路 调车	其他联锁	进路号码
正方向发车	列车进路	由Ⅰ股道		S_1LA,X_FLA		S_1	L或LU或U	B-A	23/25,17/19,13/15,9/11,1/3	D_{13},D_9,D_5,D_3,X_F,S_ID	17-23DG,9-15DG,3DG,1DG,ⅡAG			BS	14
		由Ⅱ股道		$S_Ⅱ$LA,X_FLA		$S_Ⅱ$	L或LU或U	B-A	27,17/19,1/3	D_{15},D_5,D_3,X_F,S_ID	19-27DG,1/19WG,1DG,ⅡAG			BS	15
		由 4 股道		S_4LA,X_FLA		S_4	L或LU或U	B-A	(27),17/19,1/3	D_{15},D_5,D_3,X_F,S_ID	19-27DG,1/19WG,1DG,ⅡAG			BS	16
反方向发车		由 5 股道	1	S_5LA,XLA	(5/7)	S_5	L	B-B	(21),9/11,13/15,(5/7)	D_1,D_3,$S_ⅢD$	21DG,〈23/25〉25DG,〈1/3〉3DG,ⅠAG			BS	17
		由 5 股道	2	S_5LA,D_7A或D_9A,XLA	5/7	S_5	L	B-B	(21),[13/15],(9/11),1/3,5/7	D_9,D_5,D_3,$S_ⅢD$	21DG,〈23/25〉25DG,[13/15]9-15DG,3DG,5DG,ⅠAG			BS	18
		由Ⅲ股道	1	$S_Ⅲ$LA,XLA	(23/25)	$S_Ⅲ$	L	B-B	(23/25),17/19,13/15,9/11,1/3,5/7	D_3,D_5,D_7,D_9,X,$S_ⅢD$	25DG,〈21〉21DG,17-23DG,9-15DG,3DG,5DG,ⅠAG			BS	19
		由Ⅲ股道	2	$S_Ⅲ$LA,$B_Ⅱ$A,XLA	23/25	$S_Ⅲ$	L	B-B	23/25,21,[13/15],(9/11),1/3,5/7	D_3,D_5,D_7,XS$_ⅢD$	25DG,21DG,[13/15],9-15DG,3DG,5DG,ⅠAG			BS	20
		由Ⅰ股道		S_1LA,XLA		S_1	L	B-B	23/25,17/19,13/15,9/11,1/3	D_3,D_5,D_7,D_9,X,S_ID	17-23DG,9-15DG,3DG,5DG,ⅠAG			BS	21
		由Ⅱ股道		$S_Ⅱ$LA,XLA		$S_Ⅱ$	L	B-B	27,(17/19),13/15,9/11,1/3,5/7	D_3,D_5,D_7,D_9,X,S_ID	19-27DG,17-23DG,9-15DG,3DG,5DG,ⅠAG			BS	22
		由 4 股道		S_4LA,XLA		S_4	L	B-B	(27),(17/19),13/15,9/11,1/3,5/7	D_3,D_5,D_7,D_9,X,S_ID	19-27DG,17-23DG,9-15DG,3DG,5DG,ⅠAG			BS	23
北京方面列车进路 正方向接车		至 5 股道	1	XLA,S_5LA		X	U,U		(5/7),9/11,13/15,(21)	D_3,D_{11},S_5D	ⅠAG,5DG,3DG,〈1/3〉3DG,7DG,11-13DG,21DG,〈23/25〉25DG,5G	5G	5G		24
		至 5 股道	2	XLA,D_7A或D_9A,S_5LA	5/7	X	U,U		5/7,1/3,(9/11),13/15,(21)	D_3,D_9,D_{11},S_5D	ⅠAG,5DG,3DG,9-15DG,11-13DG,〈23/25〉25DG,5G	5G	5G		25
		至Ⅲ股道	1	XLA,$S_Ⅲ$LA	(23/25)	X	U,U		5/7,1/3,9/11,13/15,17/19,〈23/25〉	D_3,D_5,D_7,D_9,$S_ⅢD$	ⅠAG,5DG,3DG,9-15DG,17-23DG,25DG,〈21〉21DG,ⅢG	ⅢG	ⅢG		26

· 81 ·

学习笔记

Study Notes

模块三 课堂练习

Module 3　In-class Exercises

在图 2-34 所示的车站中，办理下行 Ⅱ 道通过时，有关道岔、进路和信号机之间的联锁关系是什么？

In the station in Figure 2-34, what is the interlocking relations among the turnout, routes and signal machines when dealing with passing of downlink Ⅱ route?

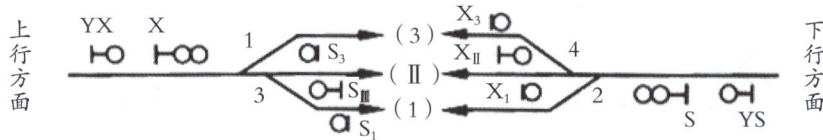

图 2-34　车站联锁示意图

Figure 2-34　Station Interlocking Diagram

课堂练习
In-class Exercises

模块四　课后拓展

熟悉联锁图表的用途，掌握联锁图表中有关列车进路和调车进路相应的联锁关系。

Module 4　After–class Activity

Understand the usage of interlocking diagram and command the interlocking relation between train routes and shunting routes in the diagram.

After–class Activity

任务五 6502电气集中联锁设备

Task 5　6502 Electric Interlocking Equipment

模块一　学前准备

搜集观看6502车站接发车作业视频、铁路总公司《接发列车作业标准》、铁路局《非正常接发列车作业标准》。

Module 1　Preparation before Class

Search and watch videos of 6502 station receiving-departure operating, Train Receiving-departure Operation Standard and Abnormal Receiving-departure Operation Standard of China Railway Corporation.

课前学习笔记
Study Notes before Class

模块二 课堂学习

知识点一：设备组成

6502电气集中联锁设备分为室内和室外两部分，其组成如图2-35所示。信号楼内设有控制台、继电器组合及组合架、电源屏、区段人工解锁盘和分线盘；室外有信号机、转辙机、轨道电路和地下电缆。

Module 2　In-class Exercises

Key Point 1：Equipment Composition

6502 electric interlocking equipment is divided into indoor and outdoor equipment as shown in Figure 2-35. Controlling platform, relay combination and shelf, power screen, section manual unlocking panel and nose plate are installed in the signal building; color light signal machine, electric point switch, track circuit and underground cables are installed outdoors.

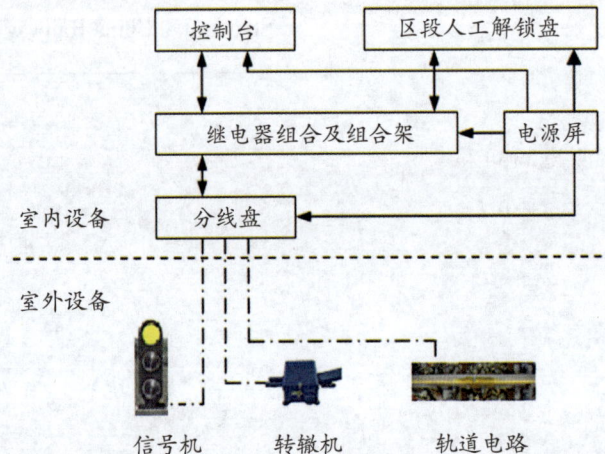

室内设备：indoor equipment　　控制台：controlling platform
区段人工解锁盘：section manual unlocking panel
继电器组合及组合架：relay combination and shelf
电源屏：power source screen　　分线盘：noseplate　　室外设备：outdoor equipment
信号机：signal machine　　转辙机：point switch　　轨道电路：track circuit

图 2-35　6502 电气集中联锁设备组成
Figure 2-35　Composition of 6502 Electric Interlocking Equipment

1. 室内设备

（1）信号楼运转室内设备。

①控制台，如图 2-36 所示。

1. Indoor Equipment

（1）Indoor equipment is run in the signal building.

① Controlling platform, as shown in Figure 2-36.

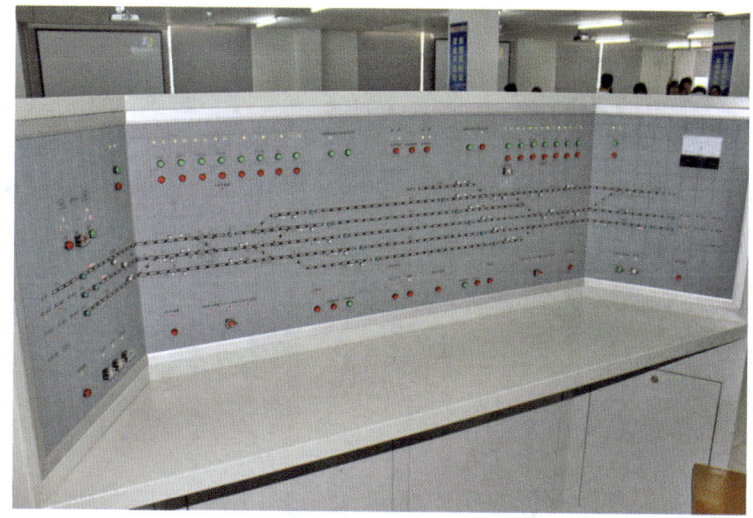

图 2-36 控制台

Figure 2-36 Controlling Platform

②区段人工解锁盘，如图 2-37 所示。

② Section manual unlocking panel, as shown in Figure 2-37.

图 2-37 区段人工解锁盘（局部）

Figure 2-37 Section Manual Unlocking Panel（part）

（2）信号楼机械室内设备。

① 继电器组合及组合架，如图2-38所示。

(2) Equipment in the machinery room of the signal building.

① Relay combination and shelf, as shown in Figure 2-38.

图2-38 继电器组合及组合架

Figure 2-38 Relay Combination and Shelf

② 电源屏，如图2-39所示。

② Power source screen, as shown in Figure 2-39.

图2-39 电源屏

Figure 2-39 Power Source Screen

③ 分线盘，如图 2-40 所示。

③ Noseplate, as shown in Figure 2-40.

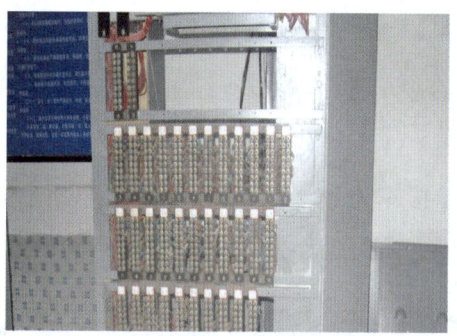

图 2-40　分线盘

Figure 2-40　Noseplate

2. 室外设备

室外设备包括信号机、转辙机、轨道电路、电缆及电缆盒等。

2. Outdoor Equipment

Outdoor equipment includes signal machine, point switch, rail circuit, cable and cable box.

知识点二：列车进路办理方法

进路办理流程如图 2-41 所示。

Key Point 2: Train Route Processing Methods

Route processing procedure is shown in Figure 2-41.

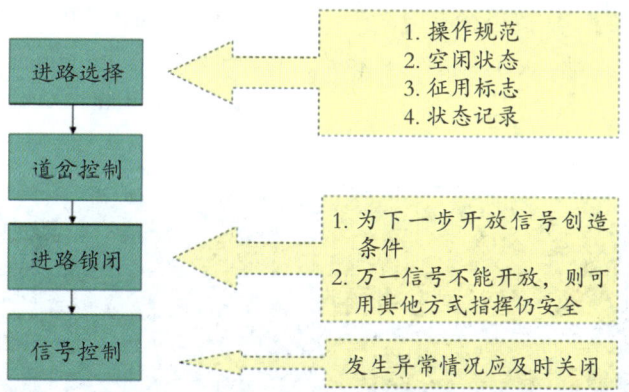

进路选择：select route　　操作规范：operation standard　　空闲状态：vacancy
征用标志：occupied mark　　状态记录：status record　　道岔控制：turnout control　　进路锁闭：route lock
为下一步开放信号创造条件：create conditions for signal open in the next step
万一信号不能开放，则可用其他方式指挥仍安全：
in case the signal can't be opened, other controlling methods are safe
信号控制：signal control　　发生异常情况应及时关闭：instant shut down in case of emergency

图 2-41　进路办理流程

Figure 2-41　Route Processing Procedure

基本进路的办理方法：顺序按压进路的始端按钮和终端按钮。

下面以列车进路中的接车进路和发车进路办理进行说明。

接车进路：例如1G接车进路。始端，X终端，S1，如图2-42所示。

Operating methods of basic route: press route starting and terminal buttons in order.

The following is the illustration of train receiving and departure routes.

Receiving route: for example, IG receiving route. Starting end, X terminal, S1, as shown in figure 2-42.

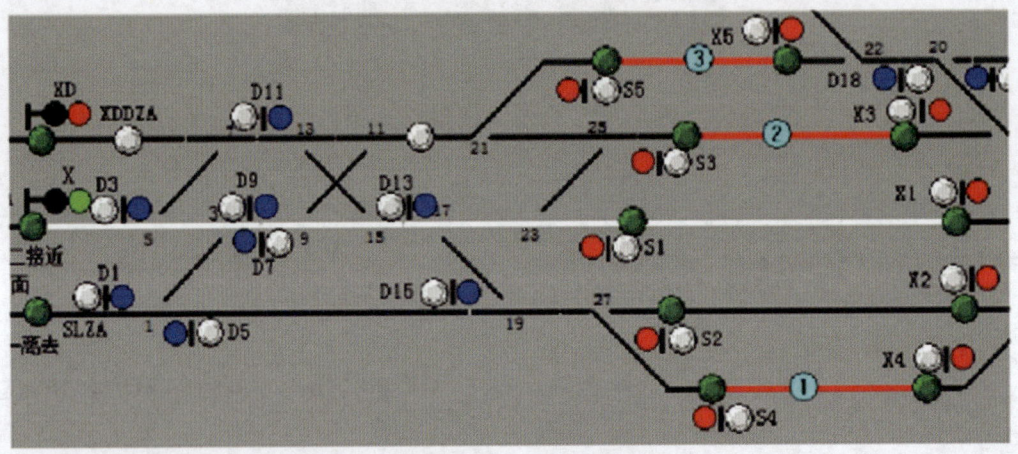

图 2-42　接车进路办理

Figure 2-42　Train Receiving Route Processing

发车进路：例，3G向东郊方向发车进路。始端，S5终端，XD，如图2-43所示。

Train departure route: example, 3G to east suburb train departure route. Starting end, S5 terminal, XD, as shown in figure 2-43.

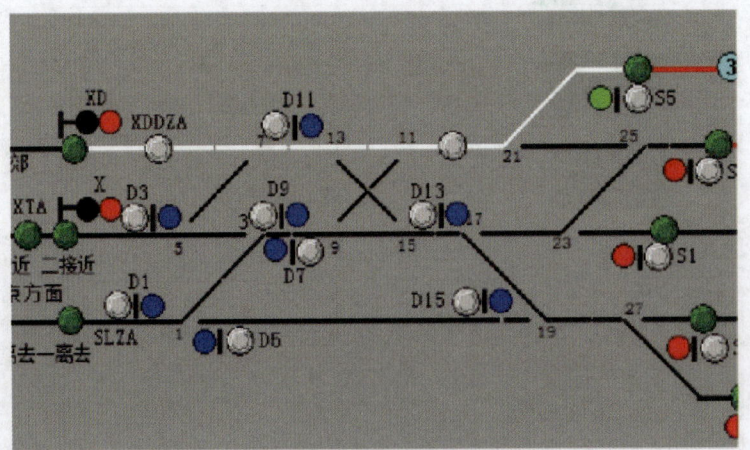

图 2-43　发车进路办理

Figure 2-43　Departure Route Processing

学习笔记
Study Notes

模块三　课堂练习

Module 3　In-class Exercises

　　分小组在6502仿真控制台上办理列车进路、调车进路。

　　Processing train departure and shunting routes in 6502 simulation controlling platform in groups.

模块四　课后拓展

（1）通过参观实训室，掌握6502设备组成。

（2）结合铁路局非正常接发车作业要求，执行6502车站的非正常接发车操作。

Module 4　After-class Activity

（1）Visit the training room and understand 6502 equipment composition.

（2）Execute abnormal receiving-departure operation in 6502 station with abnormal receiving-departure operation requirements of railway bureau.

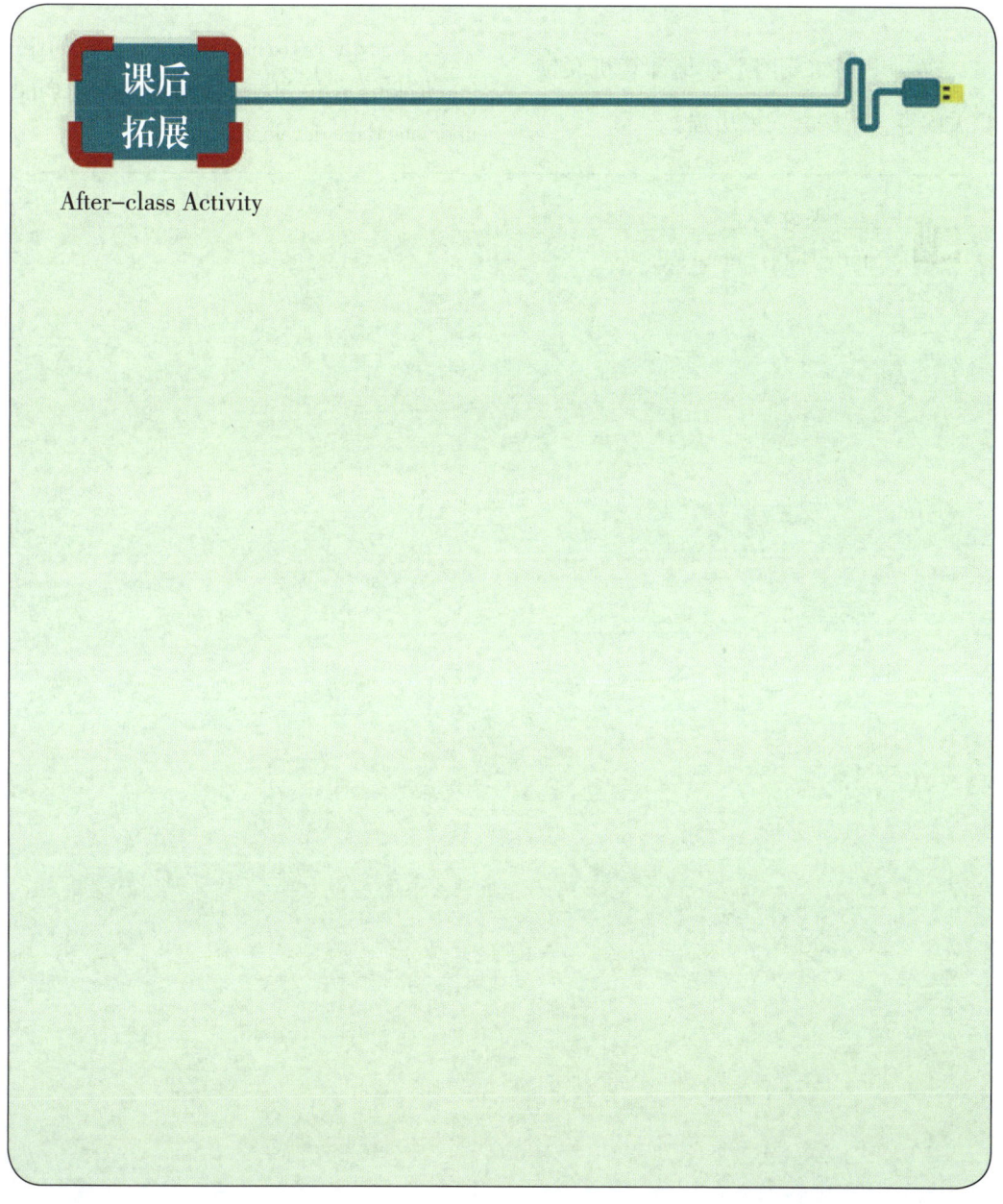

任务六 计算机联锁

Task 6　Computer Interlocking

模块一　学前准备

通过图书馆或网上搜集计算机联锁相关内容,了解其发展历程。

Module 1　Preparation before Class

Search information on computer interlocking in the library or on the Internet and understand the development process.

课前学习笔记
Study Notes before Class

模块二　课堂学习

知识点一：计算机联锁设备类型

根据计算机软件厂家的不同，计算机联锁设备主要分为以下几类：

北京交通大学研制的 JD 型（如图 2-44 所示）、卡斯柯公司研制的 VPI 型（如图 2-45 所示）、铁道科学研究院通号所研制的 TYJL 型（如图 2-46 所示）、通号公司研究设计院研制的 DS6 型（如图 2-47 所示）。

Module 2　In-class Learning

Key Point 1：Types of Computer Interlocking Equipment

Computer interlocking equipment is divided into the following types base on different software manufacturers.

JD type（Figure 2-44）developed by Beijing Jiaotong University, VPI type（Figure 2-45）developed by Casco Signal Ltd., type TYJL（Figure 2-46）developed by Communication Signal Office of Railway Scientific Research Institute, and type DS6（Figure 2-47）developed by Research and Design Institute of Communication Signal Corporation.

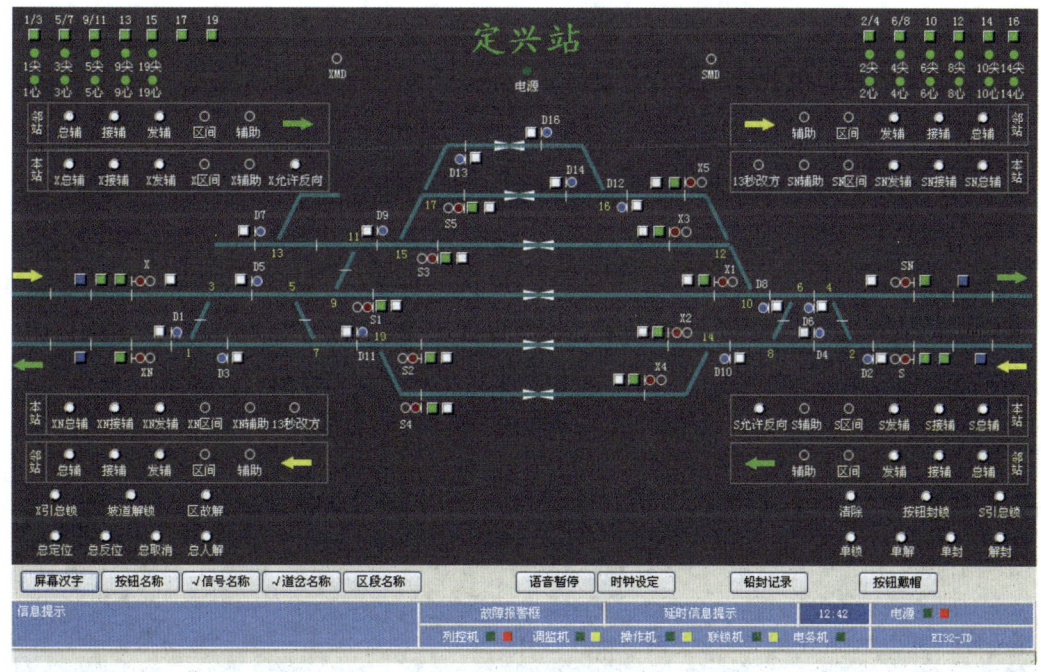

图 2-44　JD 型系统操作界面

Figure 2-44　Type JD System Operation Interface

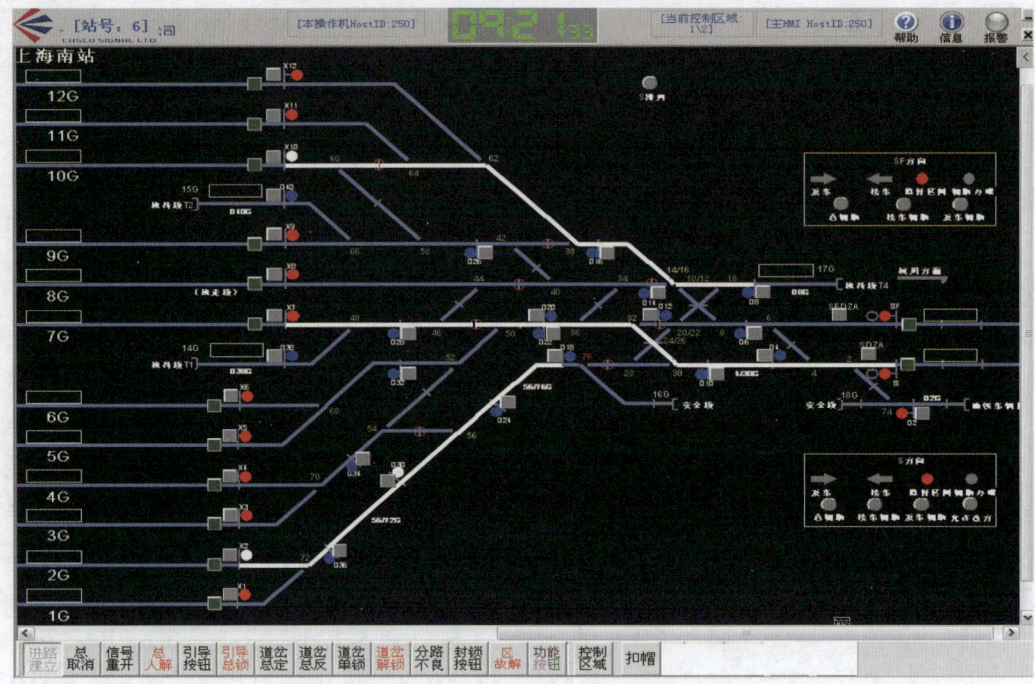

图 2-45 VPI 型系统操作界面

Figure 2-45 Type VPI System Operation Interface

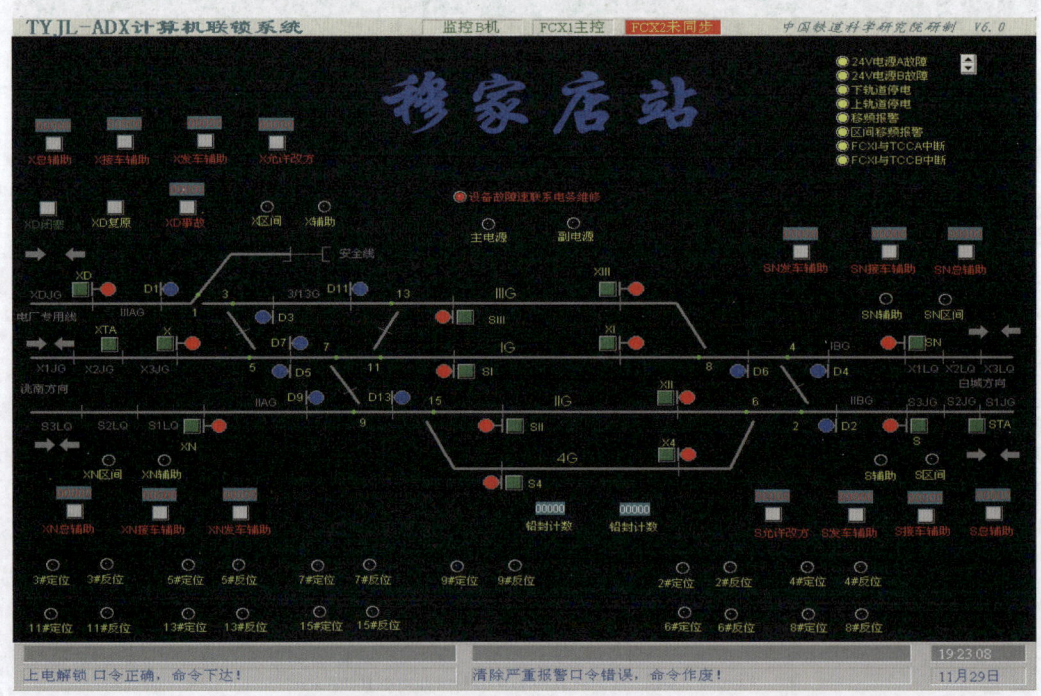

图 2-46 TYJL 型系统操作界面

Figure 2-46 Type TYJL System Operation Interface

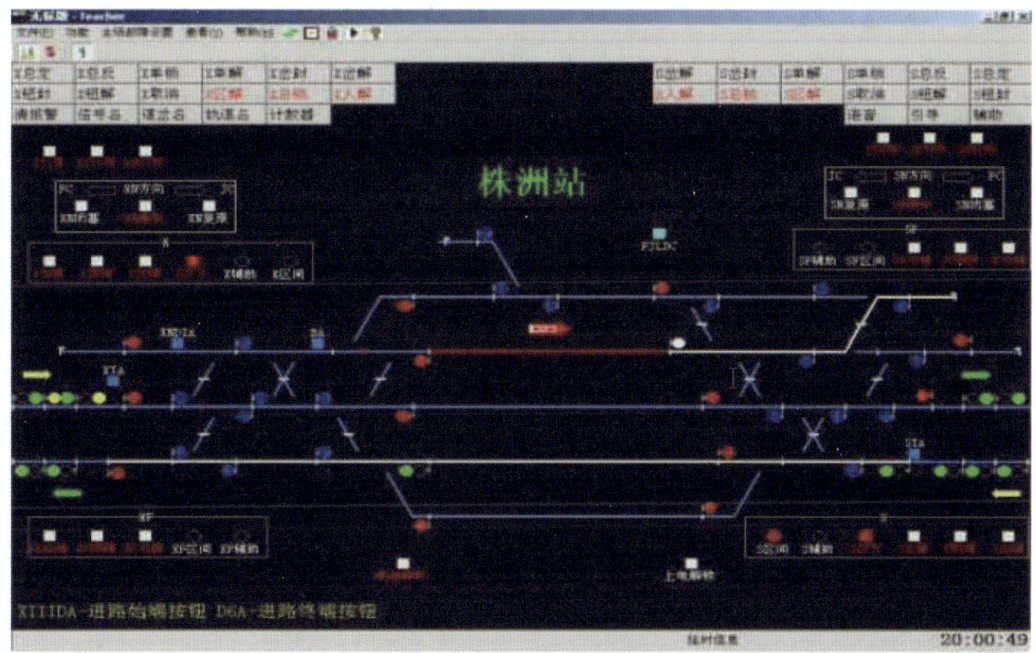

图 2-47 DS6 型系统操作界面

Figure 2-47　Type DS6 System Operation Interface

知识点二：计算机联锁设备组成

Key Point 2：Computer Interlocking Equipment Composition

计算机联锁系统的层次结构如图 2-48 所示。

Hierarchical structure of computer interlocking system is shown in Figure 2-48.

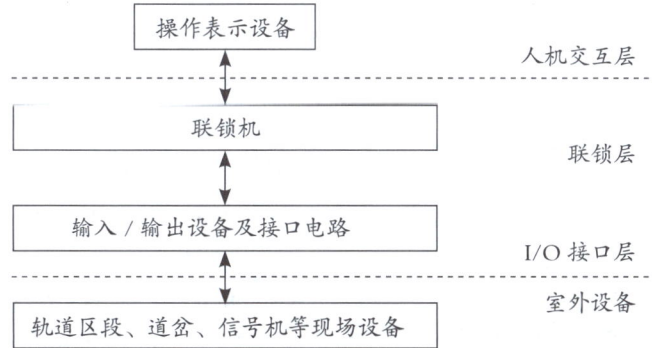

操作表示设备：operation indicating equipment　人机交互层：human-computer interaction level
联锁机：interlocking computer　输入/输出设备及接口电路：input/output equipment and port circuit
联锁层：interlocking level　I/O 接口层：I/O port level　室外设备：outdoor equipment
轨道区段、道岔、信号机等现场设备：track section, turnout, signal machine and other outdoor equipment

图 2-48　计算机联锁系统的层次结构图

Figure 2-48　Hierarchical Structure of Computer Interlocking System

1. 操作表示设备

操作表示设备又称为上位机、操作表示机、控显机、监控机等。其操作和显示部分设置于运转室。

2. 联锁机

联锁机又称为下位机,设置在车站信号楼的机械室内,是联锁系统的核心,必须具有"故障安全"性能。

3. 输入/输出设备

输入/输出设备一般由继电器电路和驱动采集电路构成。其中,继电器电路以 6502 电气集中的信号机点灯电路、转辙机控制电路等为基础。驱动采集电路又称为驱采机、执表机等。

电务维修机是专门为电务维修人员设置的计算机,其主要任务包括站场状态跟踪与回放、操作命令记录与故障记录、输入/输出故障定位等。

计算机联锁系统与 CTCS-2 的列控中心、TDCS 车站机以及 CTC 车站自律机等设备均有接口。

知识点三:DS6-K5B 型计算机联锁系统应用

教材使用的典型教学车站采用 DS6-K5B 型计算机联锁系统时,操作界面如图 2-49 所示。

1. Operation Indicating Equipment

Operation indicating equipment is also called principle computer, operation indicating computer, controlling display computer, monitoring computer and so on. The operating and indicating parts are installed in the operation room.

2. Interlocking Computer

Interlocking computer is also called sub computer and is installed in the machinery room of the station signal building. It is the core of the interlocking system and must have "fault safety" function.

3. Input/Output Equipment

Input/output equipment usually consists of relay circuit and driving acquisition circuit. Relay circuit is based on signal machine lighting circuit, point switch controlling circuit of 6502 electric interlocking. Driving acquisition circuit is called driving acquisition machine, execution indicating machine and so on.

Electric repair computer is specially set for electric repair personnel. Its major tasks are station status follow and replay, operation order record and fault record, input/output fault positioning and so on.

Ports between computer interlocking system and train control center of CTCS 2, TDCS station computer and CTC station autonomous computer are set.

Key Point 3: DS6-K5B Computer Interlocking System Application

Typical station example with DS6-K5B

下面以排列进路为例进行说明。

办理从东郊方面至 5G 的接车进路，顺序单击 XD 信号机的红色圆形表示灯和 S5 信号机的红色圆形表示灯即可。

办理从 4G 向北京方面的发车进路，顺序单击 S4 信号机的红色圆形表示灯和 XF 信号机的红色圆形表示灯。

从北京方面向天津方面的下行正线通过进路，顺序单击 X 进站信号机旁边的 XTA 按钮和 SF 信号机的红色圆形表示灯。

办理 D15 至 4G 的调车进路，顺序单击 D15 信号机的信号名和 S4 信号机的信号名。

办理从 S5 至东郊方向进站信号机的调车进路，顺序单击 S5 信号机的信号名和 XD 信号机旁蓝色的调车终端按钮。

computer interlocking system is used in the textbook and operation interface shown in Figure 2-49.

The following examples are route arrangement.

Processing receiving route from east suburb to 5G, single click red round light of XD signal machine and red round light of S5 signal machine in order.

Processing departure route from 4G to Beijing West station, single click red round light of S4 signal machine and red round light of XF signal machine in order.

Processing down link main track passing route from Beijing to Tianjin, single click XTA button by X arrival signal machine and red round light of SF signal machine in order.

Processing shunting route from D15 to 4G, single click signal name of D15 signal machine and signal name of S4 signal machine in order.

Processing shunting route of the arrival signal machine from S5 to east suburb, single click signal name of S5 signal machine and blue shunting terminal button by XD signal machine in order.

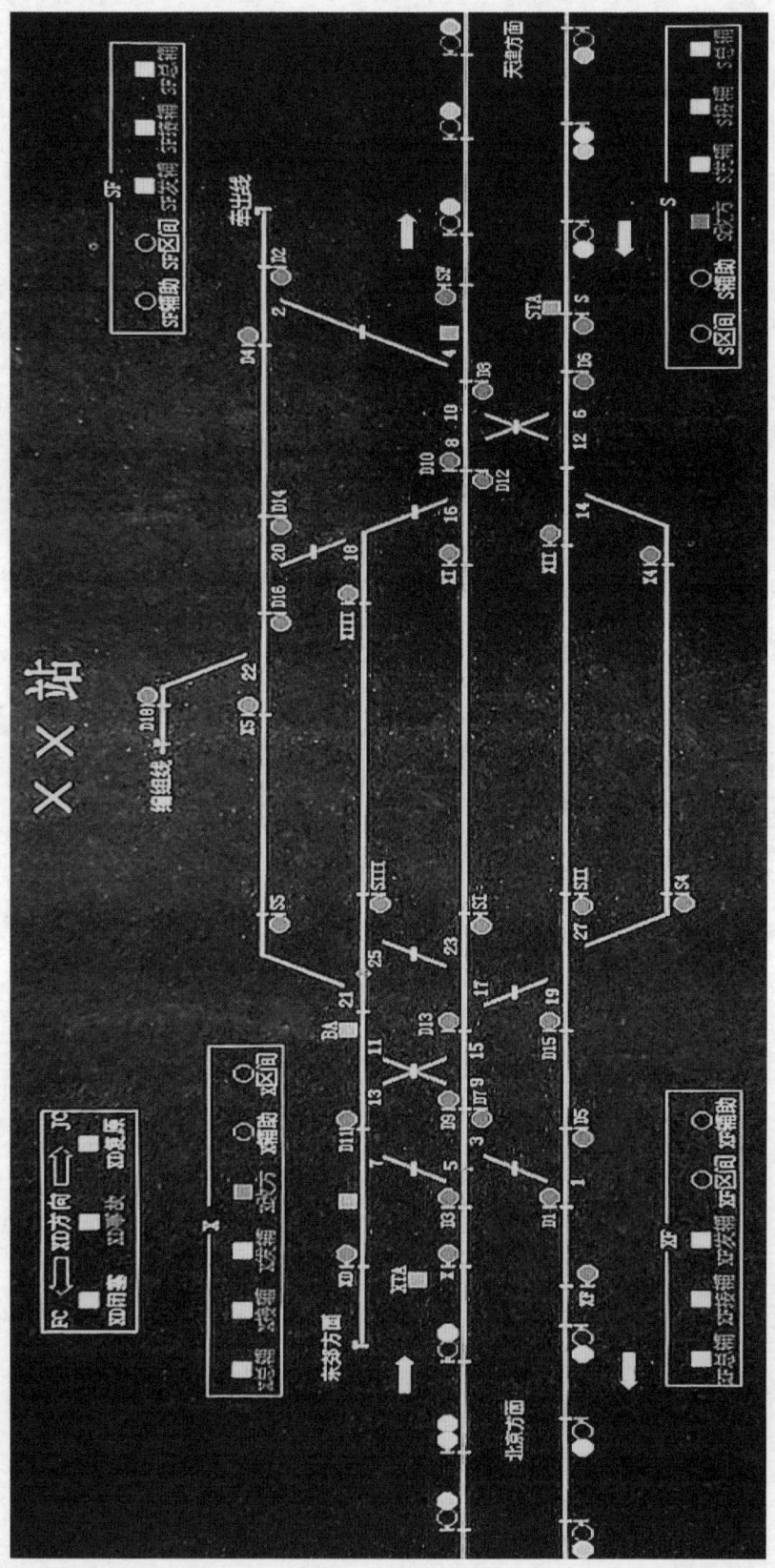

图 2-49 DS6-K5B 型计算机联锁系统应用

Figure 2-49 DS-6-K5B Computer Interlocking Operation Interface

学习笔记
Study Notes

模块三 课堂练习

分小组在 DS6 系列计算机联锁仿真软件上正常办理接发车作业、调车作业。

Module 3　In-class Exercises

Processing normal departure and shunting in DS6 series computer interlocking simulation software in groups.

课堂练习
In-class Exercises

模块四 课后拓展

参观实训室,比较计算机联锁与6502的异同。

Module 4 After-class Activity

Visit the training room and compare similarities and differences between computer interlocking and 6502.

项目三　区间闭塞设备

Project 3　Section Block Equipment

任务一　认识闭塞

Task 1　Understand Block

模块一　学前准备

Module 1　Preparation before Class

了解列车在区间（闭塞分区）内运行的特点是什么以及闭塞的基本概念。

Understand train running features in the section（block section） and the basic concept of block.

课前学习笔记
Study Notes before Class

| 模块二　课堂学习 | Module 2　In-class Learning |

| 知识点一：区间的概念 | Key Point 1：Concept of Section |

区间的定义：铁路线路以车站（线路所）为分界点划分为若干站间（所间）区间，如图 3-1 所示。

自动闭塞通过信号机将一个站间区间划分为若干闭塞分区，如图 3-2 所示。

区间（闭塞分区）界限：
进站信号机柱或站界标的中心线。
自动闭塞通过信号机柱中心线。

Definition of section：Rail track is divided into several block sections by stations（block post）, as shown in Figure 3-1.

Automatic block passing signal machine divides a section into several block sections, as shown in Figure 3-2.

Section（block section）boundary：
Center line of arrival signal machine or station boundary mark.
Automatic block passing signal machine post center line.

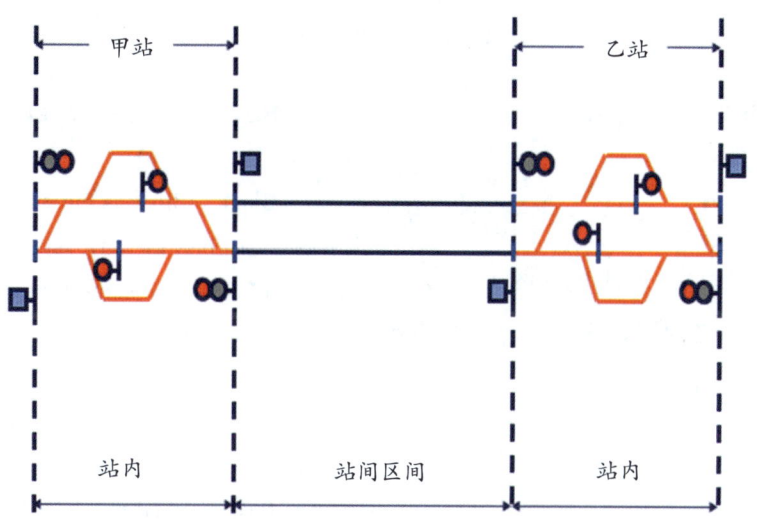

甲站：A station　乙站：B station　站内：in station　站间区间：section between stations

图 3-1　站间区间

Figure 3-1　Section between Stations

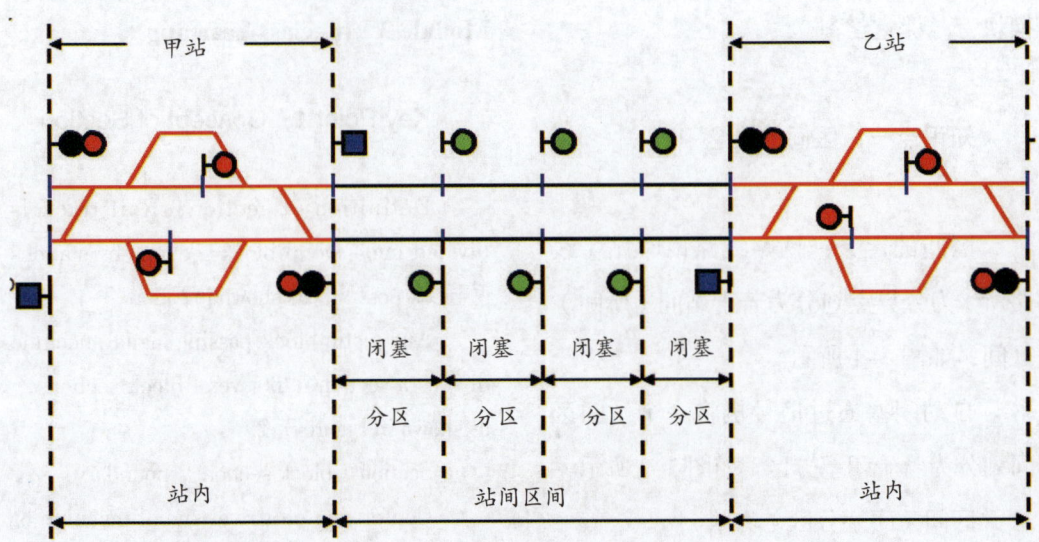

甲站：station A　乙站：station B　站内：in station　闭塞分区：block section
站间区间：section between stations

图 3-2　闭塞分区
Figure 3-2　Block Section

知识点二：闭塞的概念

闭塞：为保证列车在区间的运行安全，在同一区间（或闭塞分区），同一时间只准许一列列车运行的方法称为行车闭塞法，简称闭塞。

闭塞设备：用以完成闭塞作用的设备。

组织区间行车的基本方法如图 3-3 所示。

（1）时间间隔法：列车按照事先规定好的时间由车站发车，使前行列车和追踪列车之间必须保持一定时间间隔的行车方法。

（2）空间间隔法：将铁路线路划分为若干个段落（区间或闭塞分区），在每

Key Point 2：Concept of Block

Block：Block is the train running block method to permit only one train running in the section at the same time to ensure train running safety. The method is called block in short.

Block equipment：equipment used for block.

Basic method of organizing train running in sections is as shown in Figure 3-3.

（1）Time interval method：Trains depart at preset time to ensure certain time interval between the preceding train and the following train.

（2）Space interval method：Divide the railway into several parts (sections or block sections). Only one train runs in a section at the same time. The way to keep certain distance

个段落内同时只准许一列列车运行，这样使前行列车和追踪列车之间必须保持一定距离的行车方法称作空间间隔法。这种行车方法能严格地将列车分隔在两个空间，可以有效地防止列车追尾和正面冲突等事故的发生，确保列车运行安全。

between the preceding train and the following train is called space interval method. In this way, trains are strictly separated in two spaces to prevent rear-end collision or front collision to ensure safety.

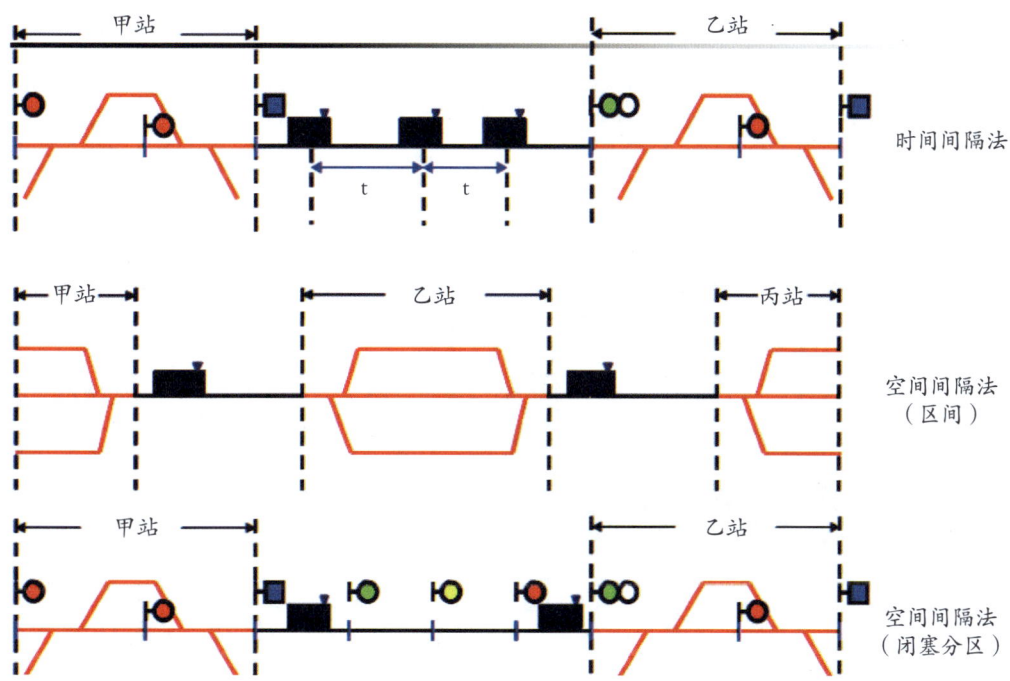

甲站：station A　乙站：station B　丙站：station C
时间间隔法：time interval method　空间间隔法（区间）：space interval method (section)
空间间隔法（闭塞分区）：space interval method (block section)

图 3-3　闭塞分类

Figure 3-3　Types of Block

学习笔记
Study Notes

模块三　课堂练习

练习1：根据已学知识说明列车在区间运行的特点。

练习2：列车在区间运行按照什么规律去组织运行？这样做的好处是什么？

练习3：区间行车的组织方法都有哪些？各自有什么优缺点？

Module 3　In-class Exercises

Exercise 1: Explain features of train running in sections.

Exercise 2: What are the rules of organizing train running in sections? What are the advantages?

Exercise 3: What are the organizing methods of train running in sections? What are their advantages and disadvantages?

课堂练习
In-class Exercises

模块四　课后拓展

简要说明闭塞对于行车的意义是什么,并且用作图的方式表现闭塞。

Module 4　After-class Activity

Explain the meaning of block for train running briefly, and represent it as a graph.

After-class Activity

任务二 半自动闭塞设备运用

Task 2　Application of Semi-automatic Block Equipment

模块一　学前准备

Module 1　Preparation before Class

查阅资料,简要说明半自动闭塞设备的特点。

Search information and briefly explain the features of semi-automatic block equipment.

课前学习笔记
Study Notes before Class

模块二 课堂学习

知识点一：半自动闭塞设备特点

1. 半自动闭塞的定义

人工办理闭塞手续，是凭出站信号机或线路所通过信号机显示的允许运行的信号发车，出站信号机自动关闭，列车出站后，区间自动转为闭塞状态的闭塞方法。如图 3-4 所示。

Module 2　In-class Learning

Key Point 1: Features of Semi-automatic Block Equipment

1. Definition of Semi-automatic Block

Block manually, train departs on the permission signal of the departure signal machine or track passing signal machine. Departure signal machine closes automatically, the section automatically is closed after train departure. See Figure 3-4.

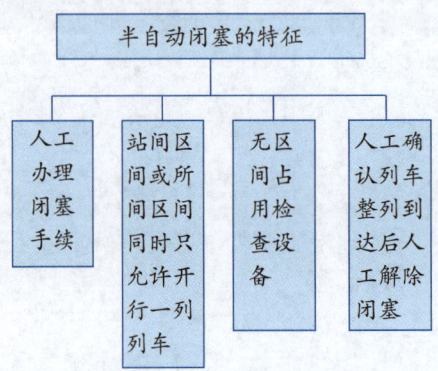

人工办理闭塞手续：manual block
站间区间或所间区间同时只允许开行一列列车：
only one train can run in sections between stations or block sections between posts
无区间占用检查设备：no occupation check equipment
人工确认列车整列到达后人工解除闭塞：manually clear block after confirming the whole arrived

图 3-4　半自动闭塞的特征

Figure 3-4　Features of Semi-automatic Block

列车占用区间的凭证是出站信号机或通过信号机的进行显示。

Section train occupation certificate is displayed by departure signal machine or passing signal machine.

2. 半自动闭塞的分类

如图 3-5 所示。

2. Classification of Semi-automatic Block

See Figure 3–5.

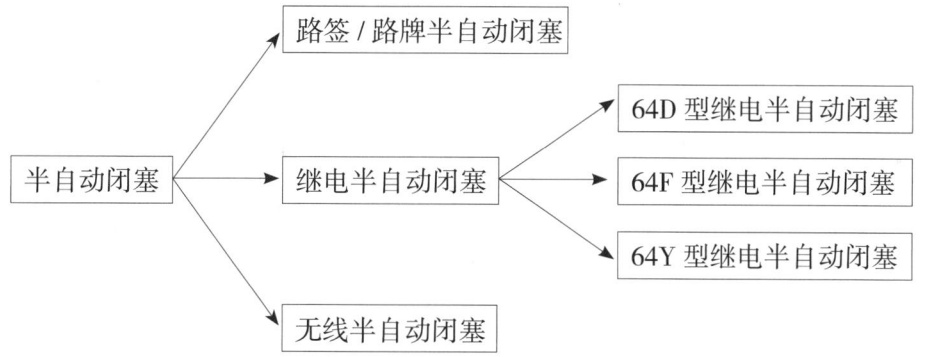

半自动闭塞：semi-automatic block
路签/路牌半自动闭塞：train staff/guide post semi-automatic block
继电半自动闭塞：relay semi-automatic block
64D 型继电半自动闭塞：64D relay semi-automatic block
64F 型继电半自动闭塞：64F relay semi-automatic block
64Y 型继电半自动闭塞：64Y relay semi-automatic block
无线半自动闭塞：wireless semi-automatic block

图 3-5 半自动闭塞的分类

Figure 3–5 Classification of Semi-automatic Block

知识点二：半自动闭塞设备以及系统构成

1. 半自动闭塞主要设备

（1）闭塞机。

采用半自动闭塞的区间两端车站上各设一台闭塞机、一段轨道电路和出站信号机。它们之间用通信线路相连接，用来控制出站信号机并实现在相邻车站之间办理闭塞。如图 3-6 所示。

Key Point 2：Semi-automatic Block Equipment and System Composition

1. Major Semi-automatic Block Equipment

（1）Block machine.

One block machine, a track circuit and signal machine are set at the both stations of the semi-automatic block section. The equipment is connected with communication link to control departure signal machine to process block in neighboring stations. See Figure 3–6.

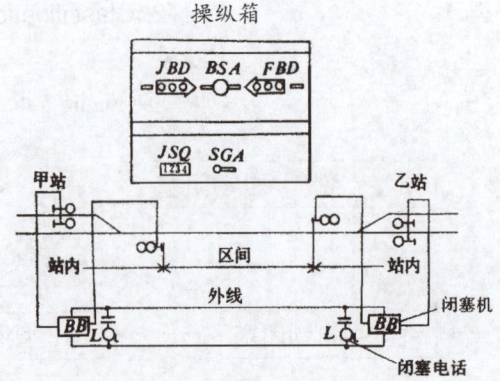

甲站：station A　乙站：station B　站内：in station　区间：section　外线：exterior line
闭塞机：block machine　闭塞电话：block telephone　操纵箱：the operation box
闭塞按钮：block button（BSA）　接车表示灯：train receiving indicating light（JBD）
事故按钮：accident button（SGA）　计数器：counter（JSQ）
发车表示灯：departure indicating light（FBD）

图 3-6　半自动闭塞原理

Figure 3-6　Semi-automatic Block Principle

（2）出站信号机。

出站信号机是指示列车能否由车站开往区间的信号机。它受到闭塞机和车站联锁设备的双重控制。如图3-7所示。

（2）Departure signal machine.

Departure signal machine is to indicate if the train can run from station to section. It is double controlled by block machine and station interlocking equipment. See Figure 3-7.

图 3-7　出站信号机

Figure 3-7　Departure Signal Machine

（3）轨道电路。

轨道电路应设在车站进站信号机内适当地点，用以监督列车的出发和到达，并使双方闭塞机的接发车表示灯有相应的表示。如图 3-8 所示。

（3）Track circuit.

Track circuit is set in a proper position in station arrival signal machine to monitor the departure and arrival of trains and make receiving-departure indicating lights at the both block machines display correspondingly. See Figure 3-8.

图 3-8 轨道电路

Figure 3-8　Track Circuit

2. 64D 型单线半自动闭塞设备

如图 3-9 所示。

2. 64D Single Line Semi-automatic Block Equipment

See Figure 3-9.

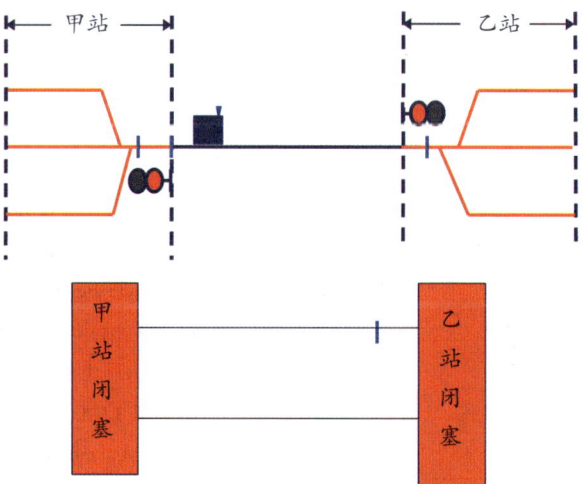

甲：A　乙：B　站闭塞：station block

图 3-9　64D 型单线半自动闭塞设备

Figure 3-9　64D Single Line Semi-automatic Block Equipment

知识点三：半自动闭塞办理方法

Key Point 3: Processing Method of Semi-automatic Block

1. 正常办理

如表 3-1 所示。

1. Normal Processing

See Chart 3-1.

表 3-1　正常办理流程
Chart 3-1　Normal Processing Procedure

甲站（发车站） station A (departure station)	乙站（接车站） station B (receiving station)
1. 车站值班员用闭塞电话请求发车 1. station attendant applies for departure by block telephone	2. 车站值班员同意接车 2. station attendant agrees with receiving
3. 按压 BSA，FBD 亮黄灯，DL 响 3. press BSA, FBD displays yellow light, DL rings	
	4. JBD 亮黄灯，DL 响 4. JBD displays yellow light, DL rings
	5. 按压 BSA，JBD 亮绿灯 5. press BSA, JBD displays green light
6. FBD 亮绿灯，DL 响 6. FBD displays green light, DL rings	
7. 开放出站信号机，列车出发进入发车轨道电路区段，FBD 亮红灯 7. open departure signal machine, trains departs and enters departure track circuit section, FBD displays red light	
	8. JBD 亮红灯，DL 响 8. JBD displays red light, DL rings
	9. 开放进站信号机，列车到达进入接车轨道电路区段，FBD 和 JBD 均亮红灯 9. open arrival signal machine, train arrives at receiving track circuit section, FBD and JBD display red light
	10. 按压 FUA，FBD 和 JBD 红灯熄灭 10. press FUA, red lights on FBD and JBD are off
11. FBD 红灯熄灭，DL 响 11. red light on FBD is off, DL rings	

2. 取消闭塞

如表 3-2 所示。

2. Clear Block

See Chart 3-2.

表 3-2 取消闭塞流程
Chart 3-2 Procedure of Block Clear

发车站出站信号机 departure signal machine at the departure station	双方站闭塞表示灯 block indicating light in both stations	发车站操作 operation at departure station	操作结果 result
关闭 off	黄 yellow	按压 FUA press FUA	双方站闭塞表示灯熄灭，闭塞设备复原 block indicating lights in both stations are off, block equipment recover
关闭 off	绿 green	按压 FUA press FUA	双方站闭塞表示灯熄灭，闭塞设备复原 block indicating lights in both stations are off, block equipment recover
开放 open	绿 green	关闭信号，解锁发车进路，按压 FUA signal off, unlock departure route, press FUA	双方站闭塞表示灯熄灭，闭塞设备复原 block indicating lights in both stations are off, block equipment recover

学习笔记

Study Notes

模块三　课堂练习

练习1：根据所学知识说明半自动闭塞的特点。

练习2：简要说明半自动闭塞的主要设备有哪些。

练习3：简述半自动闭塞的办理方法。

Module 3　In-class Exercises

Exercise 1：Explain features of semi-automatic block based on what you have learned.

Exercise 2：List major semi-automatic block equipment briefly.

Exercise 3：Explain semi-automatic block processing methods briefly.

课堂练习
In-class Exercises

模块四 课后拓展

通过学习和查阅资料说明半自动闭塞的优缺点以及实用情况。

Module 4 After-class Activity

Explain advantages, disadvantages, and application status of semi-automatic block through learning and information search.

After-class Activity

任务三 自动闭塞设备运用

Task 3　Automatic Block Equipment Application

模块一　学前准备

Module 1　Preparation before Class

查阅资料，了解什么是自动闭塞。

Search information to understand automatic block.

课前学习笔记
Study Notes before Class

模块二 课堂学习

知识点一：自动闭塞设备的特点

定义：将一个区间划分为若干个闭塞分区，根据列车运行和闭塞分区状态，自动变换通过信号机的显示，司机凭信号显示行车的闭塞方法进行操作。

分类如图 3-10 所示。

Module 2　In-class Learning

Key Point 1：Features of Automatic Block Equipment

Definition：Divide a section into several block sections. Drivers operate based on the automatic signal display on the basis of train running and block section status.

Classification as shown in Figure 3-10.

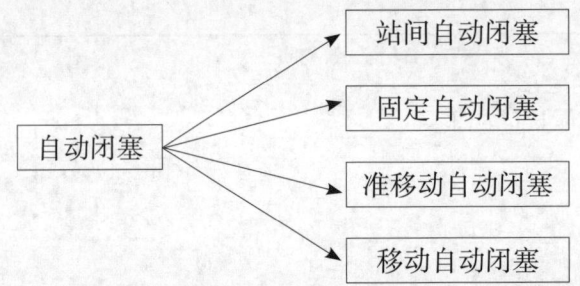

自动闭塞：automatic block　站间自动闭塞：automatic block between stations
固定自动闭塞：fixed automatic block　准移动自动闭塞：quasi-moving block
移动自动闭塞：mobile automatic block

图 3-10　自动闭塞的分类

Figure 3-10　Classification of Automatic Block

特征如图 3-11 所示。

（1）有闭塞分区占用检查设备（轨道电路）。

（2）站间能实现列车追踪。

（3）办理发车进路时自动实现闭塞。

Features as shown in Figure 3-11.

（1）With block section occupation check equipment (rail circuit).

（2）Train trace between sections.

（3）Automatic block when processing train departure route.

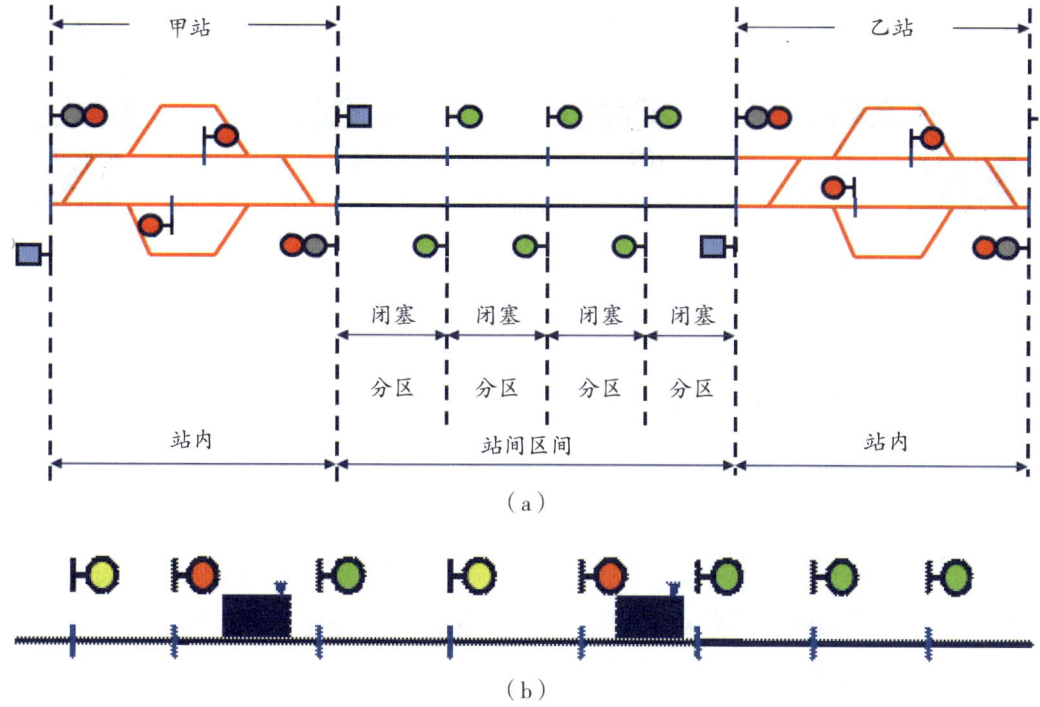

甲站：station A　乙站：station B　站内：in station　闭塞分区：block section
站间区间：section between stations

图 3-11　自动闭塞特征
Figure 3-11　Features of Automatic Block

知识点二：自动闭塞的分类

1. 按信号显示分类

三显示自动闭塞、四显示自动闭塞。

三显示自动闭塞，如图 3-12 所示。

（1）信号显示。

红、黄、绿。

（2）接近、离去区段。

进站信号机外方的两个闭塞分区，分别为一接近、二接近；发车站界外方两个闭塞分区，分别为一离去、二离去。

Key Point 2: Classification of Automatic Block

1. Classification by Signal Display

Triple display of automatic block and quadruple display of automatic block.

Triple display of automatic block as shown in Figure 3-12.

（1）Signal display.

Red, yellow, green.

（2）Approaching and leaving sections.

The two block sections outside the arrival signal machine are approaching section 1 and 2; the two block sections outside the departure stations are called departure section 1 and 2.

·123·

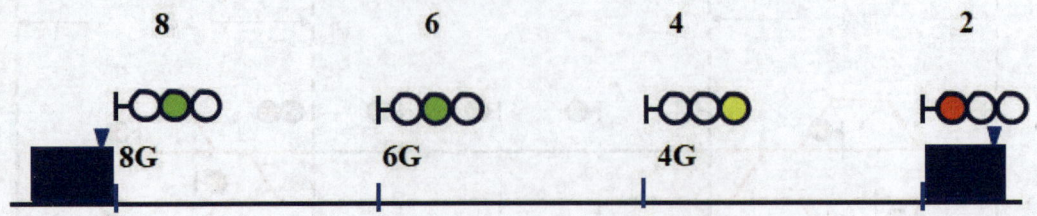

图 3-12 三显示自动闭塞

Figure 3-12　Triple Display Automatic Block

四显示自动闭塞，如图 3-13 所示。

（1）信号显示。

红、黄、绿黄、绿。

（2）接近、离去区段。

一接近、二接近、三接近。

一离去、二离去、三离去。

Quadruple display automatic block as shown in Figure 3-13.

（1）Signal display.

Red, yellow, greenish yellow, green.

（2）Approaching, leaving section.

Approaching 1, 2 and 3.

Leaving 1, 2 and 3.

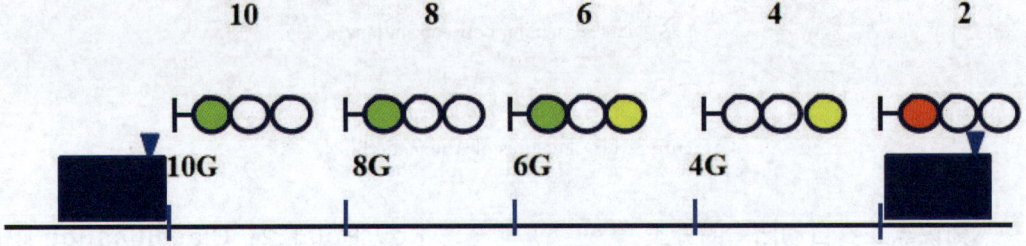

图 3-13 四显示自动闭塞

Figure 3-13　Quadruple Display Automatic Block

2. 按行车组织分类

单线、双线单向、双线双向自动闭塞。

2. Classification by Traffic Organizing

Single line, dual line single direction, dual line dual direction automatic block.

学习笔记

Study Notes

模块三　课堂练习

练习1：简要说明自动闭塞设备的特点有哪些。

练习2：自动闭塞分类有哪些。

练习3：三显示自动闭塞、四显示自动闭塞的区别是什么？

Module 3　In-class Exercises

Exercise 1：Briefly explain the features of automatic block equipment.

Exercise 2：Classifications of automatic block.

Exercise 3：What are the differences between triple and quadruple display automatic block?

课堂练习
In-class Exercises

模块四 课后拓展

收集资料了解当前铁路自动闭塞的应用和前景。

Module 4　After-class Activity

Search information to understand the application and prospect of railway automatic block.

任务四 移动闭塞设备识别

Task 4　Mobile Block Equipment Recognition

模块一　学前准备

Module 1　Preparation before Class

了解什么是移动闭塞设备、移动闭塞设备有何特点。

Understand mobile block equipment and its features.

 课前学习笔记
Study Notes before Class

模块二 课堂学习

知识点一：移动闭塞的定义

移动闭塞是相对于固定闭塞而言的。移动闭塞取消了以通过信号机分隔的固定闭塞分区，移动闭塞分区随着列车的行驶，不断地向前移动和调整。

移动闭塞方式是在列车运行中自动调整间隔，使两列车之间的间隔最小，从而提高了区间内的行车密度，大大提高区段的通过能力。

知识点二：移动闭塞的基本要素和特点

1. 移动闭塞的基本要素

（1）列车定位：能计算出后行列车距前行列车尾部距离或距进站信号点的距离。

（2）安全距离：附加在列车常用制动距离上的一段安全余量，如图 3-14 所示。

（3）目标点：列车运行的行车凭证。

Module 2　In-class Learning

Key Point 1：Definition of Mobile Block

Mobile block is defined compared with fixed block. Fixed block sections separated by passing signal machines are canceled, and the mobile block sections move and adjust with train running.

Mobile block method raises train running intensity in sections by automatic adjustment and reducing of intervals to improve section passing capacity greatly.

Key Point 2：Basic Elements and Features of Mobile Block

1. Basic Elements of Mobile Block

（1）Train positioning：calculating the distance between the following train to the rear of the preceding train or the arrival signal point.

（2）Safe distance：a safety margin added to the train normal braking distance, as shown in figure 3-14.

（3）Target point: train running certificate.

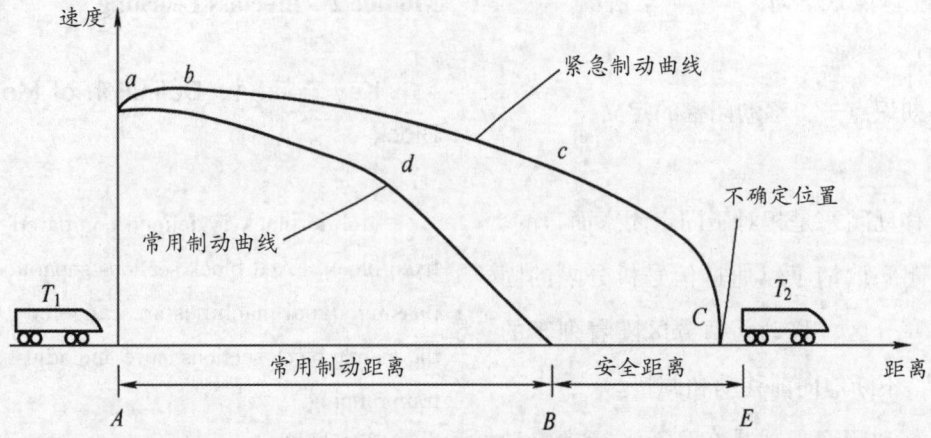

速度：speed　常用制动曲线：normal braking curve　常用制动距离：normal braking distance
紧急制动曲线：emergency braking curve　不确定位置：uncertain position
安全距离：safe distance　距离：distance

图 3-14　安全距离示意图
Figure 3-14　Safe Distance Diagram

2. 移动闭塞系统的特点

（1）没有固定的闭塞分区，列车间隔是动态的。

（2）列车间隔：制动距离 + 安全距离。

（3）制动的起点和终点是动态的。

（4）可实现较小的列车间隔。

2. Features of Mobile Block System

（1）No fixed block section, dynamic train intervals.

（2）Train intervals: braking distance + safety distance.

（3）Braking starting and ending points are dynamic.

（4）Realizing shorter train intervals.

学习笔记
Study Notes

模块三　课堂练习

练习1：什么是移动闭塞?

练习2：移动闭塞的基本要素是什么?

练习3：移动闭塞系统的特点有哪些?

Module 3　In-class Exercises

Exercise 1：What is mobile block?

Exercise 2：What are the basic elements of mobile block?

Exercise 3：What are the features of mobile block system?

课堂练习
In-class Exercises

模块四　课后拓展

收集资料，简要说明移动闭塞系统的优势是什么，以及在未来的应用前景怎么样。

Module 4　After-class Activity

Search information to explain advantages of mobile block system and its application prospect.

项目四 列车运行控制系统（CTCS）

Project 4　China Train Control System（CTCS）

任务一　机车信号认知

Task 1　Understand Locomotive Signal

模块一　学前准备

Module1　Preparation before Class

观察铁路线路中的各种信号和信号设备，挑选出你认为属于机车信号的照片。

Observe signals and signal equipment in railway route and pick those you think as locomotive signals.

课前学习笔记
Study Notes before Class

模块二 课堂学习

知识点一：机车信号

1. 什么是机车信号

机车信号又称机车自动信号，设在机车司机控制室内，用于自动反映运行条件，指示机车运行。

2. 机车信号的作用

如图 4-1 所示。

Module 2　In-class Learning

Key Point 1：Locomotive Signal

1. What is Locomotive Signal

Locomotive signal is also called locomotive automatic signal and is set in the driver's room of the locomotive to reflect operating conditions and indicate train operation automatically.

2. Function of Locomotive Signal

See Figure 4-1.

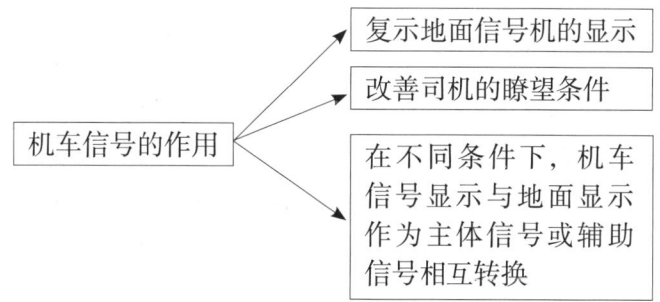

机车信号的作用：function of locomotive signal
复示地面信号机的显示：display of repeating ground signal machine
改善司机的瞭望条件：improve driver's observing condition
在不同条件下，机车信号显示与地面显示作为主体信号或辅助信号相互转换：under different conditions, locomotive signal display and ground display exchange as main signal or auxiliary signal

图 4-1　机车信号的作用
Figure 4-1　Function of Locomotive Signal

3. 机车信号的分类

如表 4-1 所示。

3. Classification of Locomotive Signal

See Chart 4-1.

表 4-1 机车信号的分类

Chart 4-1　Classification of Locomotive Signal

按照机车接收地面信息的时机分类 classification by the timing of locomotive receiving ground information	点式机车信号 intermittent locomotive signal
	接近连续式机车信号 approaching continuous locomotive signal
	连续式机车信号 continuous locomotive signal
按照机车接收地面信息的特征分类 classification by features of locomotive receiving ground information	移频制式机车信号 frequency shift system locomotive signal
	交流计数电码制式机车信号 AC counting coded system locomotive signal

知识点二：机车信号设备

Key Point 2：Locomotive Signal Equipment

1. 机车信号的设备组成

机车信号的设备组成，包含地面设备和机车设备两部分，如图 4-2 所示。

1. Equipment Composition of Locomotive Signal

Equipment composition of locomotive signal includes ground equipment and locomotive equipment, as shown in Figure 4-2.

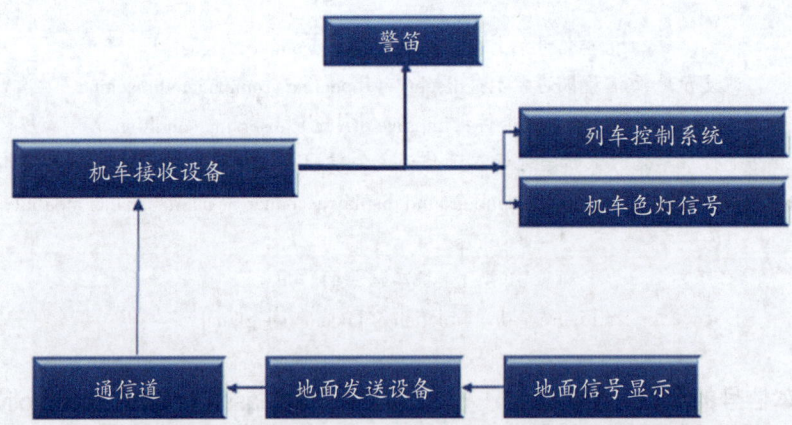

警笛：siren　机车接收设备：locomotive receiving equipment　列车控制系统：train control system
机车色灯信号：locomotive color light signal　通信道：communication channel
地面发送设备：ground sending equipment　地面信号显示：ground signal display

图 4-2　机车信号的设备组成

Figure 4-2　Equipment Composition of Locomotive Signal

2. 机车信号的显示方式

机车信号有 8 种显示方式：绿灯（L）、绿黄灯（LU）、黄灯（U）、黄2灯（U2）、红黄灯（HU）、双黄灯（UU）、红灯（H）、白灯（B）。

如图 4-3 所示。

2. Display Way of Locomotive Signal

Eight display ways of locomotive signal: green light (L), greenish-yellow light (LU), yellow light (U), two yellow light (U2), reddish-yellow light (HU), dual yellow light (UU), red light (H), white light (B).

As illustrated in Figure 4-3.

图 4-3　机车信号的显示方式

Figure 4-3　Display of Locomotive Signal

学习笔记

Study Notes

模块三　课堂练习

Module 3　In-class Exercises

练习 1：找出下列图片中机车信号的机车设备在哪里。

Exercise 1：Find out the locomotive equipment of locomotive signals in the picture.

练习 2：请写出下列机车信号从上到下的显示意义。

Exercise 2：Write down the meanings of the locomotive signals from top to bottom.

灯色 light color_____，显示意义 meaning_____

灯色 light color_____，显示意义 meaning_____

灯色 light color_____，显示意义 meaning_____

灯色 light color_____，显示意义 meaning_____

灯色 light color_____，显示意义 meaning_____

 灯色 light color＿＿＿＿，显示意义 meaning＿＿＿＿

 灯色 light color＿＿＿＿，显示意义 meaning＿＿＿＿

 灯色 light color＿＿＿＿，显示意义 meaning＿＿＿＿

课堂练习
In-class Exercises

模块四　课后拓展

如果你是一名信号员，请尝试根据机车信号判断列车的运行条件，并且条理清晰地说出判断理由。

Module 4　After-class Activity

If you are a signal man, try to judge train operating conditions based on the locomotive signals and state your reasons clearly.

After-class Activity

任务二 列车运行控制系统(CTCS)认知

Task 2　Understand China Train Control System (CTCS)

模块一　学前准备

请观察和思考高铁的运行。高铁的运行是用什么进行控制的？请简要写出你认为的列车运行控制过程。

Module 1　Preparation before Class

Observe and think about high speed train operation. What is used for control? Write down the operation control process briefly.

课前学习笔记
Study Notes before Class

模块二　课堂学习

知识点一：列车运行控制系统（CTCS）的概念

1. 列车运行控制系统

列车运行控制系统是一套信号系统，其作用是对列车运行实现自动控制。

2. CTCS 的含义

CTCS 全称为 Chinese Train Control System，即中国列车控制系统。

3. 列车运行控制系统的控制对象

列车运行控制系统的控制对象主要是列车运行速度和列车之间的距离。

4. 列车运行控制的基本过程

如图 4-4 所示。

Module 2　In-class Learning

Key Point 1: Concept of Chinese Train Control System (CTCS)

1. Train Operation Control System

Train operation control system is a set of signal system and is used for train automatic control.

2. Meaning of CTCS

The full name of CTCS is Chinese Train Control System.

3. The Controlled Objects of CTCS

Controlled objects of CTCS are train running speed and distances between trains.

4. The Basic Process of Train Operation Control

See Figure 4-4.

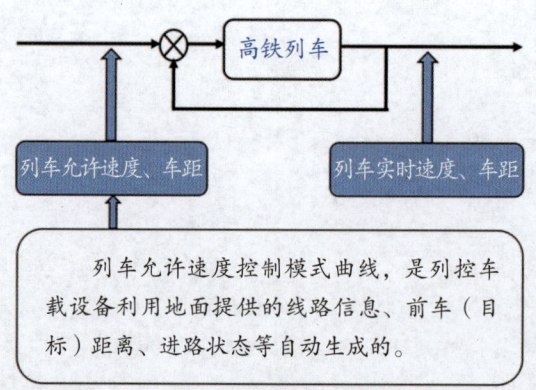

高铁列车：high speed train　列车允许速度、车距：permitted train speed and distance
列车实时速度、车距：real-time train speed and distance
列车允许速度控制模式曲线，是列控车载设备利用地面提供的线路信息、前车（目标）距离、进路状态等自动生成：permitted train speed control mode curve is automatically generated by the train control on board

equipment based on the route information, preceding (target) distance, route status provided by ground equipment

图 4-4 列车运行控制的基本过程

Figure 4-4　Basic Process of Train Operation Control

知识点二：列车运行控制系统（CTCS）的分级

CTCS 系统分为 CTCS-0 级、CTCS-1 级、CTCS-2 级、CTCS-3 级和 CTCS-4 级五个级别。如表 4-2 所示。

Key Point 2：Grading of CTCS

CTCS is divided into five grades: CTCS-0, CTCS-1, CTCS-2, CTCS-3 and CTCS-4. See Chart 4-2.

表 4-2　列车运行控制系统（CTCS）的分级

Chart 4-2　Grading of CTCS

CTCS 等级	CTCS-0 级	CTCS-1 级	CTCS-2 级	CTCS-3 级	CTCS-4 级
地面设备组成	轨道电路	轨道电路、应答器及 LEU	车站列控中心、轨道电路、应答器及 LEU	车站列控中心、GSM-R 地面设备、轨道电路、无线闭塞中心	车站列控中心、GSM-R 地面设备、无线闭塞中心
车载设备组成	通用机车信号、运行监控记录装置（LKJ）	主体机车信号、应答器信息接收模块、安全型运行监控记录装置	ATP（含机车信号、应答器信息接收功能）、LKJ	GSM-R 接收模块、ATP	GSM-R 接收模块、ATP
地对车信息传输	多信息轨道电路	多信息轨道电路+应答器	多信息轨道电路+应答器、数字轨道电路	无线通信双向信息传输	无线通信双向信息传输
适用区段	160 km/h 及以下	160 km/h 及以下	200～250 km/h 提速干线和高速新线	300～350 km/h 高速新线	特殊线路
对应欧洲标准			ETCS-1 级	ETCS-2 级	ETCS-3 级

CTCS 等级：CTCS grades　地面设备组成：composition of ground equipment　轨道电路：track circuit　应答器及 LEU：transponder and LEU　车站列控中心：station train control system　GSM-R 地面设备：GSM-R ground equipment　无线闭塞中心：wireless block center　车载设备组成：composition of on board equipment　通用机车信号：universal locomotive signal　运行监控记录装置（LKJ）：operation monitoring record device（LKJ）主体机车信号：main locomotive signal　应答器信息接收模块：transponder information receiving module　安全型运行监控记录装置：safe operation monitoring record device　ATP（含机车信号、应答器信息接收功能）：ATP（including locomotive signal, transponder information receiving function）GSM-R 接收模块：GSM-R receiving module　地对车信息传输：ground to train information transmission　多信息轨道电路：multiple information track circuit　应答器：transponder　数字轨道电路：digital track circuit　无线通信双向信息传输：wireless communication two-way information transmission　适用区段：applicable section　160 km/h 及以下：speed of 160 km/h and below　提速干线和高速新线：speed up main railways and high speed new railways　高速新线：high speed new railways　特殊线路：special railways　对应欧洲标准：corresponding European standard

知识点三：列车运行控制系统（CTCS）的分类

Key Point 3：Classification of CTCS

如图 4-5 所示。

See Figure 4-5.

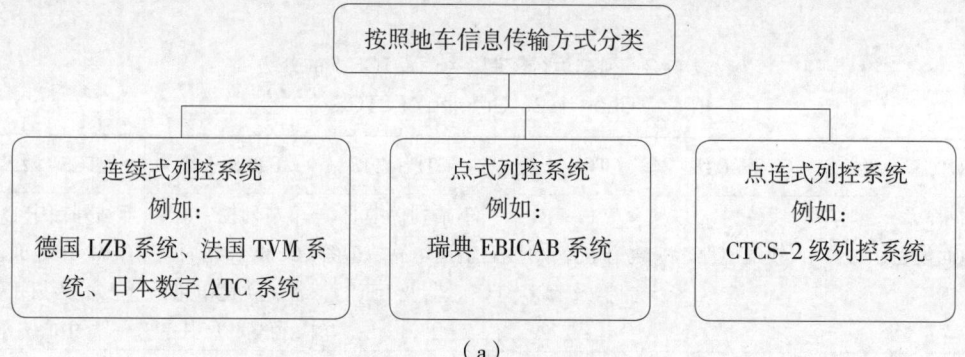

(a)

按照地车信息传输方式分类：classification by ground-train information transmission mode　连续式列控系统：continuous train control system　例如：for example　德国 LZB 系统：German LZB system　法国 TVM 系统：French TVM system　日本数字 ATC 系统：Japanese digital ATC system　点式列控系统：intermittent train control system　瑞典 EBICAB 系统：Swedish EBICAB system　点连式列控系统：intermittent-continuous train control system　CTCS-2 级列控系统：CTCS-2 train control system

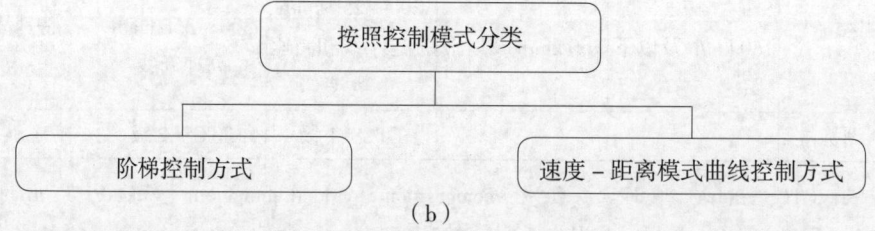

(b)

按照控制模式分类：classification by controlling mode　阶梯控制方式：ladder controlling mode　速度-距离模式曲线控制方式：speed-distance mode curve control

图 4-5　列车运行控制系统（CTCS）的分类

Figure 4-5　Classification of CTCS

知识点四：列车运行控制系统（CTCS）的构成

从系统功能的角度来看，列车运行控制系统包含三个子系统，即列车自动监控系统（ATS）、列车自动防护系统（ATP）和列车自动运行系统（ATO）。

从系统结构的角度来看，列车运行控制系统由车载子系统和地面子系统两大部分组成，如图4-6所示。

Key Point 4: Composition of CTCS

CTCS includes three subsystems in terms of system function, namely Automatic Train Supervision (ATS), Automatic Train Protection (ATP), and Automatic Train Operation (ATO).

In terms of system structure, CTCS consists of on board subsystem and ground subsystem, as shown in Figure 4-6.

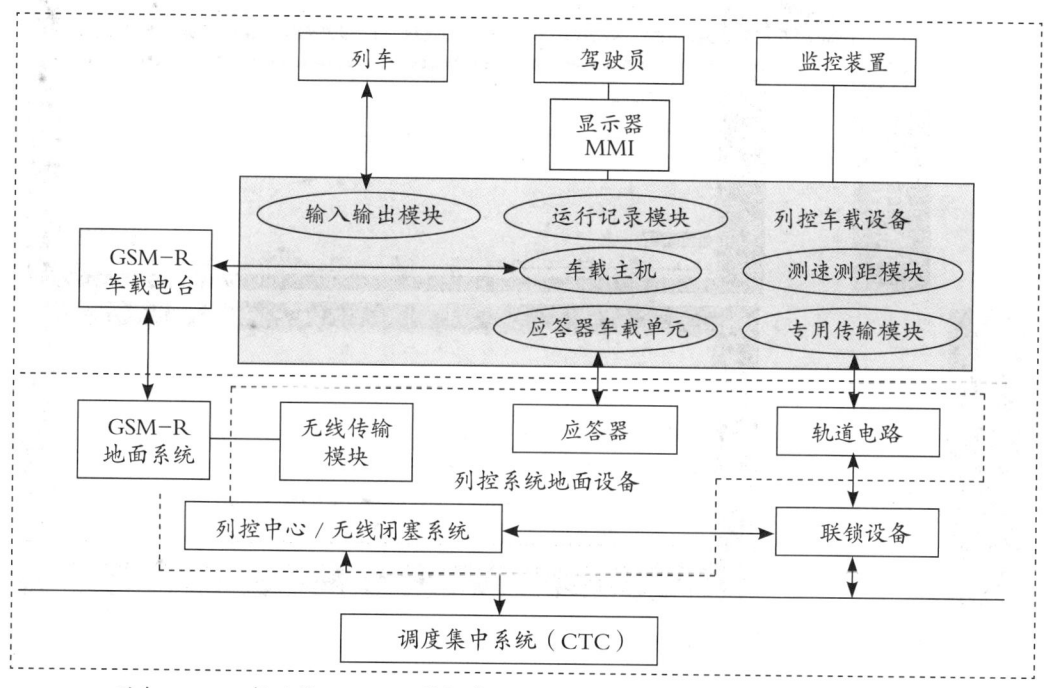

列车：train 驾驶员：driver 监控装置：supervision device 显示器MMI：display
GSM-R车载电台：GSM-R on board radio 输入输出模块：input and output module
运行记录模块：operation record module 车载主机：on board host computer
应答器车载单元：transponder on board unit 列控车载设备：train control on board equipment
测速测距模块：speed and distance measurement module 专用传输模块：specialized output module
GSM-R地面系统：GSM-R ground system 无线传输模块：wireless transmission module
应答器：transponder 轨道电路：track circuit 列控系统地面设备：train control system ground equipment
列控中心/无线闭塞系统：train control center/wireless block system 联锁设备：interlocking equipment
调度集中系统：centralized traffic control

图4-6 列车运行控制系统（CTCS）的构成
Figure 4-6 Composition of CTCS

知识点五：列车运行控制模式

Key Point 5：Train Operation Control Mode

列车运行控制模式主要有三种：一次连续模式、分级连续模式、阶梯模式，如图4-7所示。

There are three major train operation control modes: one-time continuous mode, grade continuous mode, ladder mode, as shown in figure 4-7.

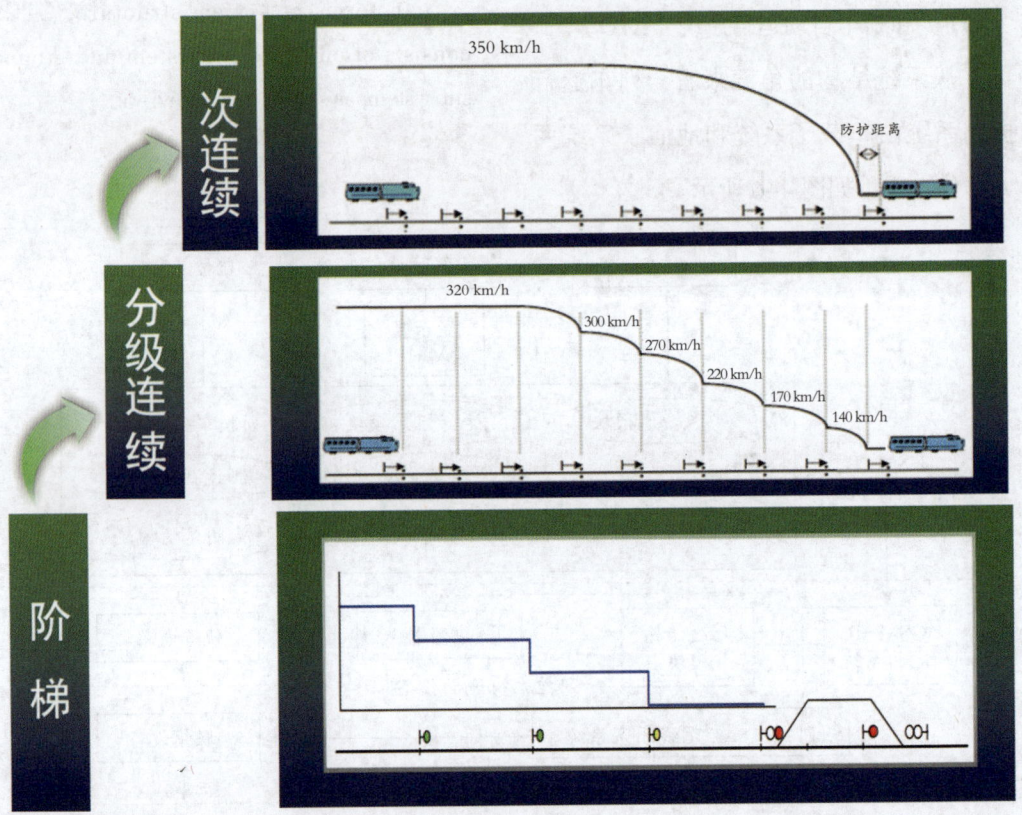

一次连续：one-time continuous 防护距离：protection distance 分级连续：grade continuous
阶梯：ladder

图4-7 列车运行控制模式

Figure 4-7 Train Operation Control Mode

学习笔记
Study Notes

模块三　课堂练习

练习1：CTCS系统分为CTCS-0级、CTCS-1级、CTCS-2级、CTCS-3级和CTCS-4级五个级别。每一个级别对应的列车运行状态分别是什么？

CTCS-0级：_____
CTCS-1级：_____
CTCS-2级：_____
CTCS-3级：_____
CTCS-4级：_____

练习2：根据如下示意图，讨论CTCS列车运行控制系统的特点。

Module 3　In-class Exercises

Exercise 1：CTCS is divided into five grades，CTCS-0，CTCS-1，CTCS-2，CTCS-3，CTCS-4. What are the corresponding train operation status of each grade?

Exercise 2：Discuss features of CTCS according to the following picture.

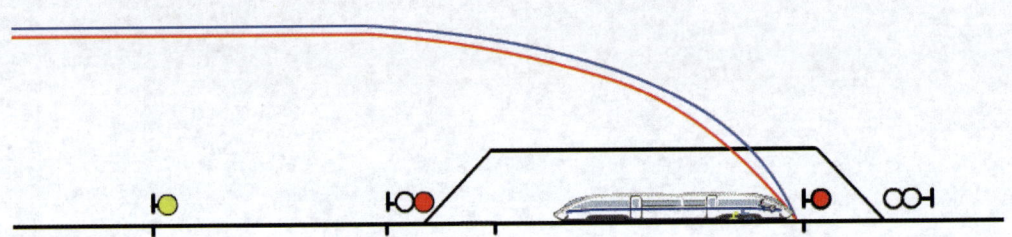

练习3：列车运行控制模式有一次连续模式、分级连续模式、阶梯模式三种。这三种控制模式有什么特点？

一次连续模式：_____
_____

Exercise 3：There are three train operation control modes：one-time continuous mode, sectional continuous mode and ladder mode. What are their features?

one-time continuous mode：_____

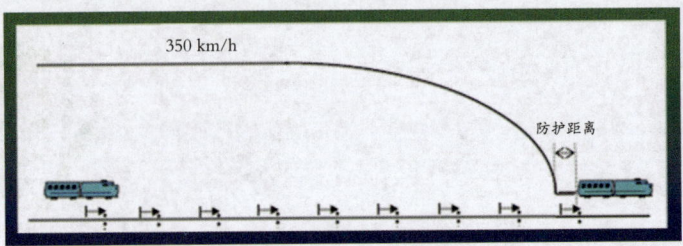

分级连续模式：_____　　　　grade continuous mode：_____

_____　　　　_____

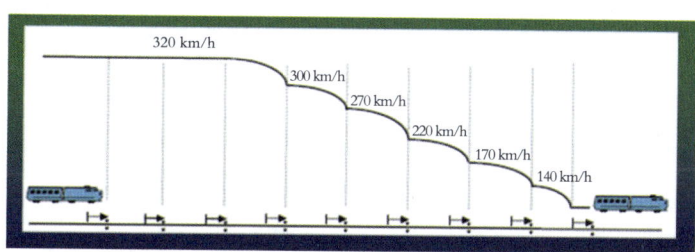

阶梯模式：_____　　　　ladder mode：_____

_____　　　　_____

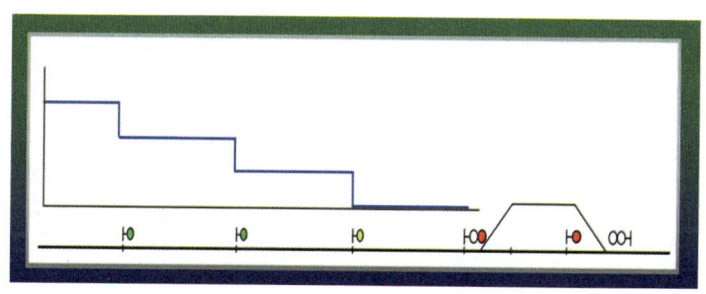

练习4：列车运行控制系统包含三个子系统。这三个子系统在列车运行控制过程中的功能分别是什么？

列车自动监控系统：_____

_____

列车自动防护系统：_____

_____

列车自动运行系统：_____

_____

Exercise 4：CTCS includes three sub systems. What are their functions?

ATS（Automatic Train Supervision）：

_____

_____

ATP（Automatic Train Protection）：

_____

_____

ATO（Automatic Train Operation）：

_____

_____

课堂练习
In-class Exercises

模块四　课后拓展

从世界范围来看，不同国家采用的列控系统是不同的，例如德国 LZB 系统、法国 TVM 系统、日本数字 ATC 系统、瑞典 EBICAB 系统、中国的 CTCS 系统等。请思考：世界各国所采用的列控系统有什么不同？

Module 4　After-class Activity

Train control systems vary in different countries all around the world, such as German LZB system, French TVM system, Japanese digital ATC system, Swedish EBICAB system and Chinese CTCS. What are the differences of the train control systems?

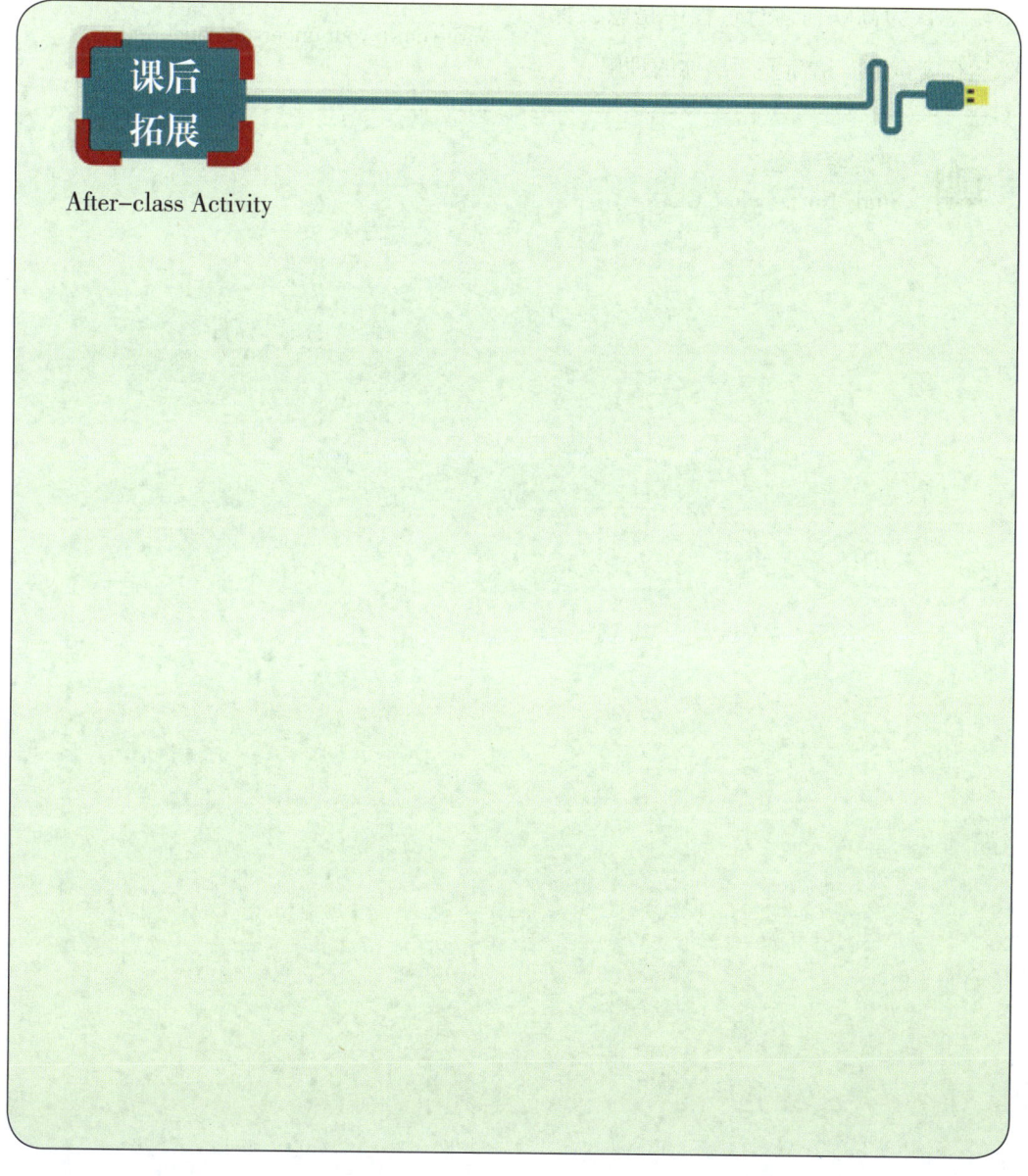

任务三 列车运行监控记录装置和列车超速防护系统

Task 3 Train Operation Supervision Record Device and Train Over-speed Protection System

模块一 学前准备

Module 1 Preparation before Class

你认为高铁在运行过程中是怎么保障运行安全的？请简要写出你的理解。

How to safeguard train operation safety? Write down your understanding briefly.

课前学习笔记
Study Notes before Class

模块二 课堂学习

知识点一：列车运行监控记录装置（LKJ-2000 型）

1. 什么是列车运行监控记录装置（LKJ-2000 型）

列车运行监控记录装置简称监控装置（LKJ），是中国自主研发的列车速度控制和运行过程记录的信号设备。

该装置在实现安全速度控制的同时，采集和记录与列车安全运行有关的各种机车运行状态信息，促进了机车运行管理的自动化。它是列车运行信息记录的黑匣子。

最高运行速度不超过 160 km/h 的列车，机车信号设备与列车运行监控记录装置结合使用，或采用列车超速防护系统。最高运行速度超过 160 km/h 的列车，应采用列车超速防护系统。

中国列车运行监控记录装置以 LKJ-2000 型为主。

2. 列车运行监控记录装置（LKJ-2000 型）的适用范围

适合于各型电力机车和内燃机车。
适应自动和半自动闭塞方式。
适应各种信号制式。
适合运行于不同速度等级的线路的各型旅客列车（包括动车组）及货物列车。
适合于调车机车。

Module 2 In-class Learning

Key Point 1: Train Operation Supervision Record Device (LKJ-2000)

1. What is Train Operation Supervision Record Device (LKJ-2000)

Train operation supervision record device is also called LKJ for short, and is the signal equipment for train speed control and operation process record developed independently by China.

The device collects and record locomotive operation status information related to train operation safety when controlling safety speed control, and it improves automatic locomotive operation management. It is the black box recording train operation information.

Locomotive signal equipment and train operation supervision record device are combined, or train over speed protection system is used for trains with the maximum speed of 160 km/h. Train over speed protection system is used for train with maximum speed over 160 km/h.

Main train operation supervision device in China is LKJ-2000.

2. Application Range of Train Operation Supervision Record Device (LKJ-2000)

Suit for various types of electric and diesel locomotive.

Suit for automatic and semi-automatic block mode.

Suit for various signal mode.

Suit for various types of passenger train (including CHR trains) and freight trains on routes of different speed grades.

Suit for shunting trains.

3. 列车运行监控记录装置（LKJ-2000型）的功能

如图4-8所示。

3. Functions of Train Operation Supervision Record Device (LKJ-2000)

See Figure 4-8.

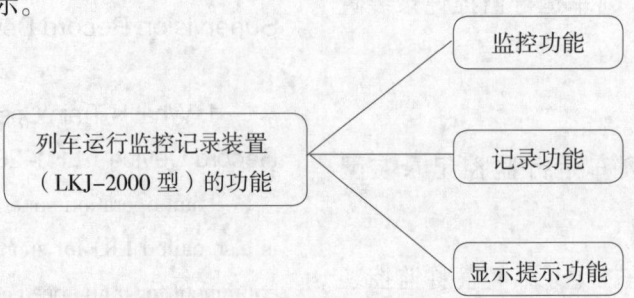

列车运行监控记录装置（LKJ-2000型）的功能：
functions of train operation supervision record device (LKJ-2000)
监控功能：supervision function　记录功能：record function　显示提示功能：display reminding function

图4-8　列车运行监控记录装置（LKJ-2000型）的功能
Figure 4-8　Functions of Train Operation Supervision Record Device (LKJ-2000)

4. 列车运行监控记录装置（LKJ-2000型）的系统构成

LKJ-2000型列车运行监控记录装置主要由主机、显示器、事故状态记录器、速度传感器、压力传感器以及双针速度表组成，如图4-9所示。

4. System Composition of Train Operation Supervision Record Device (LKJ-2000)

LKJ-2000 device consists of host computer, display, accident status recorder, speed senor, pressure sensor and twin-needles speedometer, as shown in Figure 4-9.

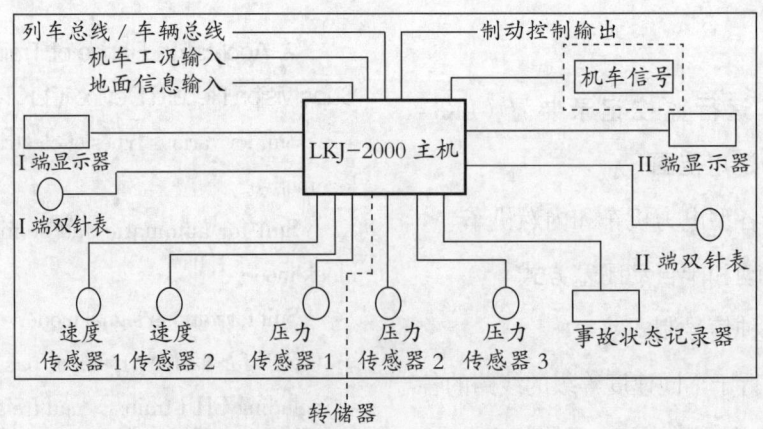

列车总线/车辆总线：train trunk　机车工况输入：locomotive operation condition input
地面信息输入：ground information input　I端显示器：terminal I display

Ⅰ端双针表：terminal Ⅰ twin-needles speedometer　速度传感器：speed sensor
压力传感器：pressure sensor　制动控制输出：brake control output　机车信号：locomotive signal
Ⅱ端显示器：terminal Ⅱ display　Ⅱ端双针表：terminal Ⅱ twin-needles speedometer
事故状态记录器：accident status recorder　LKJ-2000 主机：LKJ-2000 host computer　转储器：dumper

图 4-9　列车运行监控记录装置（LKJ-2000 型）的系统构成

Figure 4-9　System Composition of Train Operation Record Device（LKJ-2000）

知识点二：列车超速防护系统（ATP）

Key Point 2：Automatic Train Protection（ATP）

1. 什么是列车超速防护系统（ATP）

ATP 的核心是铁路信号速度化，要求信号信息具备明确的速度含义，并根据这些信息对列车运行速度进行实时的连续监控。

1. What is ATP

The core of ATP is train signal up and requires specific speed meaning of signal information and real time continuous supervision of train operation speed.

2. 列车超速防护系统（ATP）的分类

如图 4-10 所示。

2. Classification of Automatic Train Protection（ATP）

See Figure 4-10.

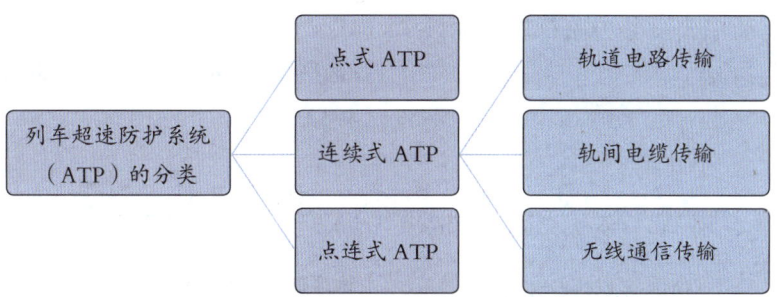

列车超速防护系统（ATP）的分类：classification of ATP　点式 ATP：intermittent ATP
连续式 ATP：continuous ATP　点连式 ATP：intermittent-continuous ATP
轨道电路传输：track circuit transmission　轨间电缆传输：inter-track cable transmission
无线通信传输：wireless communication transmission

图 4-10　列车超速防护系统（ATP）的分类

Figure 4-10　Classification of ATP

3. 列车超速防护系统（ATP）的制动模式

列车超速防护系统（ATP）的制动模式分为一级制动模式和分级制动模式，一级制动模式如图4-11所示。

3. Brake Mode of ATP

Brake mode of ATP is divided into grade one and hierarchical brake mode, grade one brake mode as shown in Figure 4-11.

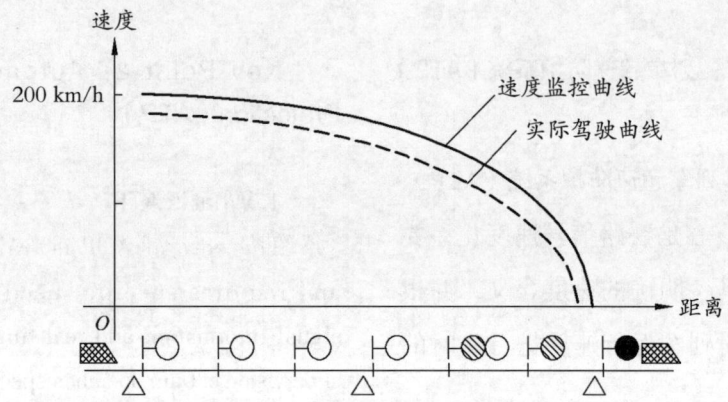

速度：speed 距离：distance 速度监控曲线：speed supervision curve
实际驾驶曲线：actual driving curve

图 4-11 一级制动模式的速度曲线

Figure 4-11 Speed Curve of Grade One Brake Mode

分级制动模式又分为阶梯型和曲线型，如图4-12所示。

Hierarchical mode is divided into ladder mode and curve mode, as shown in Figure 4-12.

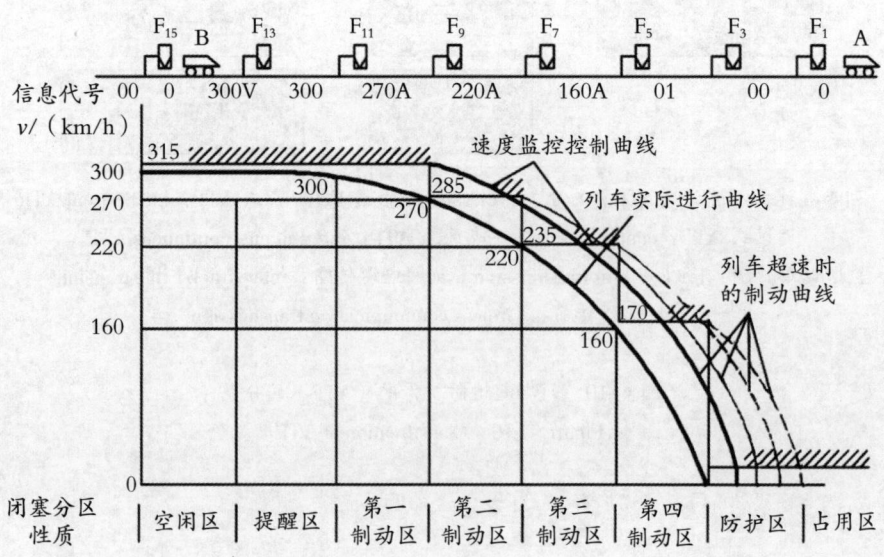

(a)

信息代号：information code　速度监控控制曲线：speed supervision control curve
列车实际进行曲线：actual train running curve　列车超速时的制动曲线：brake curve of over speeding train
闭塞分区性质：nature of block section　空闲区：vacancy area　提醒区：reminding area
第一制动区：first braking area　第二制动区：second braking area　第三制动区：third braking area
第四制动区：fourth braking area　防护区：protection area　占用区：occupied area

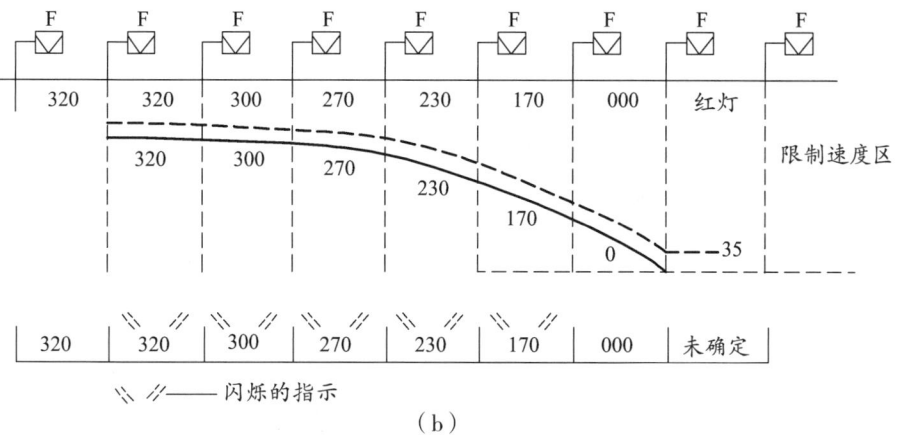

红灯：red light　限制速度区：speed limit area　未确定：uncertain　闪烁的指示：sparkling indicator

图 4-12　分级制动模式的速度曲线

Figure 4-12　Speed Curve of Hierarchical Braking Mode

学习笔记

Study Notes

模块三 课堂练习

Module 3　In-class Exercises

练习1：根据列车运行监控记录装置（LKJ-2000型）的系统构成示意图，讨论列车运行监控记录装置（LKJ-2000型）的工作原理。

Exercise 1: Discuss the working principle of train operation supervision recording device (LKJ-2000) based on its system composition figure.

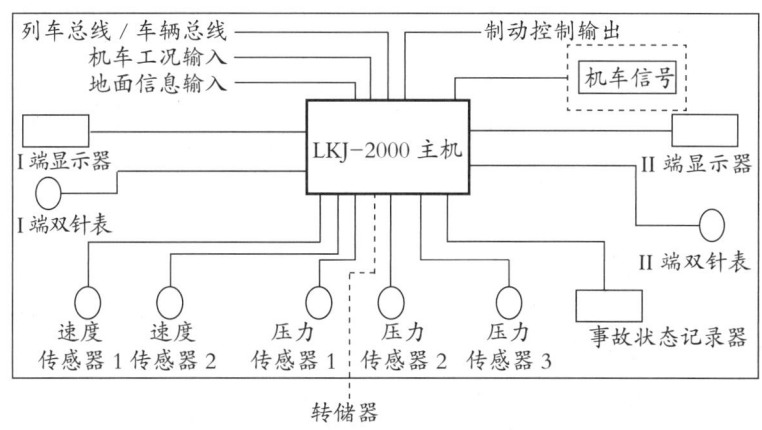

列车总线/车辆总线：train trunk　机车工况输入：locomotive operation condition input
地面信息输入：ground information input　Ⅰ端显示器：terminal Ⅰ display
Ⅰ端双针表：terminal Ⅰ twin-needles speedometer　速度传感器：speed sensor
压力传感器：pressure sensor　制动控制输出：brake control output　机车信号：locomotive signal
Ⅱ端显示器：terminal Ⅱ display　Ⅱ端双针表：terminal Ⅱ twin-needles speedometer
事故状态记录器：accident status recorder　LKJ-2000主机：LKJ-2000 host computer　转储器：dumper

图4-13　列车运行监控记录装置（LKJ-2000型）系统构成示意图

Figure 4-13　System Composition of Train Operation Record Device (LKJ-2000)

练习2：讨论列车超速防护系统（ATP）的三种制动模式，即阶梯型分级制动模式、曲线型分级制动模式和一级制动模式分别有什么特点？

（1）阶梯型分级制动模式。

Exercise 2: Discuss features of three brake modes of ATP, namely ladder hierarchical brake mode, curve hierarchical brake mode and grade one brake mode.

（1）Ladder hierarchical brake mode.

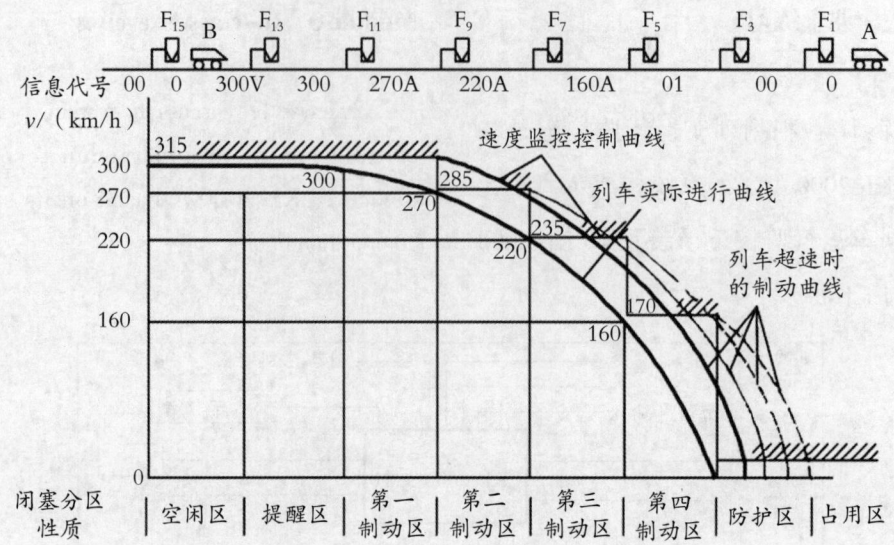

信息代号：information code 速度监控控制曲线：speed supervision control curve
列车实际进行曲线：actual train running curve 列车超速时的制动曲线：brake curve of over speeding train
闭塞分区性质：nature of block section 空闲区：vacancy area 提醒区：reminding area
第一制动区：first braking area 第二制动区：second braking area 第三制动区：third braking area
第四制动区：fourth braking area 防护区：protection area 占用区：occupied area

图 4-14 阶梯型分级制动模式曲线

Figure 4-14 Curve of Ladder Braking Mode

（2）曲线型分级制动模式。　　　　　　　　（2）Curve hierarchical brake mode.

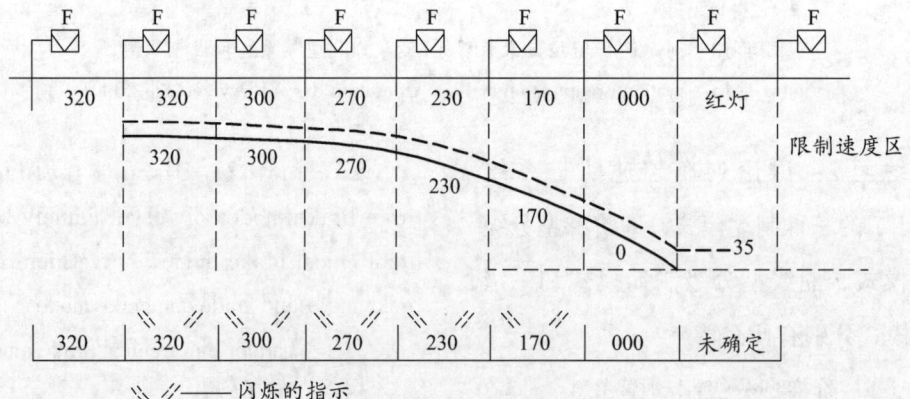

红灯：red light 限制速度区：speed limit area 未确定：uncertain
闪烁的指示：sparkling indicator

图 4-15 曲线型分级制动模式曲线

Figure 4-15 Curve of Hierarchical Braking Mode

（3）一级制动模式。　　　　　　　　　　（3）Grade one brake mode.

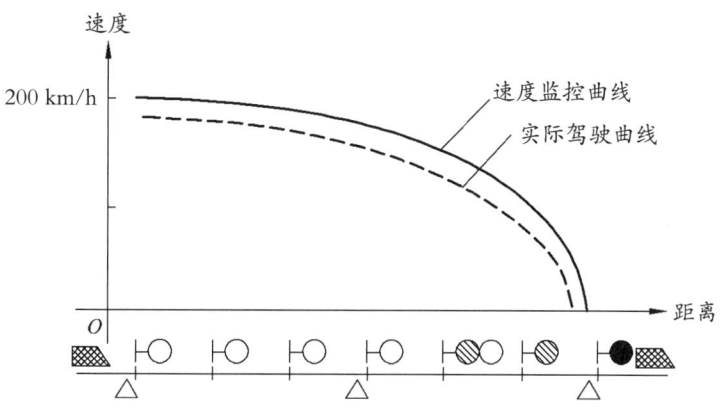

速度：speed　距离：distance　速度监控曲线：speed supervision curve
实际驾驶曲线：actual driving curve

图 4-16　一级制动模式曲线

Figure 4-16　Curve of Grade One Braking Mode

课堂练习
In-class Exercises

模块四　课后拓展

为了保障高铁的运行安全,列车运行控制系统需要运行监控记录装置和列车超速防护系统。请你在乘坐高铁的时候,观察并指出实现列车运行监控记录和列车超速防护的装置和设备。

Module 4　After-class Activity

Operation supervision record device and train over speed protection system are required to safeguard high speed train safety. Observe and point out the device and equipment.

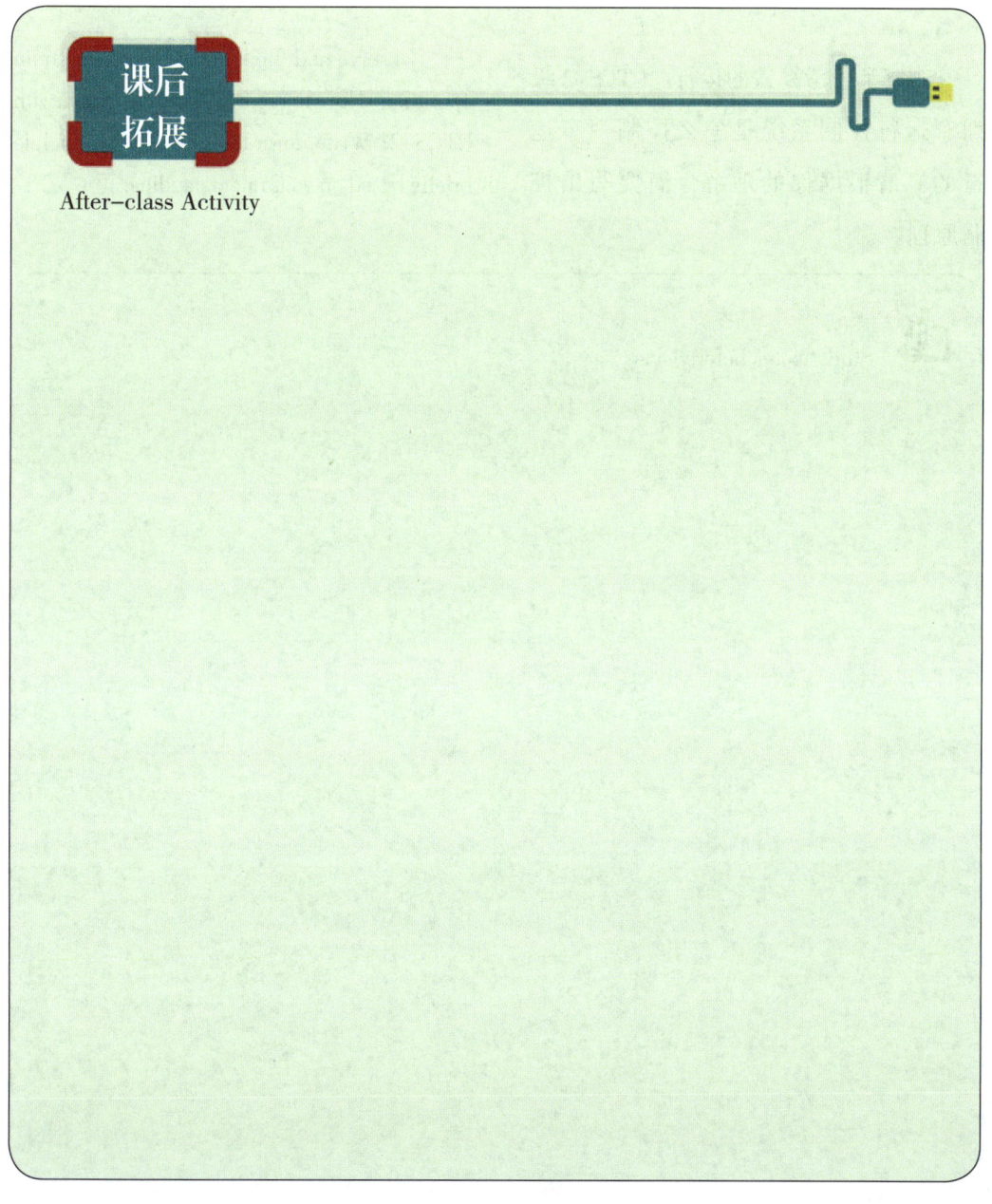

After-class Activity

任务四 CTCS-2级列车运行控制系统运用

Task 4　Application of CTCS-2

模块一　学前准备

观察和思考高铁的运行。CTCS-2级列车运行控制系统是怎么控制列车运行的？请根据你的理解，简要写出控制原理。

Module 1　Preparation before Class

Observe and think about high speed train operation. How to control train operation with CTCS-2? Write down the controlling principle briefly based on your understanding.

课前学习笔记
Study Notes before Class

模块二　课堂学习　　　　　　　　　　Module 2　In-class Learning

知识点一：CTCS-2 级列车运行控制系统的系统结构（如图 4-13）

Key Point 1: System Structure of CTCS-2 (See Figure 4-13)

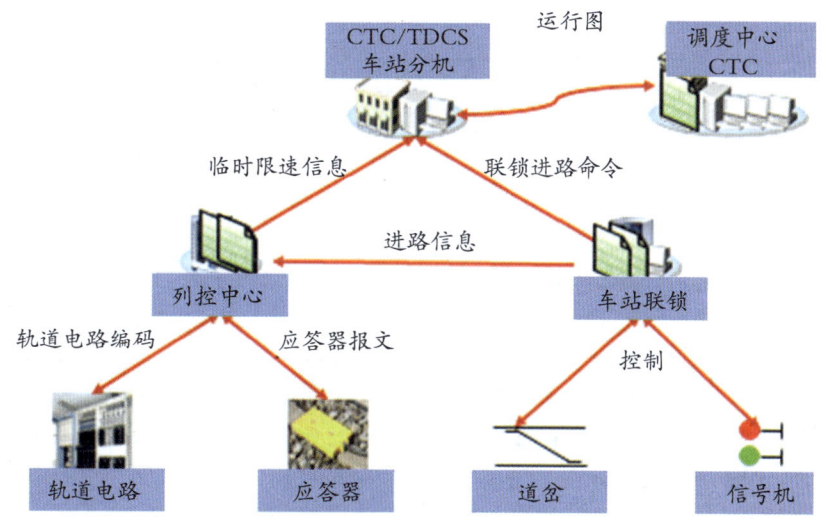

CTC/TDCS 车站分机：CTC/TDCS station extension　调度中心 CTC：dispatching center
临时限速信息：temporary speed limit information　联锁进路命令：interlock route order
列控中心：train control center　车站联锁：station interlocking　轨道电路：track circuit
轨道电路编码：track circuit coding　应答器：transponder　应答器报文：transponder information message
道岔：turnout　信号机：signal machine　控制：control

图 4-17　CTCS-2 级列车运行控制系统的系统结构图
Figure 4-17　System Structure of CTCS-2

知识点二：CTCS-2 级列车运行控制系统的设备组成

Key Point 2: Equipment Composition of CTCS-2

CTCS-2 级列车运行控制系统的设备组成包括车载设备和地面设备两部分，地面设备又分为轨旁和室内设备两部分，如图 4-14 所示。

CTCS-2 equipment includes on board equipment and ground equipment, and ground equipment is divided into track side and indoor equipment, as shown in Figure 4-14.

·165·

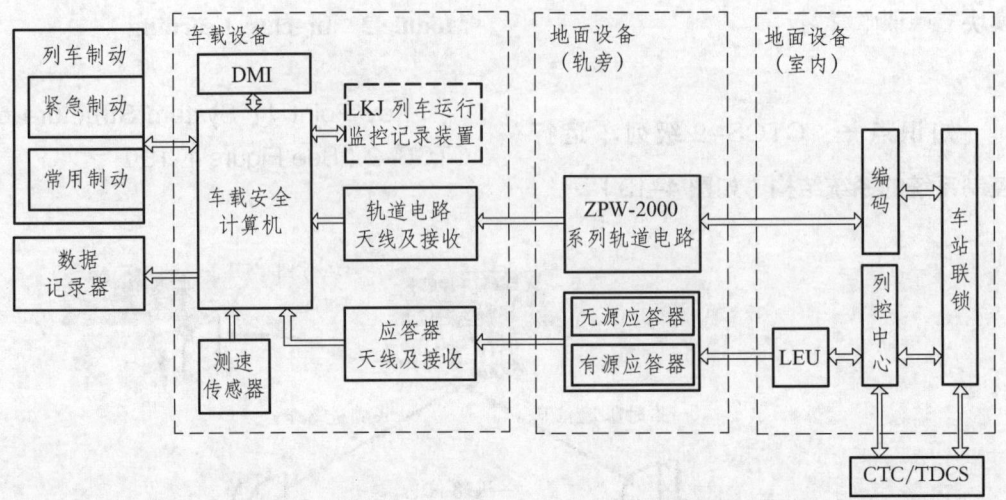

列车制动: train brake 紧急制动: emergency brake 常用制动: normal brake 数据记录器: data recorder
车载设备: on board equipment 车载安全计算机: on board safety computer 测速传感器: speedometer sensor
LKJ 列车运行监控记录装置: LKJ train operation supervision recording device
轨道电路天线及接收: track circuit antenna and receiving
应答器天线及接收: transponder antenna and receiving 地面设备（轨旁）: ground equipment (track side)
ZPW-2000 系列轨道电路: ZPW-2000 series track circuit 无源应答器: passive transponder
有源应答器: active transponder 地面设备（室内）: ground equipment (indoor) 编码: code
列控中心: CTC 车站联锁: station interlocking

图 4-18　CTCS-2 级列车运行控制系统的设备组成示意图
Figure 4-18　Equipment Composition of CTCS-2

知识点三：CTCS-2 级列车运行控制系统的工作原理

Key Point 3: Working Principle of CTCS-2

轨道电路以码序形式提供空闲闭塞分区数量，如图 4-15 所示。

应答器提供闭塞分区长度和线路允许速度。

车载设备综合计算出目标距离，生成速度曲线。

Track circuit provides the quantity of block sections in the form of code order, as shown in Figure 4-15.

Transponder provides the length of block section and permitted speed of the route.

On board equipment calculates target distance comprehensively and generates speed curve.

码序	L5	L4	L3	L2	L	LU	U	HU
空闲分区数量	7	6	5	4	3	2	1	0

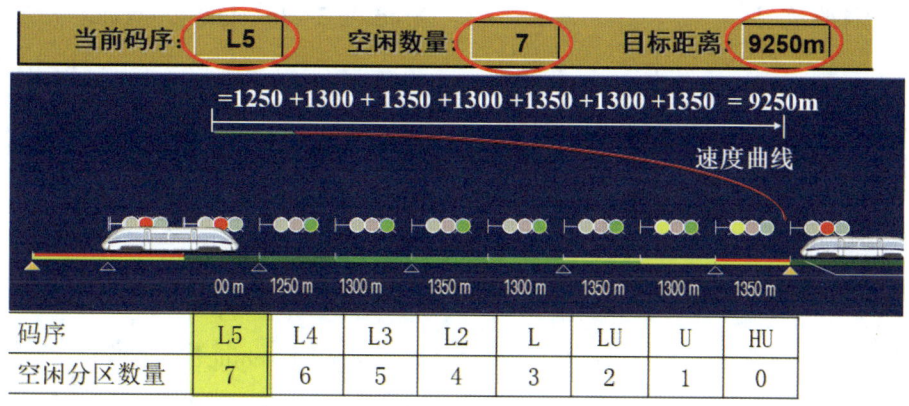

当前码序：current code order　空闲数量：vacancy quantity　目标距离：target distance

码序：code order　空闲分区数量：vacancy quantity

图 4-19　CTCS-2 级列车运行控制系统的工作原理示意图

Figure 4-19　Working Principle of CTCS-2

学习笔记

Study Notes

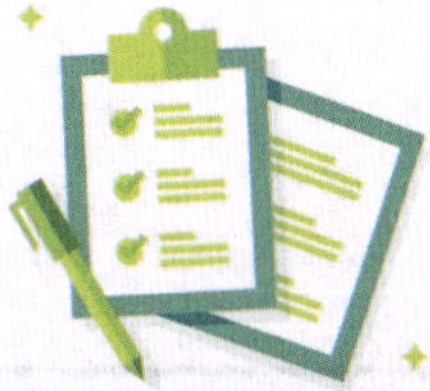

模块三　课堂练习

练习1：讨论 CTCS-2 级列车运行控制系统中各部分的作用。

轨道电路：

应答器：

道岔：

信号机：

列控中心：

车站联锁：

车站分机 CTC/TDCS：

调度中心：

练习2：讨论 CTCS-2 级列车运行控制系统的工作原理。

Module 3　In-class Exercises

Exercise 1: Discuss the functions of the components in CTCS-2.

track circuit:

transponder:

turnout:

signal machine:

train control centre:

station interlocking:

station extension CTC/TDCS:

dispatching centre:

Exercise 2: Discuss the working principle of CTCS-2.

课堂练习
In-class Exercises

模块四 课后拓展

指出你坐高铁时见到的 CTCS-2 级列车运行控制系统的控制装置和设备，并简述这些装置和设备在控制系统中的功能。

Module 4　After-class Activity

Point out the controlling device and equipment when taking high speed train and state their functions in the system.

After-class Activity

任务五　CTCS-3级列车运行控制系统运用

Task 5　Application of CTCS-3

模块一　学前准备

Module 1　Preparation before Class

思考CTCS-3级列车运行控制系统与CTCS-2级列车运行控制系统有什么异同？简要写出你认为的相同点和不同点。

Think about the similarities and differences between CTCS-3 and CTCS-2. Write down the similarities and differences briefly.

课前学习笔记
Study Notes before Class

模块二 课堂学习

知识点一：CTCS-3 级列车运行控制系统的系统构成

CTCS-3 级列控系统总体结构包括：地面设备、车载设备、GSM-R 无线通信网络、信号数据传输网络四部分，如图 4-16 所示。

CTCS-3 级列控系统与 CTCS-2 级列控系统比较，主要区别如下。

（1）地面设备增加无线闭塞中心 RBC、GSM-R 无线通信网络。

（2）车载设备增加 GSM-R 无线通信单元及天线。

（3）车载设备根据 RBC 的行车许可，生成连续速度控制模式曲线，实时监控列车安全运行。

Module 2 In-class Learning

Key Point 1：System Composition of CTCS-3

General structure of CTCS-3 includes ground equipment, on board equipment, GSM-R wireless communication network, signal data transmission, as shown in Figure 4-16.

Major differences between CTCS-3 and CTCS-2 are as follows.

（1）Wireless block center RBC and GSM-R wireless communication network are added in ground equipment.

（2）GSM-R wireless communication unit and antenna are added in on board equipment.

（3）On board equipment generates continuous speed control mode curve based on RBC train operation permission for simultaneous supervision of train operation safety.

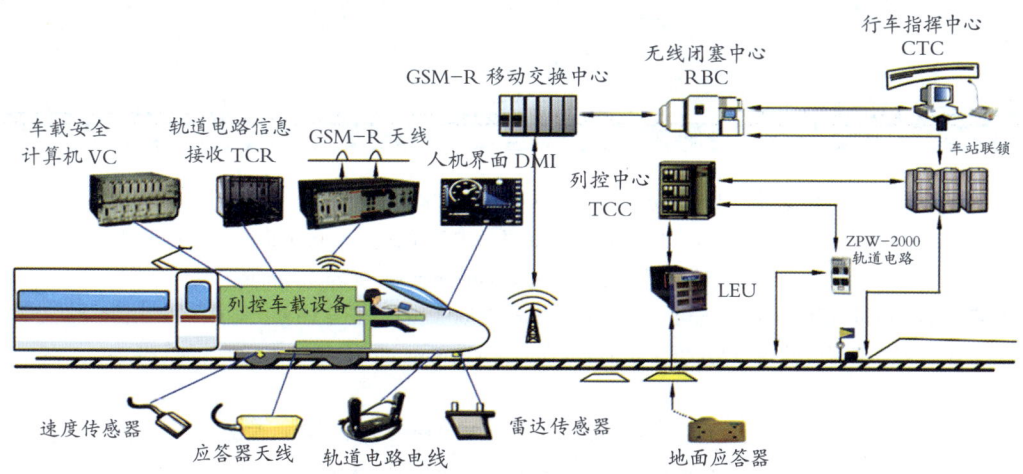

车载安全计算机 VC：on board safety computer VC　轨道电路信息接收 TCR：track circuit information receiving TCR
GSM-R 天线：GSM-R antenna　GSM-R 移动交换中心：GSM-R mobile exchange center
人机界面 DMI：human-compute interface　无线闭塞中心 RBC：wireless block center RBC

行车指挥中心 CTC：centralized traffic control　车站联锁：station interlocking
列控中心 TCC：train control center　列控车载设备：train control on board equipment
ZPW-2000 轨道电路：ZPW-2000 track circuit　速度传感器：speed sensor
应答器天线：transponder antenna　轨道电路电缆：track circuit cable　雷达传感器：radar sensor
地面应答器：ground transponder

图 4-20　CTCS-3 级列车运行控制系统的系统构成示意图

Figure 4-20　System Composition of CTCS-3

知识点二：CTCS-3 级列车运行控制系统的工作原理

Key Point 2：Working Principle of CTCS-3

如图 4-17 所示。

See Figure 4-17.

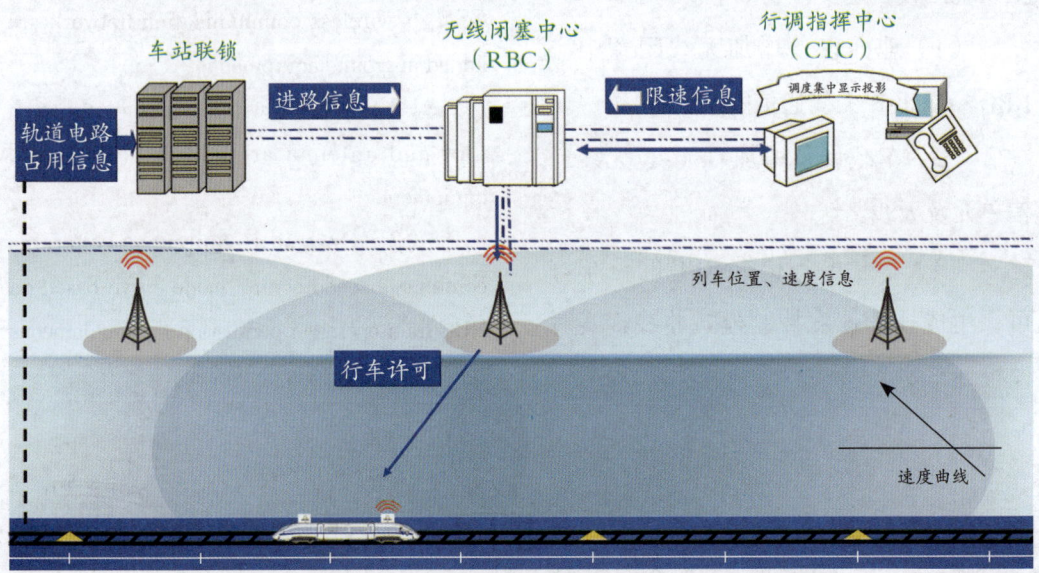

车站联锁：station interlocking　无线闭塞中心：wireless block center
行调指挥中心：centralized traffic control　调度集中显示投影：centralized projection display
轨道电路占用信息：track circuit occupation information
进路信息：route information　限速信息：speed limit information　行车许可：train operation permission
列车位置、速度信息：train location and speed information　速度曲线：speed curve

图 4-21　CTCS-3 级列车运行控制系统的工作原理示意图

Figure 4-21　Working Principle of CTCS-3

知识点三：CTCS-3 级列车运行控制系统的主要工作模式

Key Point 3：Major Working Mode of CTCS-3

如图 4-18 所示。

See Figure 4-18.

列控车载设备9种主要工作模式：nine major working modes of train control on board equipment
休眠模式：sleep mode　　完全监控模式：full supervision mode　　部分监控模式：part supervision mode
目视行车模式：visual driving mode　　引导模式：guiding mode　　调车模式：shunting mode
待机模式：standby mode　　隔离模式：separation mode　　机车信号模式：locomotive signal mode

图 4-22　CTCS-3 级列车运行控制系统的主要工作模式
Figure 4-22　Major Working Mode of CTCS-3

学习笔记
Study Notes

模块三 课堂练习

练习1:讨论CTCS-3级列车运行控制系统各部分的功能分别是什么?

地面设备:

车载设备:

GSM-R无线通信网络:

信号数据传输网络:

练习2:讨论CTCS-3级列车运行控制系统的工作原理。

练习3:讨论CTCS-3级列车运行控制系统的9种主要工作模式分别有什么特点。

Module 3　In-class Exercises

Exercise 1:Discuss the functions of the components in CTCS-3.

ground equipment:

on board equipment:

GSM-R wireless communication network:

signal data transmission network:

Exercise 2:Discuss the working principle of CTCS-3.

Exercise 3:Discuss the features of the nine major working modes of CTCS-3.

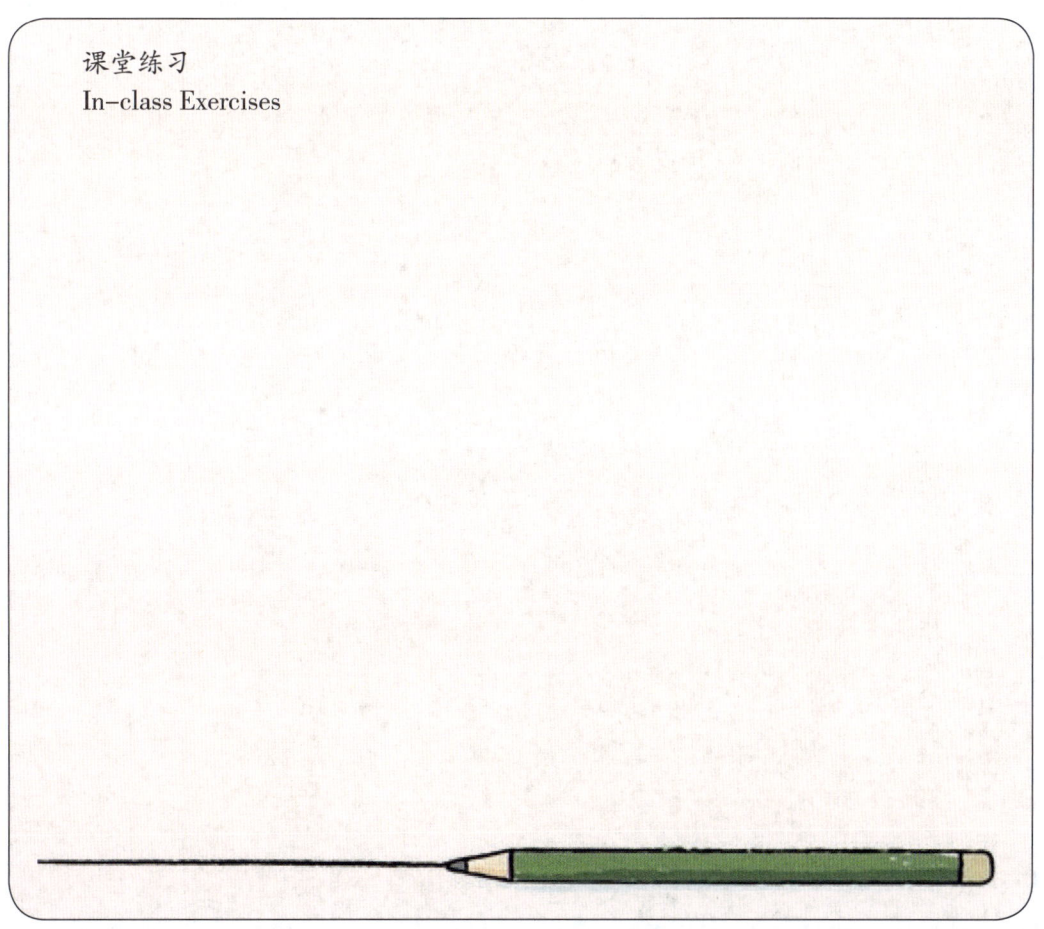

课堂练习
In-class Exercises

模块四 课后拓展

识别出你坐高铁时列车运行控制运用的是哪级系统（CTCS-2 或 CTCS-3）？这两级控制系统在设备构成方面有什么区别？

Module 4　After-class Activity

Recognize the train operation control system（CTCS-2 or CTCS-3） when taking high speed train? What are the differences of the two systems in terms of equipment composition?

After-class Activity

项目五 列车调度指挥系统（TDCS）和分散自律调度集中系统（CTC）

Project 5　Train Operation Dispatching and Command System（TDCS）and Decentralized Autonomous Dispatching and Command System（CTC）

任务一　铁路列车调度指挥系统（TDCS）

Task 1　Railway Train Operation Dispatching and Command System（TDCS）

模块一　学前准备

Module 1　Preparation before Class

中国铁路列车调度系统发展历程。

1962 年，我国铁路在宝成线宝凤段首次安装调度集中，为继电式极性频率制。又相继在其他线路采用晶体管分立元件的 DD1 型、集成电路的 DD4、D4 等调度集中。但是由于设备不配套、系统本身不稳定、设备可靠性不高等众多原因，这一时期的调度集中系统未能达到理想的效果，于 20 世纪 70 年代末相继停止使用。进入 20 世纪 80 年代，随着技术的进步，微机化调度集中和调度监督取得了突破性的成果。尽管这一阶段的调度监督系统有了较快的发展，但是调度集中仍然没有解决调车作业对行车的影响。

Development of Chinese railway dispatching system.

In 1962, first centralized dispatching was installed in Baoji-Chengdu railway, and it was relay polarity frequency system. DD1 type with transistor discrete part, DD4 of integrated circuit, D4 and so on were used in other railways consequently. Centralized dispatching system did not achieve expected results due to lack of complete set of equipment, unstable system and unreliable equipment. The use of the system stopped gradually by the end of 1970s. Micro-computerized centralized dispatching and dispatching supervision made breakthrough with the development of technology in 1980s. However, the affection of shunting over train operation was not solved in spite of the fast development of dispatching supervision system.

1996年，在吸取国外先进经验的基础上，铁道部批准实施铁路运输调度指挥管理信息系统（DMIS）的工程建设。采用现代信息技术改造传统的落后铁路调度方式，逐步推进TDCS一期工程的建设。主要包括京沪全线、京广、京九、京哈、京秦、胶济等干线，7个铁路局、18个局间接口、21处主要枢纽。一期工程的实施，带动了整个铁路信号系统向网络化、智能化方向的发展，从根本上解决了我国铁路信号系统落后的面貌，使整个路网的运输能力、效率以及行车安全程度得到了全面的提高。

TDCS二期工程包括16条干线、33个局间分界口、1984个车站，新建7个铁路局调度指挥中心。2005年，根据《铁路信息化总体规划》，DMIS更名为TDCS。明确TDCS覆盖全路70条干线和全部铁路局，建成以行车调度为核心的现代化铁路运输调度指挥控制管理信息系统。

In 1996, the Ministry of Railway approved the construction of train transportation dispatching and command management information system (DMIS) based on the experiences adopted from foreign countries. Traditional and outdated railway dispatching mode was replaced by modern information technology and phase one TDCS construction was carried forward gradually. The railways included the trunk railways of Beijing-Shanghai railway, Beijing-Guangzhou railway, Beijing-Kowloon railway, Beijing-Harbin railway, Beijing-Qinhuangdao railway, Qingdao-Jinan railway, 7 railway bureaus, 18 inter bureau ports, and 21 major hubs. The implement of phase one project promotes the network and intelligent development of the entire railway signal system, fundamentally improves the outdated status of the railway signal system, and greatly improves transportation capacity, efficiency and safety of the entire railway network.

Phase two TDCS project included 16 trunk railways, 1984 stations in 33 inter bureau boundary ports and 7 newly built railway bureau dispatching commanding centers. In 2005, DMIS was changed into TDCS according to General Planning of Railway Informatization. TDCS was used in 70 trunk railways and all railway bureau to build modern railway transportation dispatching commanding and control management information system focusing on train operation dispatching.

课前学习笔记
Study Notes before Class

模块二　课堂学习

知识点一：TDCS 构成及网络体系结构

TDCS（列车调度指挥系统）是我国铁路调度指挥现代化进程中的重要环节。它是采用现代信息技术改变传统落后的行车调度方式，以通信、信号、计算机网络、数据传输、多媒体等多学科为基础的一套分散控制、集中管理的综合性现代化运输调度指挥系统。全路 TDCS 系统三层网络结构如图 5-1 所示。

Module 2　In-class Learning

Key Point 1：TDCS Composition and Network System Structure TDCS

TDCS（Train Operation Dispatching and Command System）is an important part in the railway dispatching and commanding modernization in China. Modern information technology is used to replace the traditional and outdated dispatching mode. It is a comprehensive and modern dispatching system for separated control and centralized management combining communication, signal, computer network, data transmission, multimedia. Entire TDCS three level network structure is shown in Figure 5-1.

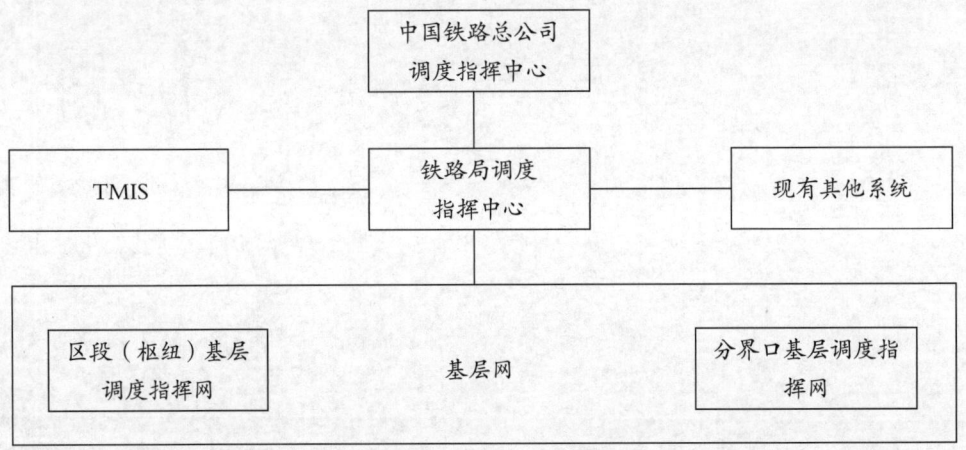

中国铁路总公司调度指挥中心：Dispatching and Commanding Center in China Railway Corporation

铁路局调度指挥中心：dispatching and commanding center in railway bureau

现有其他系统：other existing systems

区段（枢纽）基层调度指挥网：section（hub）base level dispatching and commanding network

基层网：base level network

分界口基层调度指挥网：ports base level dispatching and commanding network

图 5-1　全路 TDCS 系统三层网络结构图

Figure 5-1　Railway Bureau Dispatching and Commanding Center TDCD Network Structure

1. **中国铁路总公司调度中心**

中国铁路总公司调度中心运输调度管理系统是铁路运输调度指挥管理信息系统（TDCS）的重要组成部分，如图 5-2 所示。它是 TDCS 的核心。调度中心是现代化铁路运输调度指挥的心脏，位于整个 TDCS 的最高层。

1. **Dispatching Center in China Railway Corporation**

Transportation Dispatching Management System is a significant component part in TDCS, as shown in Figure 5-2. It is the core of TDCS. Dispatching center is the heart of modern railway transportation dispatching and commanding, located in the highest level of TDCS.

图 5-2　中国铁路总公司调度中心
Figure 5-2　Dispatching Center of China Railway Corporation

2. **铁路局调度中心**

铁路局调度中心通过专线通道、数据网链路、路由器与铁路总公司及其所属各车站远程连接，进行信息交换，如图 5-3 所示。

2. **Railway Bureau Dispatching Center**

Dispatching center in the railway bureaus connects with the railway corporation and the stations with specialized channel, data network, and routers for information exchange, as shown in Figure 5-3.

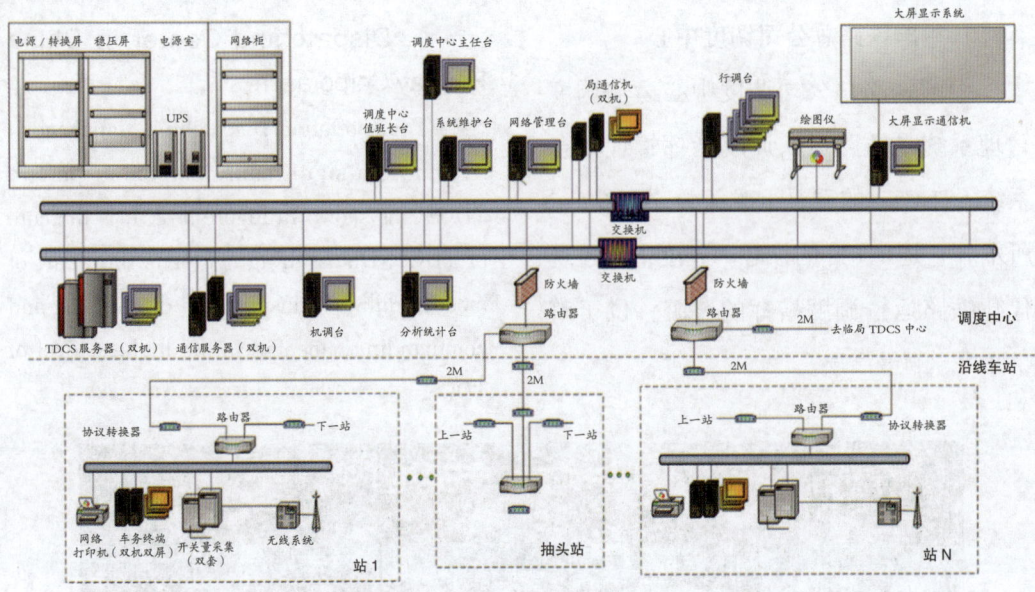

电源/转换屏：power source/conversion screen 稳压屏：voltage stabilization screen 电源室：power source room 网络柜：network cabinet 调度中心值班长台：dispatching center shift foreman platform 调度中心主任台：dispatching center director platform 系统维护台：system maintenance platform 网络管理台：network management platform 局通信机（双机）：bureau communication computer (double computer) 行调台：train operation dispatching platform 绘图仪：plotting instrument 大屏显示系统：big screen display system 大屏显示通信机：big screen display communication instrument 交换机：switch TDCS服务器（双机）：TDCS server (double instrument) 通信服务器（双机）：communication server (double instrument) 机调台：locomotive dispatching platform 分析统计台：analysis and statistics platform 防火墙：firewall 路由器：router 去临局TDCS中心：outgoing temporary bureau TDCS center 调度中心：dispatching center 协议转换器：protocol converter 下一站：next station 网络打印机：network printer 车务终端（双机双屏）：traffic terminal (double computer and double screen) 开关量采集（双套）：switching value collection (double set) 无线系统：wireless system 上一站：previous station 抽头站：tap station 沿线车站：track side stations

图 5-3 铁路局调度指挥中心 TDCS 网络结构图

Figure 5-3 Railway Bureau Dispatching and Commanding Center TDCS Network Structure

3. 基层网

铁路沿线的各站、场、段组成 TDCS 的基层网，由车站分机和车站站机组成，主要包括车站联锁系统、区间闭塞系统、调度监督系统、无线车次号自动校核系统、车站值班员终端设备等，如图 5-4 所示。

3. Base Level Network

The base level network of TDCS with stations, parking lots and sections along the railway consists of station extensions and locomotives, it includes station interlocking system, section block system, dispatching supervision system, wireless train number automatic check system, station shift terminal equipment and so on, as shown in Figure 5-4.

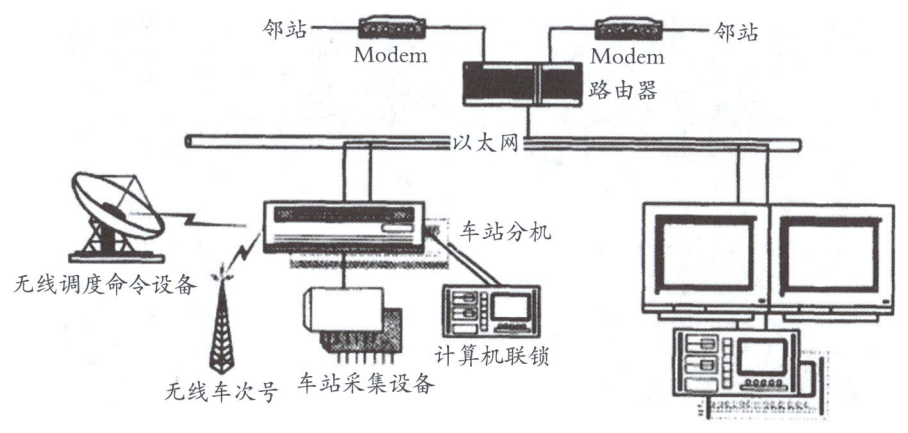

邻站：neighbor station　路由器：router　以太网：ethernet
无线调度命令设备：wireless dispatching order equipment　无线车次号：wireless train number
车站采集设备：station collection equipment　计算机联锁：computer interlocking
车站分机：station extension　车站值班员终端：station shift terminal

图 5-4　TDCS 基层网络结构图

Figure 5-4　TDCS Base Level Network Structure

知识点二：铁路局调度指挥中心 TDCS 功能

Key Point 2：Railway Bureau Dispatching and Commanding Center TDCS Function

1. 干线列车运行秩序的宏观监视

1. Macroscopic Supervision of Trunk Railway Train Operation Order

如图 5-5、5-6、5-7 和 5-8 所示。

See Figures 5-5, 5-6, 5-7 and 5-8.

图 5-5　列车运行秩序宏观监视

Figure 5-5　Train Operation Order Macro-monitoring

图 5-6 列车跟踪显示

Figure 5-6 Train Track Display

路局干线重点列车跟踪显示：bureau trunk railway important trains track display：

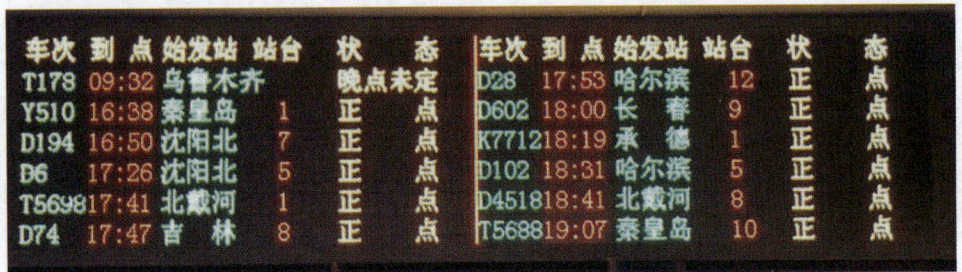

图 5-7 列车运行正点宏观显示

Figure 5-7 Train Operation Punctuality Macroscopic Display

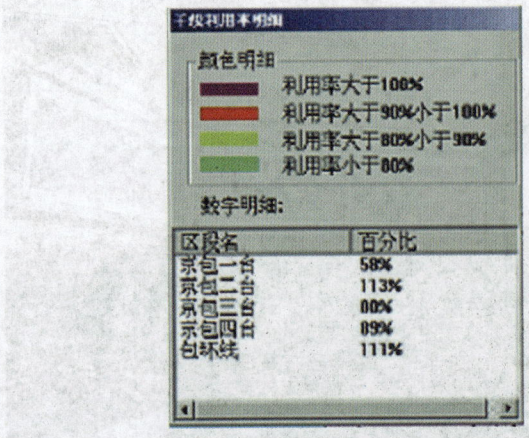

图 5-8 主要干线基本图利用率宏观显示

Figure 5-8 Major Trunk Railway Basic Use Ratio Macroscopic Display

2.列车运行实时监视和历史查询

（1）站场实时表示信息显示，如图5-9所示。

（2）区段透明，如图5-10所示。

（3）列车运行回放，如图5-11所示。

2. Train Operation Simultaneous Supervision and History Inquiry

（1）Station and parking lot simultaneous information display, as shown in Figure 5-9.

（2）Section transparency, as shown in Figure 5-10.

（3）Train operation replay, as shown in Figure 5-11.

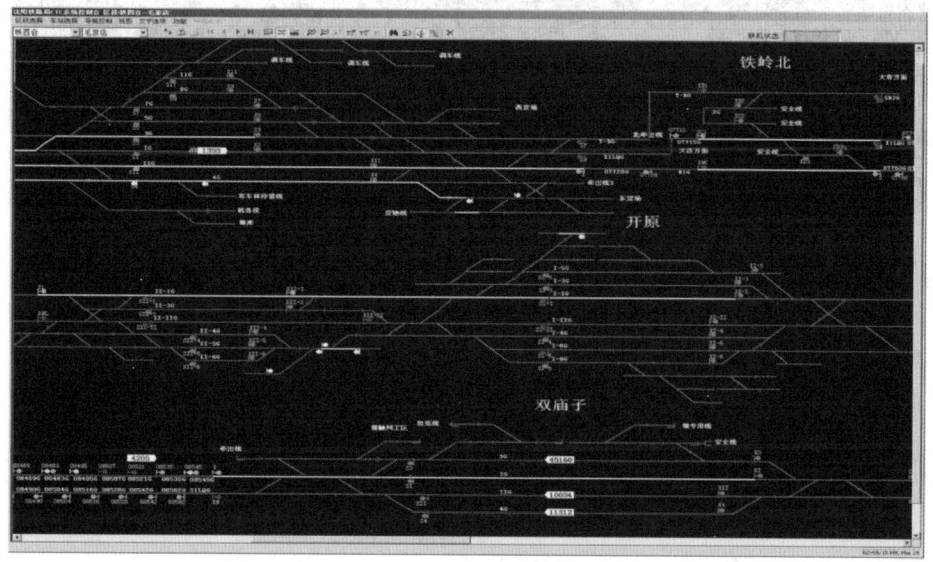

图 5-9 显示站场图画面

Figure 5-9　Picture Display Station and Parking Lot

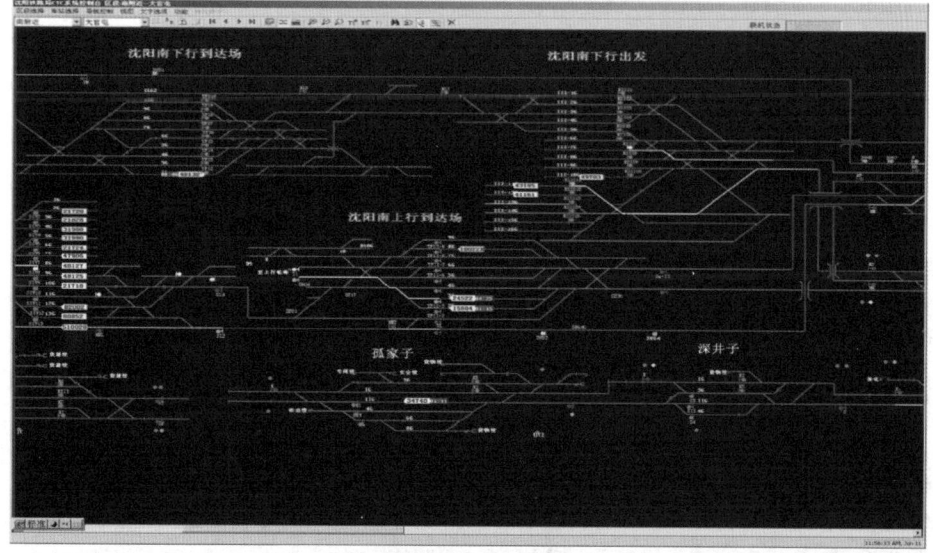

图 5-10 调度台区段画面

Figure 5-10　Dispatching Platform Section Picture

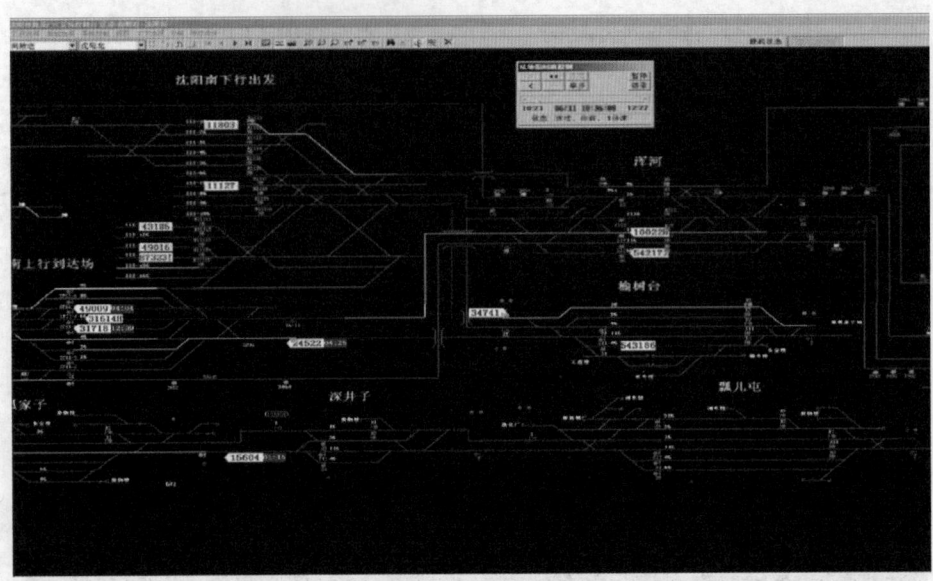

图 5-11 历史再现控制画面

Figure 5-11 History Replay Control Picture

3. 列车追踪

（1）车次号自动追踪。

（2）无线车次号校核。

（3）车次号显示，如图 5-12 所示。

3. Train Track

（1）Train number automatic track.

（2）Wireless train number check.

（3）Train number display, as shown in Figure 5-12.

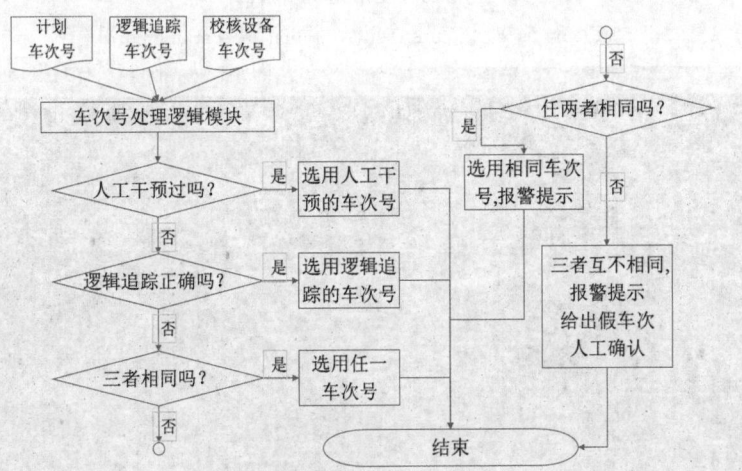

计划车次号：planned train number　逻辑追踪车次号：logical tracking train number
校核设备车次号：check equipment train number　车次号处理逻辑模块：train number processing logic module
人工干预过吗：have you ever done manual intervention　否：no　逻辑追踪正确吗：is logic tracing correct
三者相同吗：are the three the same　是：yes　选用人工干预的车次号：choose the method of manual intervention
选用逻辑追踪的车次号：select the number of vehicles tracked by logic

选用任一车次号：select any number of vehicles　任两者相同吗：is any of the two the same　选用相同车次号，报警提示：select the same train number and give an alarm　三者互不相同，报警提示给出假车次人工确认：the three are different from each other, and the false train number is manually confirmed by the alarm prompt　结束：end

图 5-12　车次号显示流程图

Figure 5-12　Train Number Display Procedure

4. 列车运行图管理

（1）基本运行图维护，如图 5-13 所示。

（2）日班计划的生成及调整，如图 5-14 所示。

（3）阶段计划的生成及调整，如图 5-15 所示。

（4）阶段计划下达，如图 5-16 所示。

（5）实际运行图绘制和输出。

（6）统计分析，如图 5-17 所示。

4. Train Operation Chart Management

（1）Basic operation chart maintenance, as shown in Figure 5-13.

（2）Day shift plan generation and adjustment, as shown in Figure 5-14.

（3）Stage plan generation and adjustment, as shown in Figure 5-15.

（4）Stage order assign, as shown in Figure 5-16.

（5）Actual operation chart making and output.

（6）Statistics analysis, as shown in Figure 5-17.

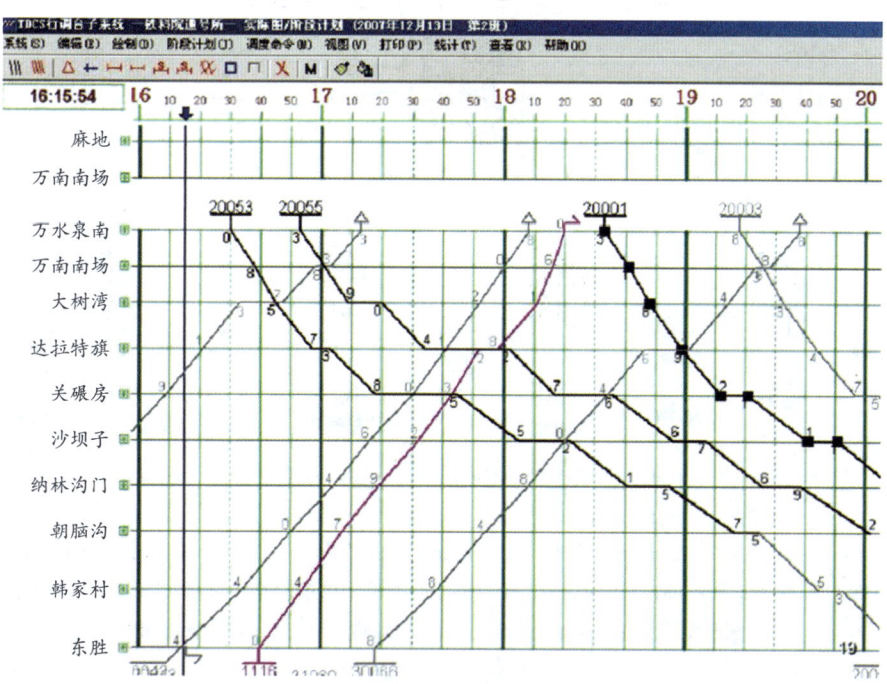

图 5-13　基本图

Figure 5-13　Basic Chart

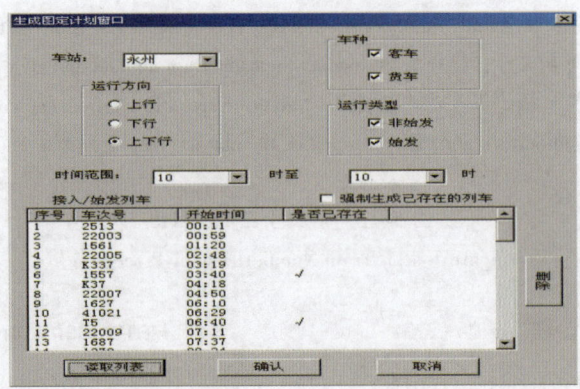

车站：station　运行方向：running direction　上行：uplink　下行：downlink　上下行：up and down link
车种：train type　客车：passenger train　货车：truck　运行类型：running type　非始发：not originating
始发：originating　时间范围：time range　时至：to　接入/始发列车：joining/originating train
强制生成已存在的列车：compulsory generating of existing train　序号：order　车次号：train number
开始时间：starting time　是否已存在：existing or not

图 5-14　生成图定计划窗口

Figure 5-14　Plan Generating Window

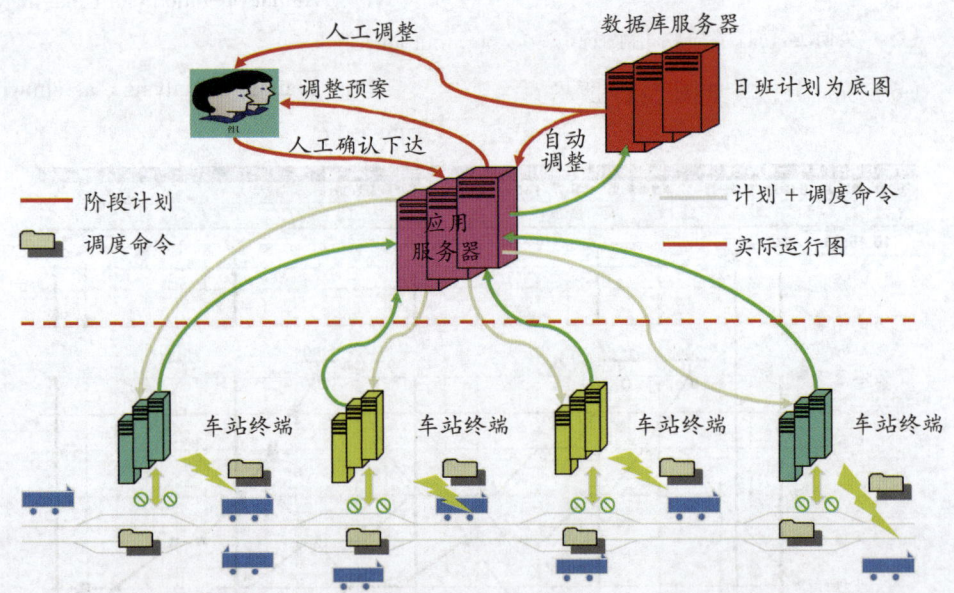

阶段计划：stage plan　调度命令：dispatching order　人工调整：manual adjustment
调整预案：adjust pre-arranged plan　人工确认下达：manual confirmation assign
自动调整：automatic adjustment　应用服务器：application server　数据库服务器：data base server
日班计划为底图：day shift plan as base chart　计划+调度命令：plan+dispatching order
实际运行图：actual running chart　车站终端：station terminal

图 5-15　阶段计划生成原理图

Figure 5-15　Stage Plan Generating Principle

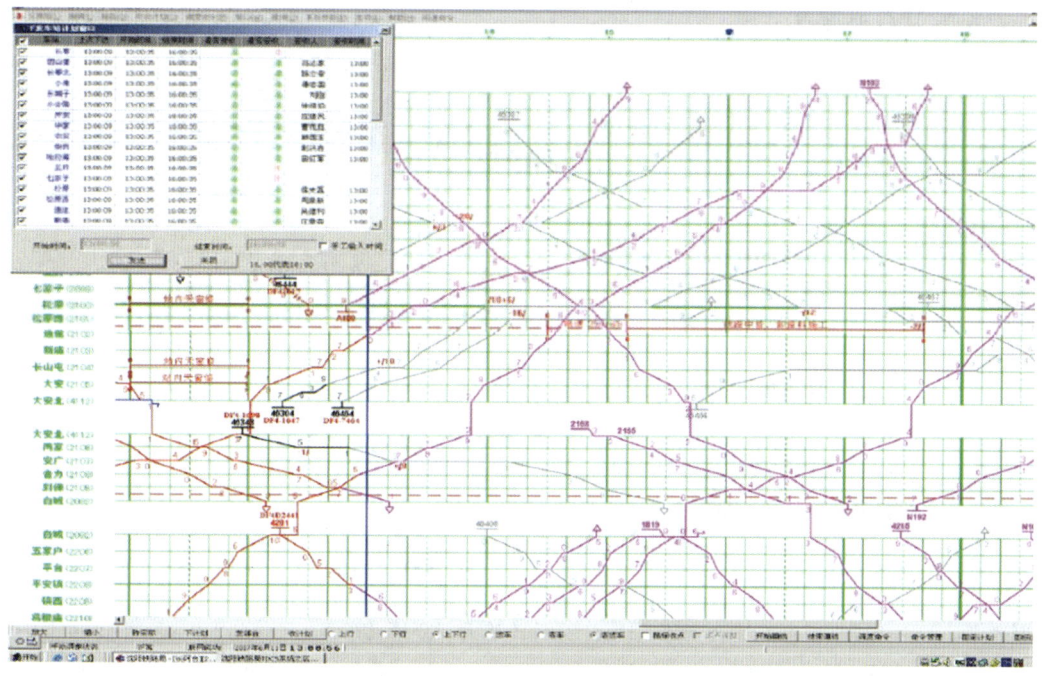

图 5-16 下发计划至车站窗口

Figure 5-16 Giving Order to Station Windows

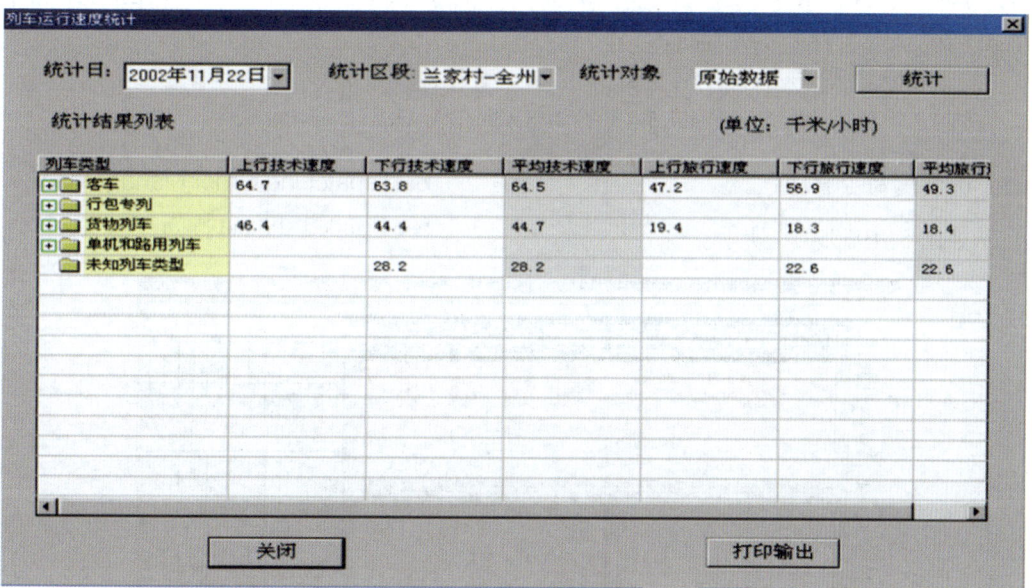

图 5-17 列车运行速度报表

Figure 5-17 Train Running Speed Statement

·189·

5. 车站自动采点

如图 5-18 所示。

5. Station Automatic Acquisition

See Figure 5-18.

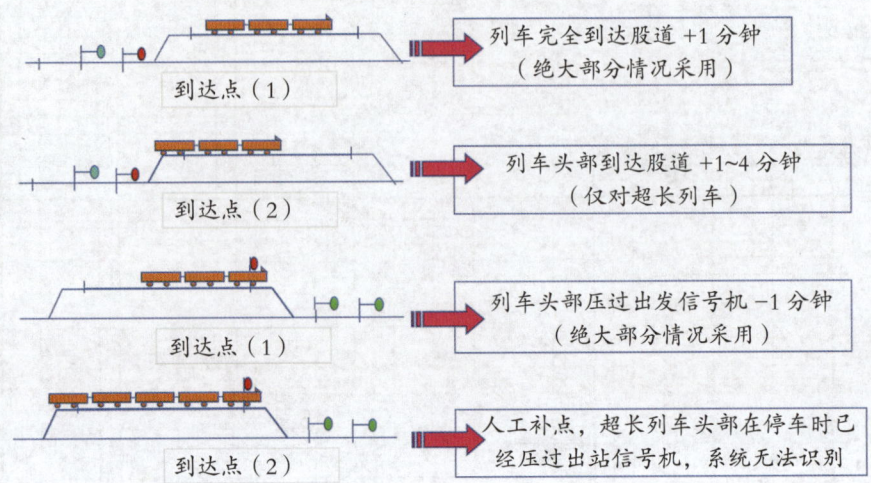

到达点：point of arrival 列车完全到达股道 +1 分钟（绝大部分情况采用）：train full arrival at the track +1minute (used in most cases) 列车头部到达股道 +1~4 分钟（仅对超长列车）：head of train arrives at the track +1~4 minutes (only for over-length trains) 列车头部压过出发信号机 -1 分钟（绝大部分情况采用）：head of train surpasses signal machine -1 minutes (used in most cases) 人工补点，超长列车头部在停车时已经压过出站信号机，系统无法识别：Manual acquisition, over-length trains stops and surpasses departure signal machine, system recognition failure

图 5-18　车站自动采点

Figure 5-18　Station Automatic Acquisition

6. 调度命令管理

如图 5-19、5-20 所示。

6. Dispatching Order Management

See Figure 5-19 and Figure 5-20.

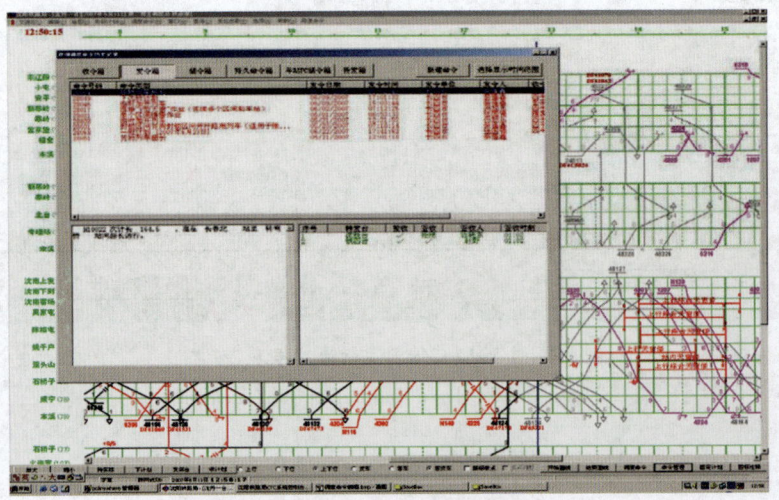

图 5-19　调度命令管理窗口

Figure 5-19　Dispatching Order Management Window

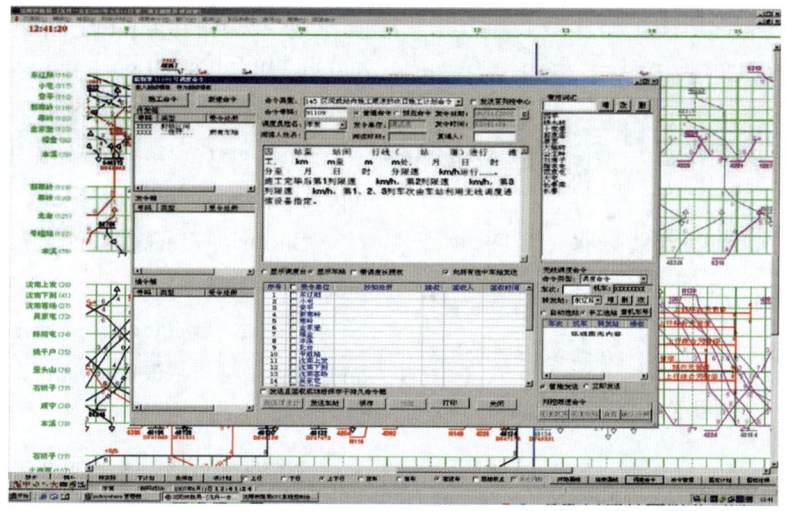

图 5-20 调度命令编辑及下达窗口

Figure 5-20　Dispatching Order Editing and Assign Window

7. 与 TMIS 的界面和接口

知识点三：车站 TDCS 功能

车站端 TDCS 系统可实现以下功能。

本站和相邻站站场与区间显示，如图 5-21 所示。

运统二和运统三的显示和打印，如图 5-22 所示。

用户管理，如图 5-23 所示。

列车运行状态信息的采集及分机码位的显示，如图 5-24 所示。

无线调度命令编辑、保存、转发及发送，如图 5-25、5-26 所示。

与无线车次号校核系统接口，无线车次号校核、车次号人工输入及跟踪，如图 5-27 所示。

站存车、甩挂车及小编组信息输入，

7. Interface with TMIS and Ports

Key Point 3：Station TDCS Functions

Station terminal TDCS system realizes the following functions.

Station, neighboring station and section display, as shown in Figure 5-21.

Display and Print in Overall Running Two and Three, as shown in Figure 5-22.

User management, as shown in Figure 5-23.

Train running status information collection and display of extension code position, as shown in Figure 5-24.

Editing, saving, transfer and sending of wireless dispatching order, as shown in Figures 5-25 and 5-26.

Port with wireless train number check system, wireless train number check, and train number manual input and track, as shown in Figure 5-27.

如图 5-28、5-29 所示。

列车自动报点和人工报点，如图 5-30 所示。

阶段计划的接收、显示和打印。

调度命令的显示、签收、打印、查询，如图 5-31 所示。

限速命令发送，车站直接限速命令编辑、保存、查阅及发送。

Station parking train, trailor and small marshaling information input, as shown in Figure 5-28 and Figure 5-29.

Automatic and manual train point report, as shown in Figure 5-30.

Receiving, display and printing of stage plan.

Display, signing for receiving, printing and inquiry of dispatching order, as shown in Figure 5-31.

Speed limit order sending, speed limit order editing, saving, inquiry and sending at station.

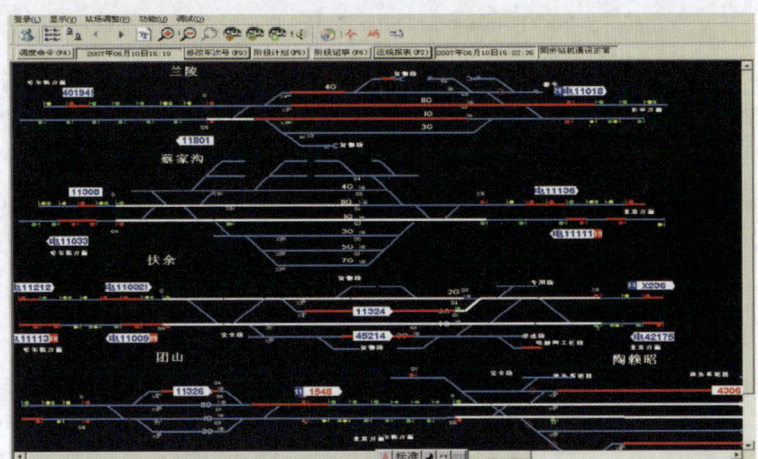

图 5-21　车站 PC 站间透明界面

Figure 5-21　Station PC Inter Station Transparent Interface

图 5-22　车站 PC 运统二界面

Figure 5-22　Station PC Overall Running Interface Two

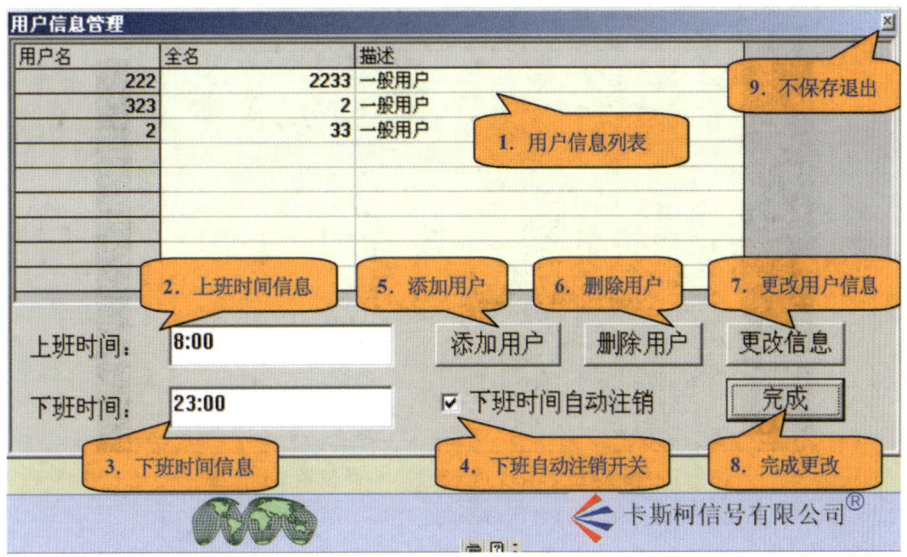

用户信息管理：user information management　　用户名：user name　　全名：full name　　描述：describe

一般用户：general users　　上班时间：work shift　　下班时间：closing time

下班时间自动注销：auto logout at off hours　　卡斯柯信号有限公司：Casco signal Co., Ltd

用户信息列表：user information list　　上班时间信息：on duty time information

下班时间信息：off duty time information　　下班自动注销开关：off duty automatic log off switch

添加用户：add user　　删除用户：cancel user　　更改用户信息：revise user information

更改信息：revise information　　完成：complete　　完成更改：revision complete

不保存退出：log out without saving

图 5-23　车站 PC 用户管理界面

Figure 5-23　Station PC User Management Interface

图 5-24　车站 PC 显示码位状态界面

Figure 5-24　Station PC Display Code Position Status Interface

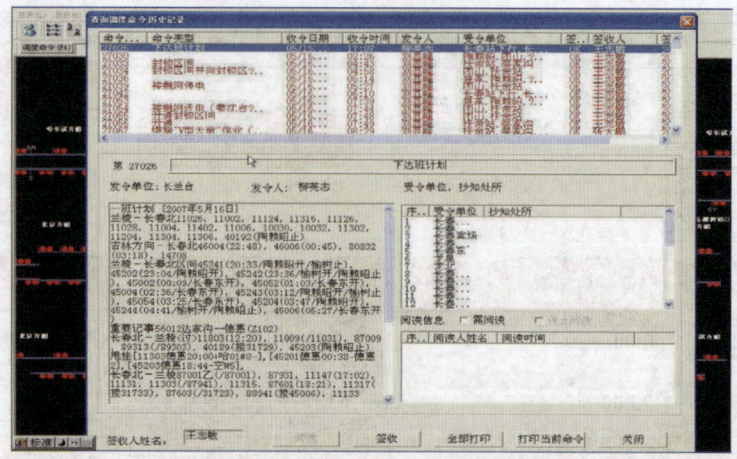

图 5-25 车站 PC 调度命令管理界面
Figure 5-25 Station PC Dispatching Order Management Interface

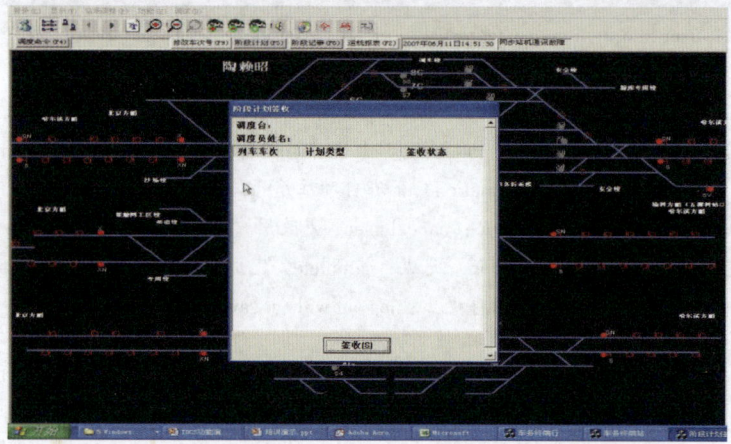

图 5-26 车站 PC 签收阶段计划
Figure 5-26 Station PC Signing for Receiving Stage Plan

车次号操作：train number operation　车次窗名：train number window name
原车次号：original train number　新车次号：new train number　确认：confirm　取消：cancel

图 5-27 车次号人工输入及修改
Figure 5-27 Train Number Manual Input and Revision

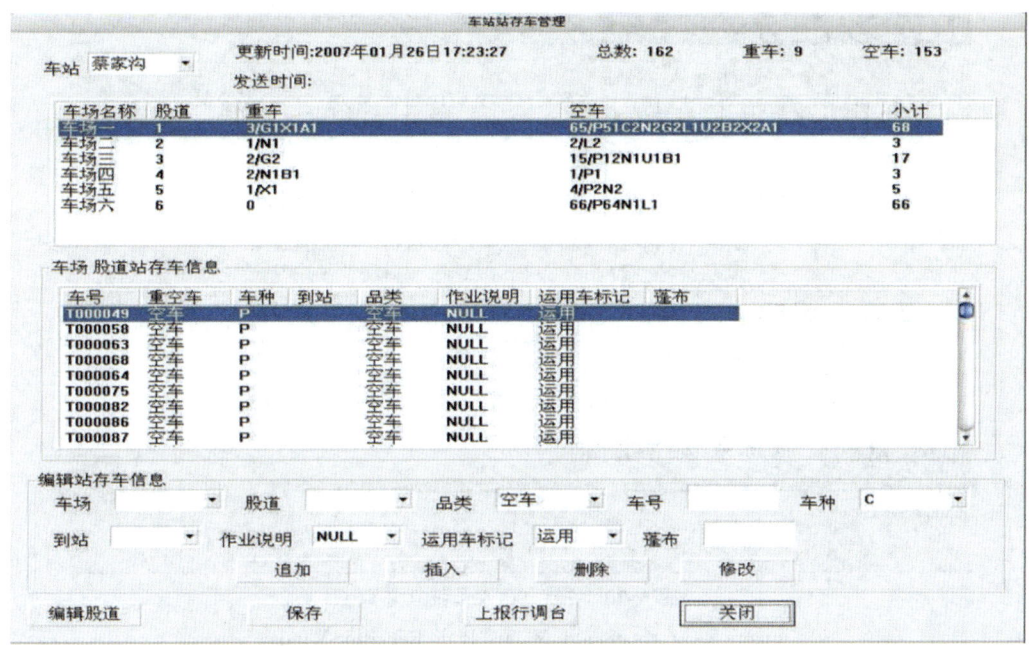

图 5-28 车站 PC 编辑站存车界面

Figure 5-28   Station PC Editing Station Parking Lot Interface

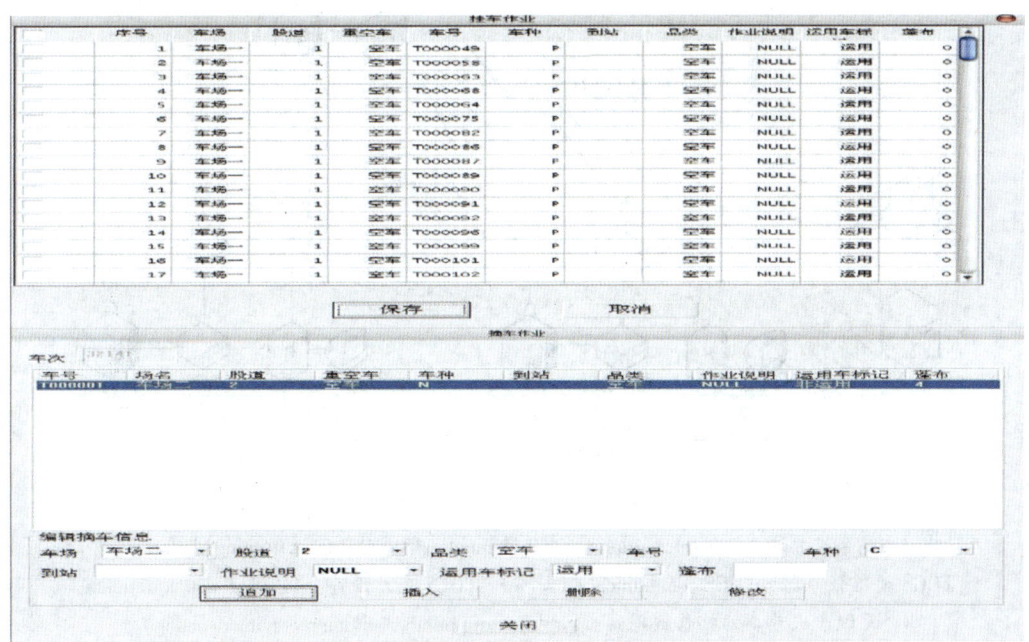

图 5-29 车站 PC 编辑列车编组界面

Figure 5-29   Station PC Editing Train Marshaling Interface

·195·

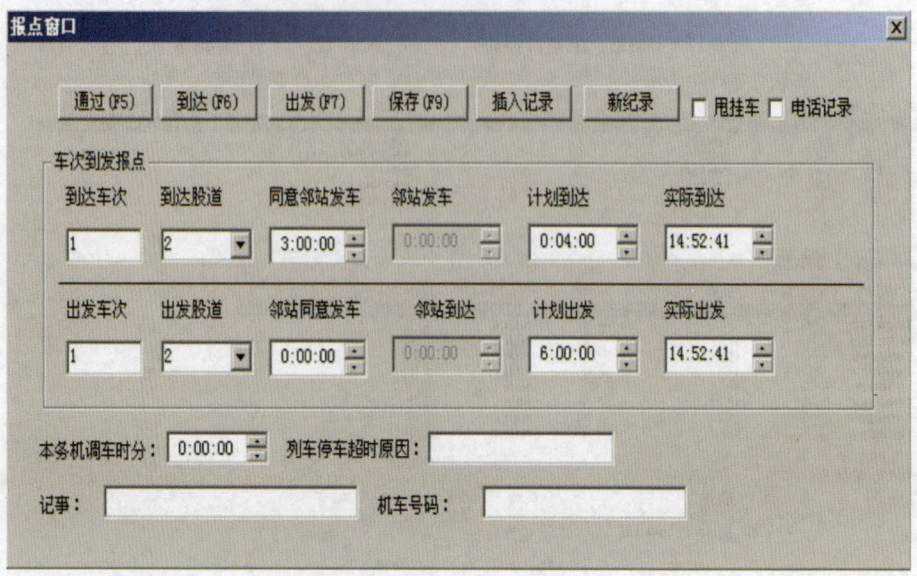

图 5-30　车站 PC 人工报点窗口

Figure 5-30　Station PC Manual Point Reporting Window

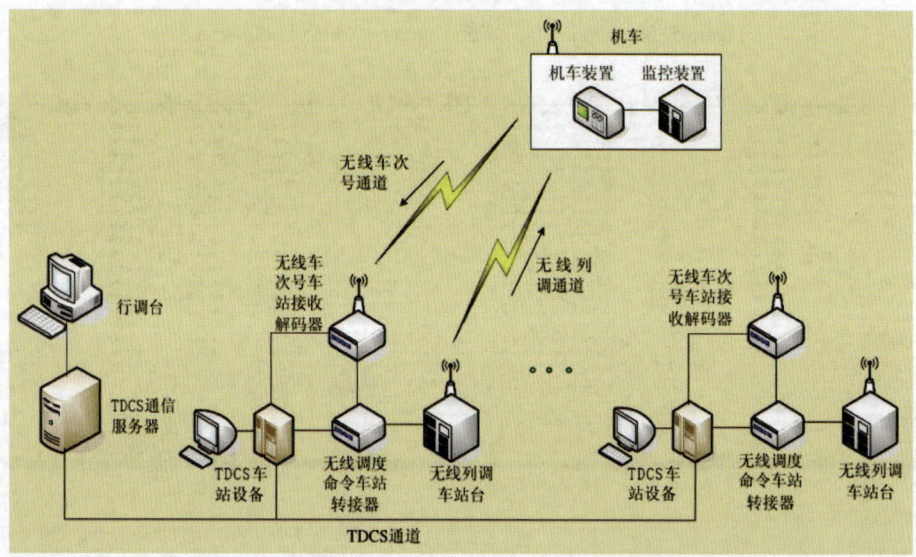

机车：locomotive　机车装置：locomotive device　监控装置：supervision device
无线车次号通道：wireless train number channel　行调台：train running platform
TDCS 通信服务器：TDCS communication server　TDCS 车站设备：TDCS station equipment
无线车次号车站接收解码器：wireless train number station receiving decoder
无线调度命令车站转接器：wireless dispatching order station converter
无线列调车站台：wireless train dispatching platform　无线列调通道：wireless train dispatching channel
TDCS 通道：TDCS channel

图 5-31　无线车次／无线调度命令示意图

Figure 5-31　Wireless Train Number/Wireless Dispatching Order

学习笔记

Study Notes

模块三　课堂练习

练习1：什么是TDCS？简述TDCS的系统结构。

练习2：简述车站自动采点原理。

Module 3　In-class Exercises

Exercise 1：What is TDCS? State system structure of TDCS briefly.

Exercise 2：State station automatic point reporting briefly.

课堂练习
In-class Exercises

模块四 课后拓展

阅读相关国内外文献,分析目前运用的 TDCS 系统存在的问题。

Module 4　After-class Activity

Read domestic and foreign documents and analyze questions in current TDCS.

任务二　分散自律调度集中系统（CTC）

Task 2　Centralized Traffic Control（CTC）

模块一　学前准备

分散自律调度集中系统的发展。

分散自律调度集中为了解决行车和调车相互干扰的问题，必须在不影响列车运行的原则下，允许调度中心和车站通过调度集中自主实现调车功能。这对于调度集中来讲是一种功能的分散，不同于传统意义上调度集中系统的集中控制，出现了分布式控制的功能。因此，如果通过在车站设立自律机来完成按照列车运行计划和站细正常接发列车以及协调列车、调车冲突的功能，将完全可以实现列车和调车作业的统一控制。这一原则叫作"分散自律控制原则"。

中国调度集中的发展经历了漫长而曲折的过程。自20世纪70年代以来中国先后自主研制了 DD-1、DD-2、DY-1、D4、D5 型调度集中系统。1991年12月23日，卡斯柯信号有限公司引进美国技术，结合中国铁路运营特点成功开发 CTC-4000 调度集中系统并在柳园—哈密调度区段开通运行。虽然这些系统都取得了一定的成功，但应用效果

Module 1　Preparation before Class

Development of CTC.

CTC shall realize the function of independent shunting of dispatching center and stations without affecting train operation and solve the mutual intervention of train operation and shunting. It is the function allocation of centralized dispatching and different from traditional control of the centralized dispatching. It is the function of distributed control. Therefore, the installation of autonomous machine in stations for train operation based on plans, normal train receiving and departure and coordination of train operation and shunting will realize unified control of train operation and shunting. The principle is called "decentralized and self disciplined control principle".

Development of centralized dispatching in China has undergone a long and tortuous process. Since 1970s, DD-1, DD-2, DY-1, D4 and D5 systems have been researched and developed in China. On 23rd, December 1991, CSACO introduced American technology and developed CTC-4000 system based on train operation characters in China and applied it in Liuyuan–Hami dispatching section. The systems were successful to some extent, but the effect was

都不明显。

直至 2004 年 5 月 23 日兰州铁路局在青藏线西宁—哈尔盖段率先开通新一代 CTC 系统（Centralized Traffic Control）。

通过学习以上材料，描述分散自律调度集中系统与 TDCS 系统的区别。

not obvious.

Till 23rd, May 2005, Lanzhou Railway Bureau took the lead in starting using the new generation of Centralized Traffic Control (CTC) system in Xining-Hargai section of Qinghai-Tibet railway.

Describe the differences between CTC and TDCS based on the above materials.

课前学习笔记
Study Notes before Class

模块二 课堂学习

知识点一：基本概念

1. 传统调度集中存在的主要问题

如图 5-32 所示。

Module 2 In-class Learning

Key Point 1：Basic Concept

1. Major Problems in Traditional Centralized Dispatching

See Figure 5-32.

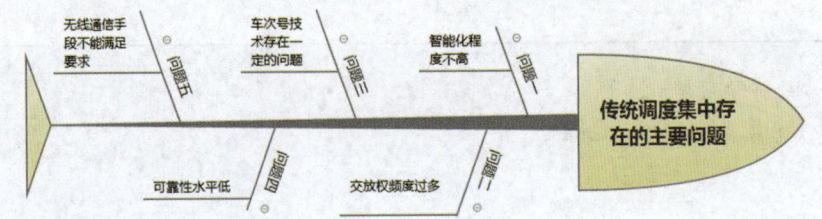

无线通信手段不能满足要求：wireless communication failing to meet the requirement
问题五：question five 车次号技术存在一定的问题：certain problems in train number technology
问题三：question three 智能化程度不高：low intelligent level 问题一：question one
传统调度集中存在的主要问题：major problems in traditional centralized dispatching
可靠性水平低：low reliability 问题四：question four 交放权频度过多：hand over frequency too high
问题二：question 2

图 5-32 传统调度集中存在的主要问题

Figure 5-32 Major Problems in Traditional Centralized Dispatching

2. 分散自律概念

（1）分散。

车站可以在自律条件下进行调车。

车站系统具备自律控制的功能。

（2）自律。

按照运行计划和站细规定接发列车。

列车进路和调车进路可靠隔离。

分散自律调度集中的主要特点。

如图 5-33 所示。

2. Concept of Decentralized Autonomous Control

（1）Decentralization.

Autonomous shunting of stations.

Autonomous control function of station system.

（2）Automation.

Train receiving and departure according to operation plan and detailed station regulations.

Reliable separation of train routes and shunting routes.

3. Major characters of decentralized autonomous control.

See Figure 5-33.

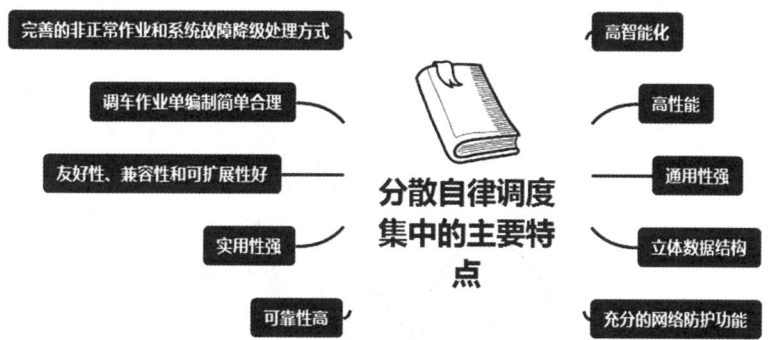

完善的非正常作业和系统故障降级处理方式：complete degraded handling of abnormal working and system error
调车作业单编制简单合理：simple and reasonable compilation of shunting assignment
友好性、兼容性和可拓展性好：good friendliness, compatibility and expansibility
实用性强：high practicability　可靠性高：high reliability　高智能化：high intelligence level
高性能：good performance　通用性强：high universality　立体数据结构：dimensional data structure
充分的网络防护功能：adequate network protection

图 5-33　分散自律调度集中的主要特点

Figure 5-33　Major Features of Decentralized Autonomous Control

知识点二：铁路 CTC 系统技术介绍

Key Point 2：Introduction to Railway CTC Technology

1. 铁路 CTC 总体结构

分散自律调度集中体系结构包括铁路局调度中心系统及车站调度集中分机系统两个层次，如图 5-34、5-35 所示。

2. CTC 控制模式

调度集中有分散自律控制模式和非常站控模式。

分散自律控制的基本模式是用列车运行调整计划自动控制列车运行进路，同时在分散自律条件下调度中心具备人工办理列车、调车进路，车站具备人工办理调车进路的功能。

非常站控模式是指当调度集中设备故障、发生危及行车安全的情况或设备

1. Overall Structure of Railway CTC Structure

Systematic structure of decentralized autonomous dispatching system includes railway bureau dispatching central system and station centralized dispatching extension system, as shown in Figure 5-34 and Figure 5-35.

2. CTC Control Mode

There are decentralized autonomous control mode and abnormal station control mode in centralized dispatching.

Basic mode of decentralized autonomous control is autonomous control of train routes with train operation plan and the dispatching center with manual train route and shunting function in decentralized autonomous conditions.

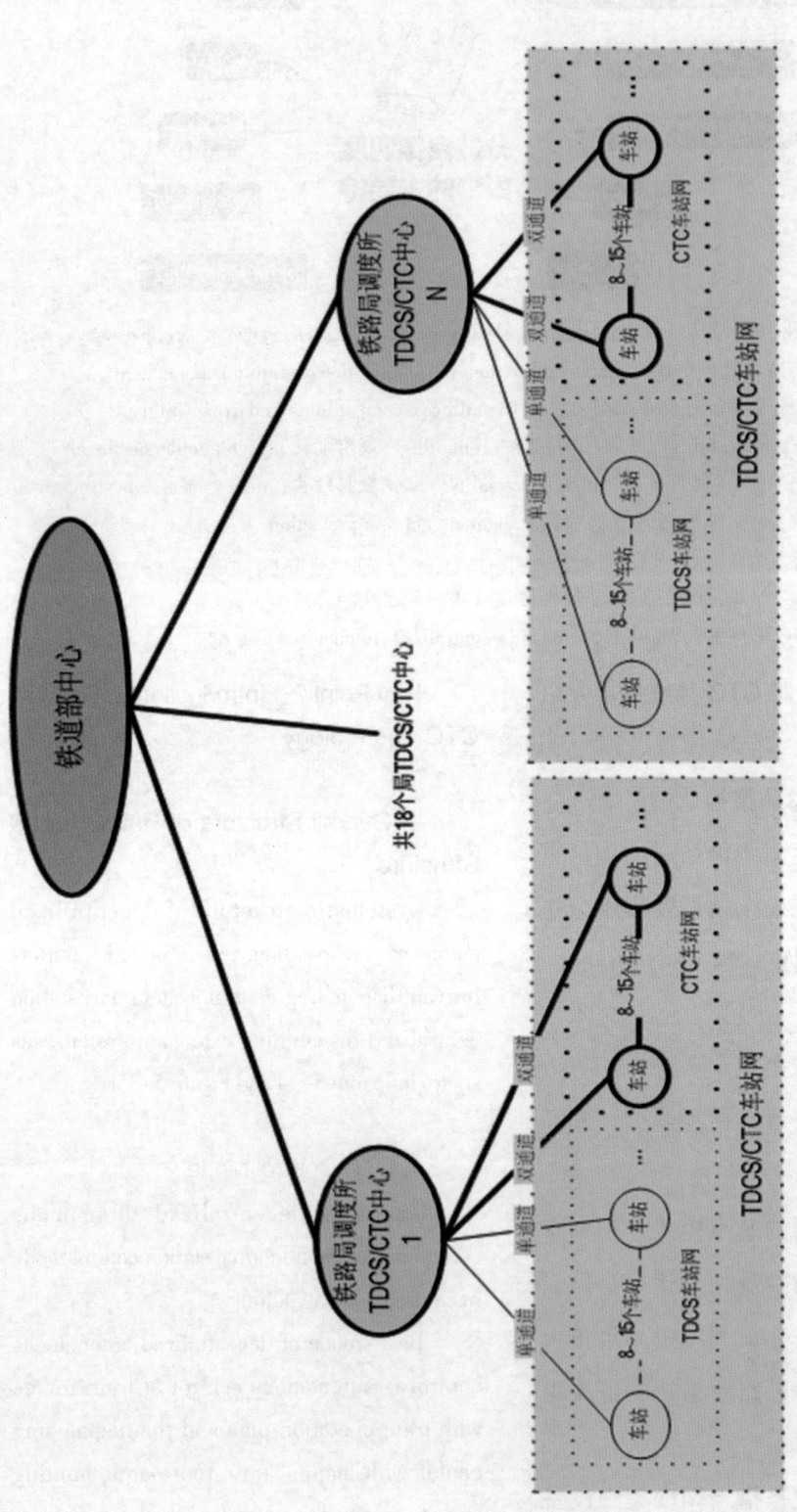

图 5-34 CTC 总体结构

Figure 5-34 CTC Overall Structure

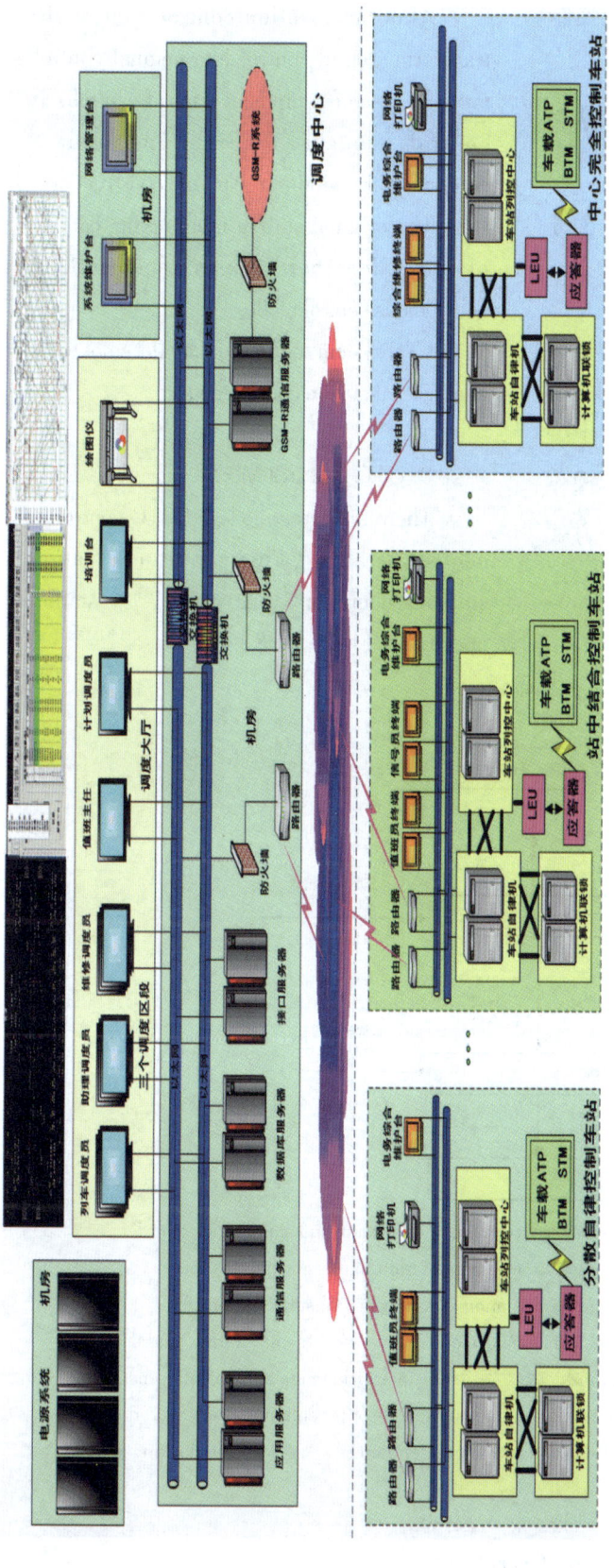

电源系统：power system　机房：computer room
三个调度区段：three dispatching sections　列车调度员：train dispatch man　助理调度员：assistant dispatch man　维修调度员：repair dispatch man
培训台：training platform　绘图仪：plotting instrument　值班主任：director on duty　计划调度员：plan dispatch man　调度大厅：dispatching hall
机房：computer room　交换机：switch　应用服务器：application server　系统维护台：system maintenance platform　网络管理台：network management platform
防火墙：firewall　路由器：router　GSM-R通信服务器：GSM-R communication server　通信服务器：communication server　数据库服务器：data base server　接口服务器：port server
值班员终端：duty man terminal　网络打印机：network printer　电务综合维护台：comprehensive electric maintenance platform　GSM-R系统：GSM-R server　调度中心：dispatching center
车站自律机：station autonomous machine　计算机联锁：computer interlocking　车站列控中心：station train control center　应答器：transponder
车载ATP：on board ATP　分散自律ATP：decentralized autonomous control station　信号员终端：signalman terminal
站中结合控制车站：in-station comprehensive control station　中心完全控制车站：central overall control station

图 5-35 调度集中总体结构图

Figure 5-35 Overall Structure of Centralized Dispatching

天窗维修、施工需要时，脱离系统控制转为车站传统人工控制的模式。

在分散自律控制模式下，原车站联锁控制台不起作用。

在非常站控模式下，CTC 系统车务终端不起作用。

3. CTC 控制方式

CTC 控制方式有三种，分别为中心操作方式（如图 5-36）、车站调车操作方式（如图 5-37 所示）、车站操作方式（如图 5-38 所示）。

Abnormal station control mode is to transform station control into manual control mode in case of equipment error of centralized control, dangers for train operation, equipment sky window repair and construction.

The original station interlocking control platform does not work in decentralized autonomous control mode.

CTC system traffic terminal does not work in abnormal station control mode.

3. CTC Control Mode

There are three modes of CTC control: center operation (Figure 5-36), station shunting operation (Figure 5-37), station operation (Figure 5-38).

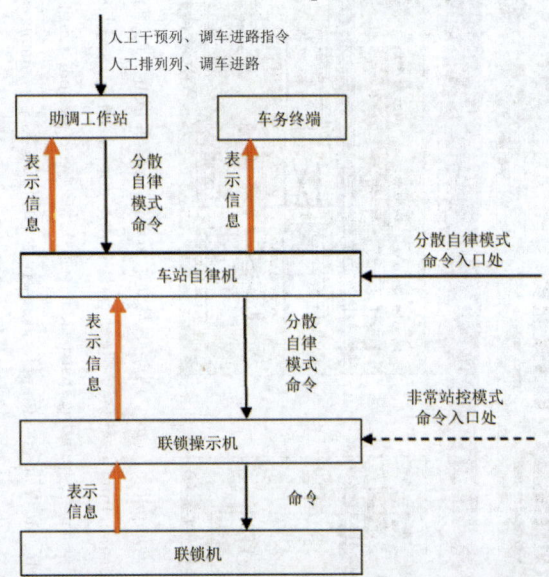

人工干预列、调车进路指令：human intervention of train route and shunting route order
人工排列列、调车进路：manual arrangement of train route and shunting route
助调工作站：shunting assistant work station　　表示信息：display information
分散自律模式命令：decentralized autonomous mode order　　车务终端：traffic terminal
车站自律机：station autonomous machine　　联锁操示机：interlocking operation display machine
分散自律模式命令入口处：decentralized autonomous mode order entrance　　命令：order
非常站控模式命令入口处：abnormal station control order entrance　　联锁机：interlocking machine

图 5-36　中心操作方式

Figure 5-36　Center Operation Mode

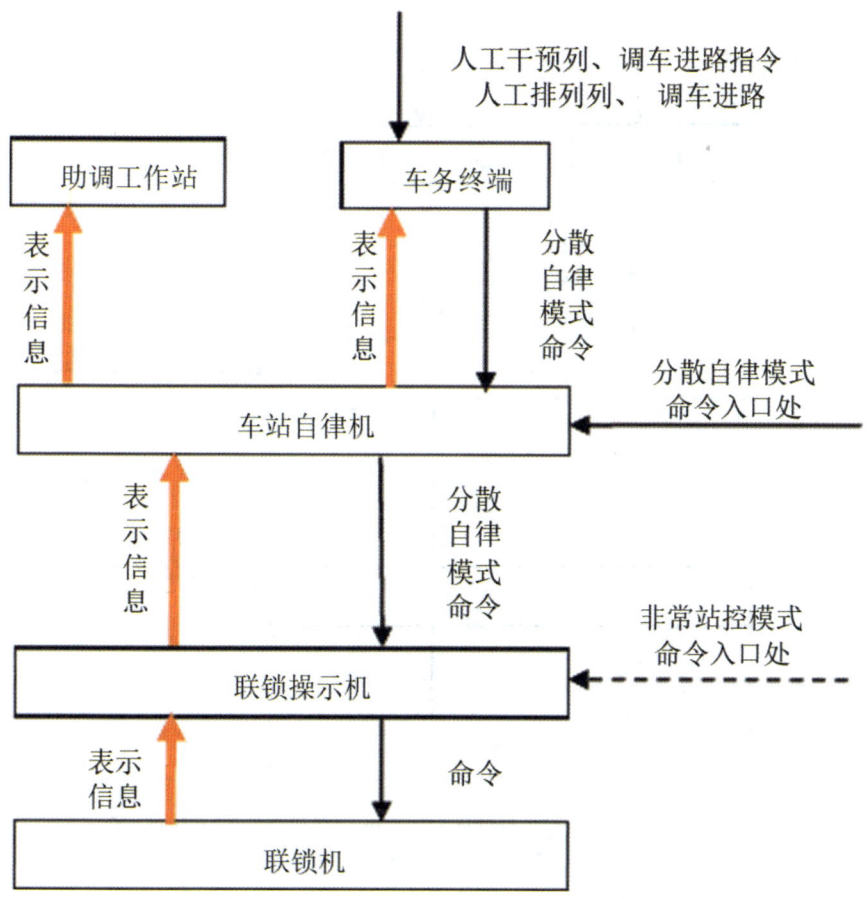

人工干预列、调车进路指令：human intervention of train route and shunting route order
人工排列列、调车进路：manual arrangement of train route and shunting route
助调工作站：shunting assistant work station　表示信息：display information
分散自律模式命令：decentralized autonomous mode order　车务终端：traffic terminal
车站自律机：station autonomous machine
分散自律模式命令入口处：decentralized autonomous mode order entrance
联锁操示机：interlocking operation display machine
非常站控模式命令入口处：abnormal station control order entrance　命令：order
联锁机：interlocking machine

图 5-37　车站操作方式

Figure 5-37　Station Operation Mode

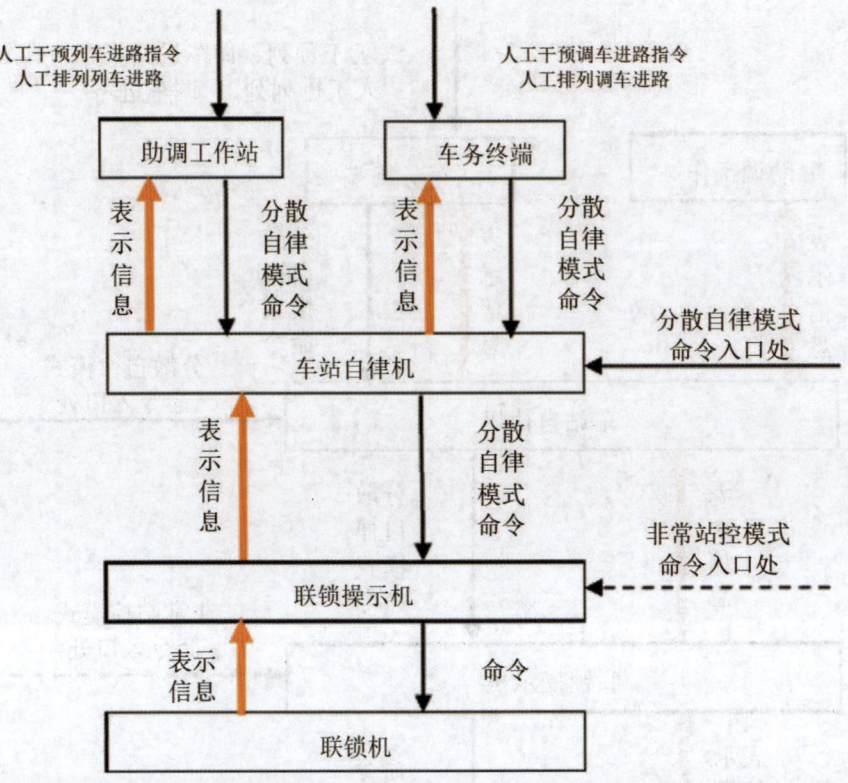

人工干预列车进路指令: manual intervention of train route instruction
人工排列列车进路: manual train routing
人工干预调车进路指令: manual intervention of shunting route instruction
人工排列调车进路: manual arrangement of shunting route
助调工作站: shunting assistant work station   表示信息: display information
分散自律模式命令: decentralized autonomous mode order   车务终端: traffic terminal
车站自律机: station autonomous machine
分散自律模式命令入口处: decentralized autonomous mode order entrance
联锁操示机: interlocking operation display machine
非常站控模式命令入口处: abnormal station control order entrance   命令: order
联锁机: interlocking machine

图 5-38　车站调车操作方式
Figure 5-38　Station Shunting Operation Mode

4. 分散自律 CTC 列车作业流程

分散自律 CTC 列车调度台作业流程如图 5-39 所示。

4. Decentralized Autonomous CTC Train Operation Procedure

Decentralized autonomous CTC train operation procedure is shown in Figure 5-39.

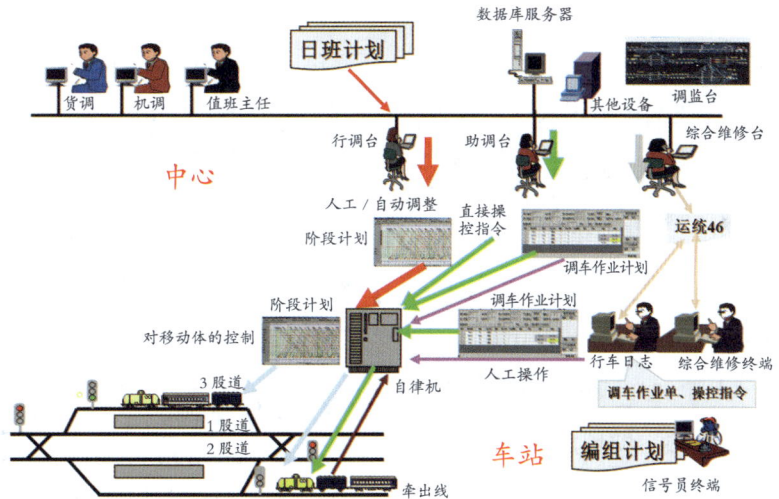

货调: freight allocation　机调: locomotive allocation　值班主任: director on duty
日班计划: day shift plan　数据库服务器: data base server　其他设备: other equipment
调监台: shunting supervision platform　中心: centre　行调台: train operation shunting platform
助调台: assisting shunting platform　综合维修台: comprehensive repair platform
人工/自动调整: manual/automatic adjustment　阶段计划: stage plan　直接操控指令: direct operation order
运统46: operation coordination 46　调车作业计划: shunting plan
对移动体的控制: control over mobile object　自律机: autonomous machine　人工操作: manual operation
行车日志: train operation log　综合维修终端: comprehensive repair terminal　股道: station track
牵出线: shunting track　车站: station　调车作业单、操控指令: shunting assignment, operation order
编组计划: marshaling plan　信号员终端: signalman terminal

图 5-39　CTC 系统运输指挥流程

Figure 5-39　CTC System Transportation Command Procedure

知识点三: 铁路 CTC 系统基本功能

调度集中系统功能主要包括行车指挥功能（TDCS 功能）、调度集中控制功能和 CTC 配套系统功能。

1. 自动排列进路

按计划自动排列进路是 CTC 的核心功能：自动排列进路具体讲就是分析列车运行计划，然后查找联锁进路表，生成包含始终端按钮的进路序列，并且在站细规定的时间进行触发（发往联锁系统执行）。

Key Point 3: Basic Functions of CTC System

CTC functions include TDCS, shunting centralized control and CTC supporting system function.

1. Autonomous Route Arrangement

Automatic route arrangement as planned is the core function of CTC. To be specific, it is the analysis of train operation plan and looking for interlocking route diagram, generating route order including terminal button and trigger at the station detailed time (send to the interlocking system for implementing).

2. 车次号处理技术

车次号处理技术包括车次窗的设置、车次号的显示、车次号的来源及优先级；车次号自动跟踪；列车车次号校核。

3. 调车作业

如图 5-40、5-41 所示，调车作业被纳入 CTC 控制范畴，助理调度员或车站值班员可编制调车作业单。

调车作业单可编辑、保存、打印，如图 5-42 所示。

调车作业单可管理行车调度进路序列，供调度员或车站值班员执行，界面如图 5-43、5-44、5-45、5-46、5-47 所示。

2. Train Number Processing Technology

The technology includes setting of train number window, display of train number, source and priority of train number; automatic track of train number; check and correction of train number.

3. Shunting

As shown in Figures 5-40 and 5-41, shunting is included in CTC. Assistant dispatch man or station watch man can compile shunting assignment.

Shunting assignment can be edited, saved and printed as shown in Figure 5-42.

Shunting assignment manages train operation dispatching route order for the execution by dispatch man or station watch man, the interface is shown in Figures 5-43, 5-44, 5-45, 5-46 and 5-47.

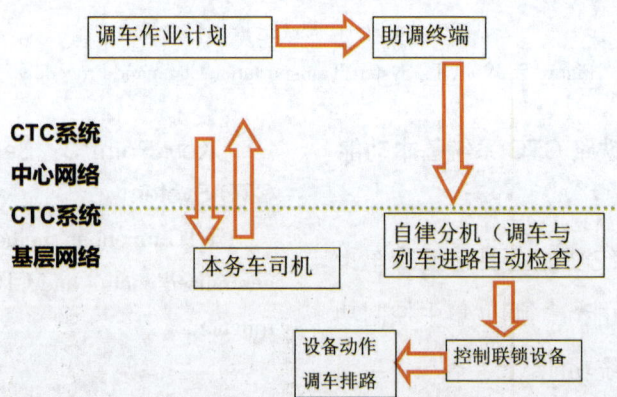

调车作业计划：shunting plan　　助调终端：assisting shunting terminal
CTC 系统中心网络：CTC system central network　　CTC 系统基层网络：CTC system basic network
本务车司机：leading locomotive driver　　自律分机（调车与列车进路自动检查）：automatic extension machine (shunting and automatic route check)　　控制联锁设备：interlocking control equipment
设备动作调车排路：equipment operation shunting route

图 5-40　助理调度台（本务机）作业流程
Figure 5-40　Working Procedure of Assisting Dispatch Platform (Leading Locomotive)

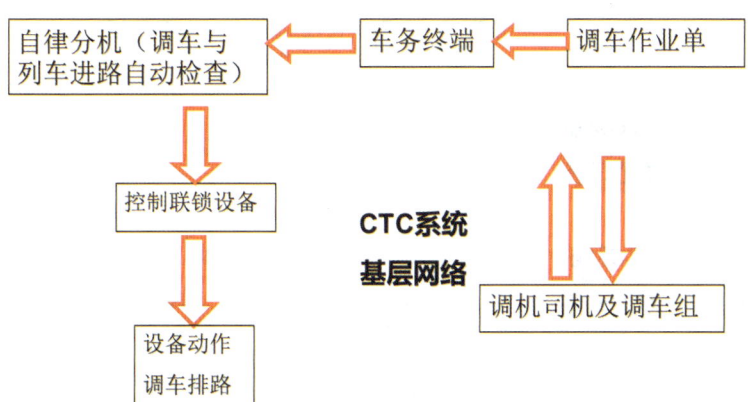

自律分机（调车与列车进路自动检查）：automatic extension machine (shunting and automatic route check)
车务终端：traffic terminal　　调车作业单：shunting assignment　　控制联锁设备：interlocking control equipment
设备动作调车排路：equipment operation shunting route　　CTC 系统基层网络：CTC system basic network
调车司机及调车组：shunting driver and shunting team

图 5-41　有专用调机车站调车作业流程

Figure 5-41　Shunting Procedure with Specialized Shunting Station

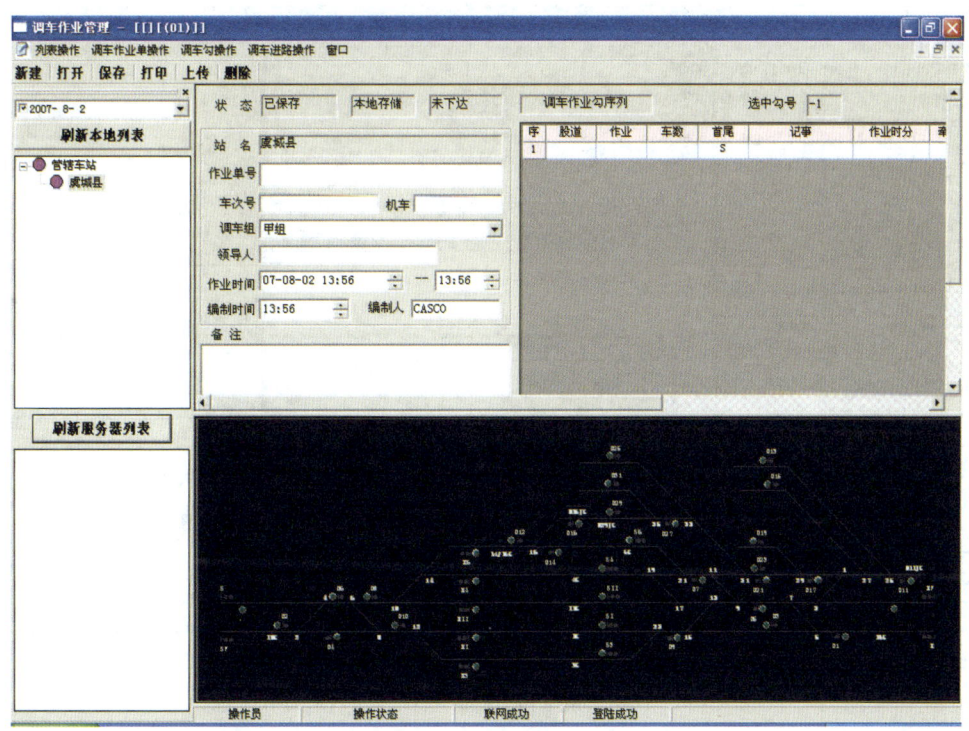

图 5-42　调车作业单

Figure 5-42　Shunting Assignment

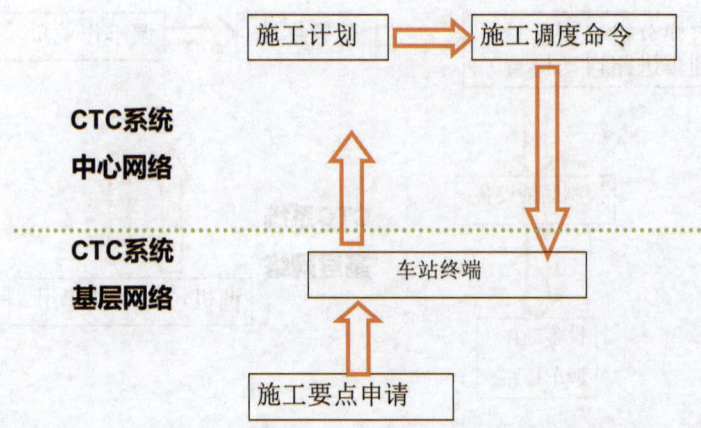

施工计划：construction plan 施工调度命令：construction dispatching order
CTC 系统中心网络：CTC system central network CTC 系统基层网络：CTC system basic network
车站终端：station terminal 施工要点申请：construction key point application

图 5-43 调度终端—施工维修调度台作业流程
Figure 5-43 Dispatching Terminal-construction Repair Dispatching Platform Procedure

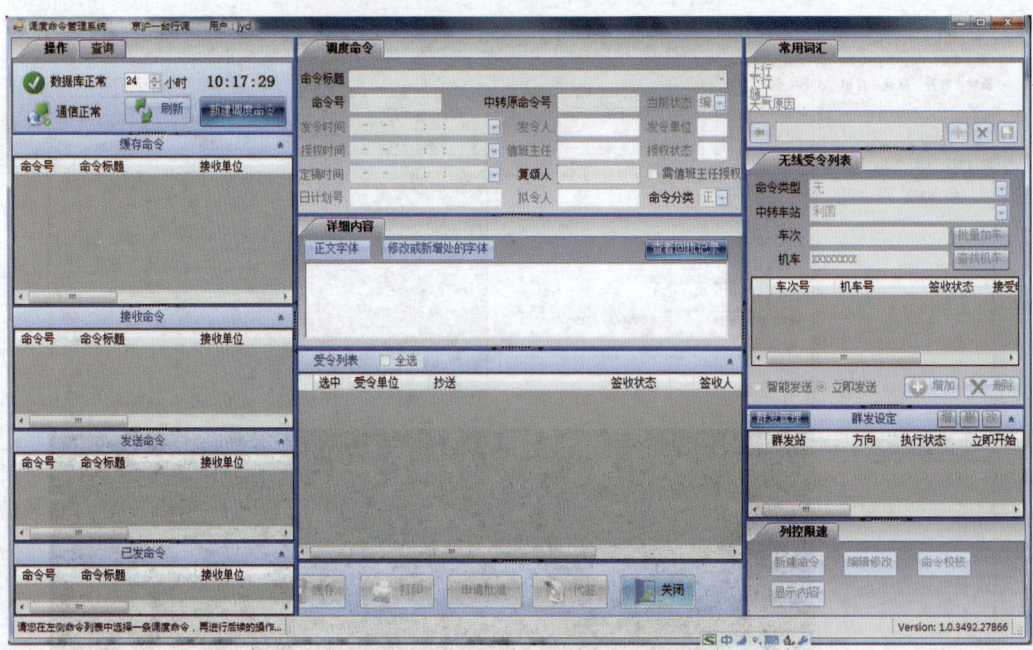

图 5-44 调度台—调度命令界面
Figure 5-44 Dispatching Platform-dispatching Order Interface

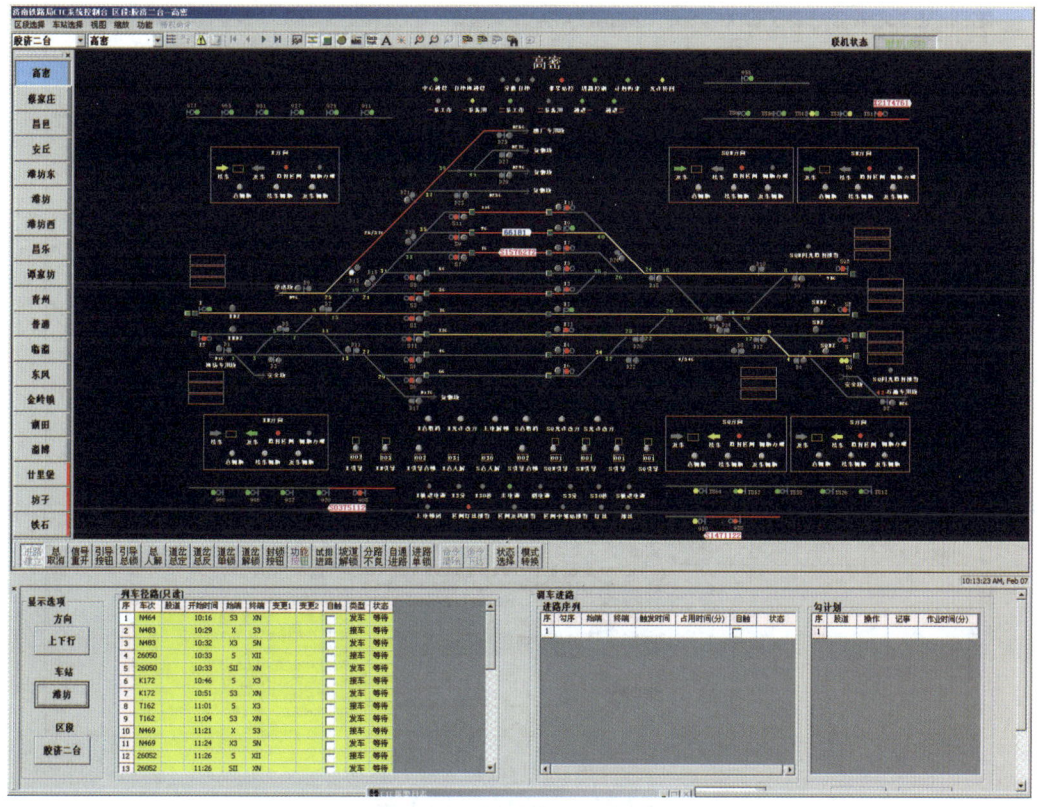

图 5-45 调度中心助调画面

Figure 5-45 Dispatching Center Assisting Dispatching Interface

图 5-46 进路序列画面

Figure 5-46 Route Order Interface

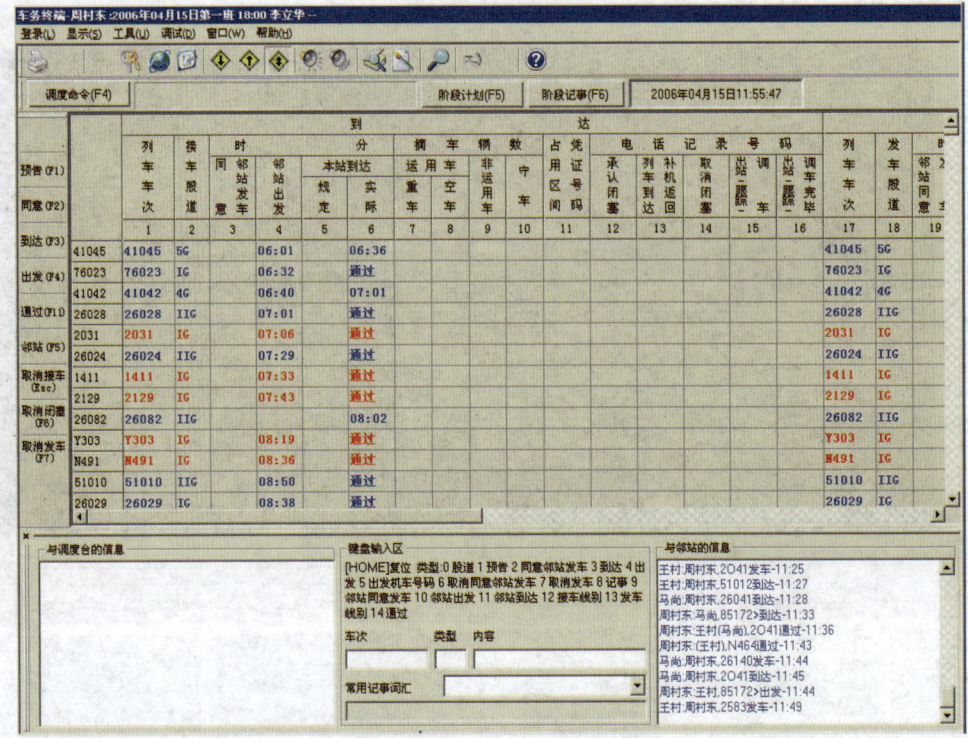

图 5-47 行车日志画面

Figure 5-47　Train Operation Interface

知识点四：调度集中主要功能——行车指挥

1. 调度中心行车指挥

调度中心行车指挥功能包含列车运行监督及运行图两个方面的内容，具体如下。

（1）列车运行实时监督功能。

（2）自动完成列车车次号追踪功能。

（3）列车紧跟踪报警功能。

（4）车站列车到发、通过自动报点功能。

（5）列车运行图管理功能，主要包

Key Point 4: Major Functions of Centralized Dispatching—Train Operation Command

1. Dispatching Center Train Operation Command

The commanding functions include train operation supervision and operation chart, the details are as follows.

(1) Real time supervision of train operation.

(2) Automatic train number track.

(3) Train tight tracking alarm.

(4) Station train arrival and departure, passing automatic point report.

(5) Train operation chart management

括确保查询、基本图接收、阶段计划生成及自动调整、实迹运行图自动绘制、行车计划下达、调度命令下达到车站及机车（通过 GSM-R 网络）、各类统计、记录信息。

2. 车站行车指挥功能

车站行车指挥功能包括列车运行监督及车站行车管理两个方面的内容，具体如下。

（1）列车运行实时信息采集及列车运行监督：通过采集系统实时采集列车运行状况及信号设备状态信息，监视本站及邻站列车运行状况及信号设备状况。

（2）车站行车业务管理：调度命令、阶段计划的签收和打印，车站行车日志的自动生成和管理，车次号修正和到发点的管理，车站现在车管理，甩挂车作业和列车速度报表管理，用户管理及其他辅助功能。

functions include ensure query, basic chart receiving, stage plan generation and automatic adjustment, actual track operation chart automatic plotting, train operation plan assign, dispatching order assign to station and locomotive (through GSM-R network), various kinds of statistics, information recording.

2. Station Train Operation Command

The command functions include train operation supervision and management, the details are as follows.

(1) Train operation real time information collection and supervision: collect real time train operation status and signal equipment information, and supervise train operation status and signal equipment status of the home station and neighboring station.

(2) Station train operation management: signing for receiving and printing of dispatching order, stage plan, automatic generation and management of train operation log, train number revision and management of arrival and departure station, station existing trains management, trailer operation and speed reporting statement management, user management and other auxiliary functions.

学习笔记
Study Notes

模块三 课堂练习

在分散自律控制模式下,调车进路的控制流程是怎样的?画图说明。

Module 3　In-class Exercises

What is the shunting route control procedure in decentralized automatic control mode?

课堂练习
In-class Exercises

模块四　课后拓展

阅读相关国内外文献，简述 CTC 系统的发展趋势。

Module 4　After-class Activity

Read domestic and foreign documents and state development trend of TCT system briefly.

After-class Activity

任务三　行车凭证和调度命令的发送

Task 3　Train Operation Certificate and Dispatching Order Sending

模块一　学前准备

Module 1　Preparation before Class

通过互联网自学国家铁路局颁布的《铁路运输调度规则》标准内容。

Study Railway Transportation Dispatching Rules issued by national railway bureau by yourself on the Internet.

课前学习笔记
Study Notes before Class

模块二 课堂学习

Module 2　In-class Learning

知识点一：调度命令认知

Key Point 1: Understanding Dispatching Order

1. 调度命令的基本概念

（1）调度命令。

各级调度在组织指挥日常运输工作中对下级调度或站调，以及有关人员所发布的有关完成日常运输生产的具体部署和指挥行车工作的指令。调度命令是编有调度命令号码并在《调度命令登记簿》上登记的书面命令。如图 5-48、5-49 所示。

1. Basic Concept of Dispatching Order

（1）Dispatching Order.

It is the order sent by the dispatching centers at different levels to the subordinates or stations for daily transportation and specific arrangement and train operation command issued for daily transportation. It is the written order of Dispatching Order Registration with dispatching order number. See figures 5-48 and 5-49.

20____年____月____日____时____分　　第____号

受　令　处　所		调度员姓名	
内　容			

（规格：110 mm×160 mm）

受令车站_____　　车站值班员_____

受令处所：ordered place　　调度员姓名：name of dispatch man　　内容：content
受令车站：ordered station　　车站值班员：station watchman

图 5-48　调度命令

Figure 5-48　Dispatching Order

月 日	发出时刻	命令			复诵人姓名	接收命令人姓名	调度员姓名	阅读时刻（签名）
		号码	受令及抄知处所	内 容				

（规格：190 mm×265 mm）

月：month　日：day　发出时刻：time of sending　命令：order　号码：number
受令及抄知处所：ordered and forwarding place　内容：content　复诵人姓名：name of repeater
接收命令人姓名：name of order receiver　调度员姓名：name of dispatch men
阅读时刻（签名）：time of reading (signature)

图 5-49　调度命令登记簿

Figure 5-49　Dispatching Order Registration

（2）口头指示。

除调度命令外，调度员在日常生产指挥中向有关人员发布的完成运输生产任务的具体部署和指挥行车工作的指令，称为口头指示。口头指示和调度命令具有同等作用，有关人员必须坚决执行。发布口头指示，应正确、及时、清晰、完整。

（3）运行揭示调度命令。

运行揭示调度命令是指由施工调度室编制的涉及限速、行车方式变化和设备变化的调度命令，如图5-50所示。

（2）Oral instruction.

Apart from dispatching orders, instruction of specific arrangement and train operation command sent by dispatch man is oral instruction. It bears the same effect as dispatching order and receivers shall carry it out resolutely. Oral instruction shall be correct, instant, clear and complete.

（3）Operation revealing dispatching order.

It is the dispatching order compiled by construction dispatching room involving speed limit, change of train operation modes and change of equipment, as shown in Figure 5-50.

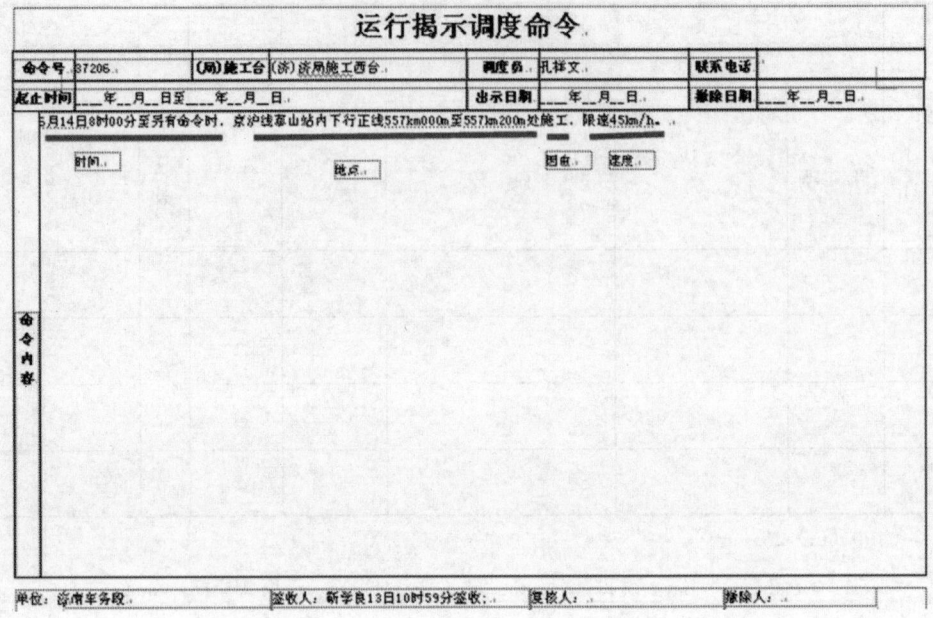

图 5-50 运行揭示调度命令
Figure 5-50 Operation Revealing Dispatching Order

2. 调度命令的发布权限

调度命令的发布必须贯彻行车工作集中统一指挥的原则，各级调度机构和各工种调度的调度命令只能在规定的权限范围内发布，不得越级或越权。

3. 发布调度命令的基本规定

（1）调度命令发布前，列车调度员应详尽了解现场情况，听取有关人员的意见，书写命令内容、受令处所必须正确、完整、清晰。

（2）采用计算机发布调度命令时，必须严格遵守"一拟、二审核（按规定须监控人审核的）、三签（按规定须领导、值班主任签发的）、四发布、五确认签收"的发布程序。受令人必须认真

2. Dispatching Order Issuance Authority

Sending of dispatching order shall follow the principle of centralized command, dispatching offices at various levels and work types shall be issued within regulated authorities.

3. Basic Rules for Dispatching Order Sending

（1）Train dispatch man shall understand site situations comprehensively and listen to the advice from relevant staff before sending dispatching order. Written content and ordered place of the order shall be correct, complete and clear.

（2）Sending procedure of computer dispatching order shall follow the principle of "draft firstly, revise secondly (for orders requiring revision by supervisor) and sign

核对命令内容并及时签收。

（3）采用电话发布调度命令时，必须严格遵守"一拟、二审核（按规定须监控人审核的）、三签（按规定须领导、值班主任签发的）、四发布、五复诵核对、六下达命令号码和时间"的发布程序。发布、接收调度命令时，应填记《调度命令登记簿》，并记明发、收人员姓名及时刻。

（4）采用常用行车调度命令用语（《铁路运输调度规则》附件2）拟写的命令，计算机编辑时"用语"中未用到的字句删除，书面拟写时"用语"中未用到的字句圈掉。

（5）调度命令书写不正确时，应重新书写。

（6）已发布的调度命令，遇有错、漏或变化时，必须取消前发命令，重新发布全部内容的调度命令。

（7）使用调度命令无线传送系统、计算机或传真机发布行车调度命令，必须认真执行确认和回执制度。

（8）发布运行揭示调度命令，不准夹带与受令处所无关的内容和命令。

（9）发布有关线路、道岔限速的调度命令，必须注明具体地点（包括站内线别、道岔号码）、起止里程及时间。发布事故救援命令，有关线路、道岔必须注明里程。

（10）指定时间段内的维修作业，

thirdly (for orders requiring sign by leader, director on duty), issue fourthly, and sign for receiving fifthly". Order receiver shall check the content carefully and sign the order in time.

(3) Sending dispatching order by phone shall follow the principle of "draft firstly, revise secondly (for orders requiring revision by supervisor), sign thirdly (for orders requiring signature by leader, director on duty), issue fourthly, and signe for receiving fifthly". Order receiver shall check the content carefully and sign the order in time.

(4) Orders written with common dispatching words (appendix 2, Railway Transportation Dispatching) shall delete words that are not used in the "common words", and cross words in written orders that are not used in "common words".

(5) Incorrect dispatching orders shall be re-written.

(6) In case the issued orders are incorrect, missed or changed, the original orders shall be canceled and re-issued.

(7) Confirmation and receipt system shall be carried out strictly when issuing orders with wireless transmission system, computers or fax machine.

(8) Irrelevant content or order shall not be included.

(9) Specific location (including in-station line types, number of turnout), starting and ending mileage and time shall be noted carefully when issuing dispatching orders related to lines and turnout speed limit. Mileage shall be marked clearly for relevant lines and turnouts when issuing accident rescue orders.

车站值班员在维修作业完毕销记后，应立即报告列车调度员。列车调度员不再发布维修作业结束恢复行车的命令。如需延长作业时间须列车调度员发布调度命令批准。

知识点二：调度命令编制与下达

1. 常用行车调度命令用语（举例）

（1）封锁区间。

_____站至_____站间_____行线因_____，自接令时（_____次列车到_____站）起，（至___时___分止），区间封锁。

（2）开通封锁区间。

根据_____站报告，_____站至_____站间，行线_____完毕，区间已空闲。自接令时起区间开通。

（3）限速。

_____月_____日_____时_____分至_____月_____日_____时_____分（另有命令时），_____线_____站（含_____道、___号道岔）至_____站（含_____道、___号道岔）间_____行线___km___m至___km___m处施工（灾害、故障），限速___km/h。

（10）Repair in designated period shall be registered for cancellation and report to train dispatch man instantly. Train operation recovery order shall not be issued again after repair ends. Extension of the repair requires approval of dispatching orders.

Key Point 2: Compilation and Assignment of Dispatching Orders

1. Common Dispatching Order Words (Examples)

（1）Section block.

____station to____inter station_____ route as_____, since receiving order (_____train number to_____station),（till_____time），section blocked.

（2）Open blocked section.

According to the report of____station, _____staion to_____station, line_____end, section is vacant. Section is open since receiving the order.

（3）Speed limit.

____month____date_____time_____minute to_____month_____date_____time____minute（if ordered otherwise），_____line____station（including____track, ____turnout number）to____station（including____track, ____turnout number）_____line ____km____m to____km____m is under construction（disaster/failure），speed limit____km/h.

2. 常用行车调度命令的标准格式

行车调度员必须了解调度命令发布的有关规定，熟悉常用调度命令的标准格式与调度命令的交付方法。

3. 调度命令的发布

（1）调度命令发布的工作要求。

按照规范化、标准化的要求，行车调度员发布调度命令应把握住六个环节。

① 情况清楚。

② 规章明确。

③ 受令人齐全。

④ 内容确切。

⑤ 措辞简明。

⑥ 记载完整。

（2）利用计算机按给定的条件下达调度命令。

熟练使用计算机按给定的条件下达调度命令大大减轻了行车调度员的劳动强度，提高了调度命令编制质量和下达效率。

2. Standard Format of Common Train Dispatching Order

Dispatch man shall be familiar with rules regarding dispatching order issuance, standard format and delivery means of common dispatching order.

3. Issuance of Dispatching Order

（1）Working requirement of dispatching order issuance.

Six points shall be focused according to normal and standard requirement.

① Clear situation.

② Specific rule.

③ Complete order receiver.

④ Accurate content.

⑤ Brief words.

⑥ Complete record.

（2）Send dispatching order as required with computer.

Good command of dispatching order sent with computers greatly relieves labor intensity of dispatcher and improves compilation quality and sending efficiency of dispatching orders.

学习笔记
Study Notes

模块三 课堂练习

练习1：讨论封锁昆明南—昆明区间的调度命令的发布。

练习2：讨论开通昆明—大理封锁区间的调度命令的发布。

练习3：讨论普通调度命令与运行揭示调度命令的区别。

Module 3　In-class Exercises

Exercise 1：Discuss sending dispatching order to block section from South Kunming Railway station to Kunming Railway station.

Exercise 2：Discuss sending dispatching order to block section from Kunming Railway station to Dali Railway station.

Exercise 3：Discuss the differences between common dispatching order and operation revealing order.

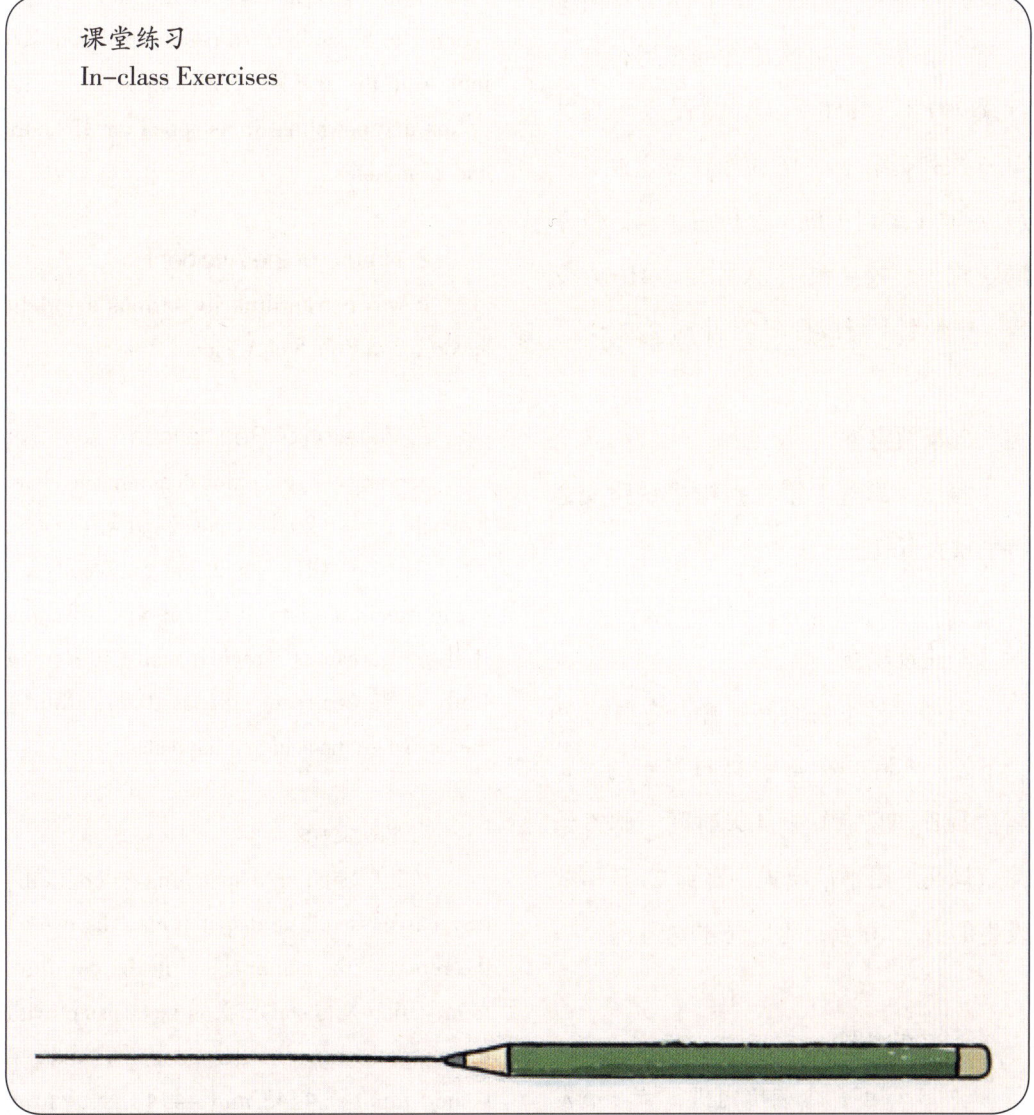

课堂练习
In-class Exercises

模块四　课后拓展

X 局"4.28"事故。

1. 事故概况

2008 年 4 月 28 日 4 时 38 分，由北京开往青岛的 T195 次旅客列车运行至 X 铁路局管内 A 线 B 站至 C 站间 290 千米 800 米处，因超速，机后 9 至 17 位车辆脱轨，并侵入上行线。4 时 41 分，由烟台开往徐州的 5034 次旅客列车运行至上行线 290 千米 850 米处，与侵入限界的 T195 次列车第 15、16 位车辆发生冲突，造成 5034 次列车机车及机后 1 至 5 位车辆脱轨。事故导致 70 人死亡，416 人受伤，中断上下行线行车 21 小时 22 分。

2. 事故定性

根据《事规》第八条构成铁路交通特别重大事故。

3. 违反规章

调图文件下发时间过晚，应提前 20 天下发，实际是在 4 月 24 日发布的，距离执行日期只有短短 4 天时间。邮寄给北京局又采用平信模式，直到 28 日事故发生的当日 10 点，北京局才收到。

4. 存在问题

（1）调度命令漏传司机，调度员发

Module 4　After-class Activity

X railway bureau "April 28th" accident.

1. General Situation of the Accident

At 4:38, April 28th, 2008, coach 9-17 of passenger train T195 from Beijing to Qingdao derailed at 290km+800m between station X to A of line B of C railway bureau as a result of over speed and invaded the uplink line. It crashed with coach 15 and 16 of train T195 that invaded in the boundary, then train 5034 and coach 1 to 5 derailed. 70 people died and 416 injured in the accident. Train operation in the uplink and downlink line stopped for 21 hours and 22 minutes.

2. Nature of the Accident

It was extraordinarily serious accident according to Rule 8 of Accident Rule.

3. Violation of Regulations

Sending of dispatching diagram is too late. It should be sent 20 days ahead and was sent on April 24th actually, which was only four days to the execution date. It was posted to Beijing Railway Bureau as a regular mail and Beijing Railway Bureau received it at 10:00, 28th, the day when the accident happened.

4. Problems

（1）Sending dispatching orders to the driver is missed. The dispatch man discovered the report "the actual speed in the downlink from station X to station X is inconsistent with the approved speed in the monitor", and re-issued number 4443 and 4444 dispatching

现"X站至X站间下行线实际运行速度与运监器允许速度不符"的报告后，根据文件重新发布了4443、4444号调度命令，要求B站、C站、D站分别交上下行各次列车，在上述不符地点限速80千米/时。

（2）对在途列车没有指定交令处所，命令不完整。车站值班员未按总公司要求与司机执行车机联控核对限速调度命令。

通过分析X局"4.28"事故报告，总结教训，认识调度命令发布工作的重要性。

orders to demand station B, station C and station D to require the downlink and uplink trains the speed limit of 80 km/h in the above-mentioned inconsistent locations.

（2）The order to the trains on route was not clear in terms of locations and incomplete. Station watchman did not check the speed limit dispatching order with the driver using train-computer co-control.

Lessons shall be learned through analyzing X Bureau "April 28th" Accident Report to realize the significance of dispatching order sending.

课后拓展

After-class Activity

项目六　驼峰信号设备

Project 6　Hump Signal Equipment

任务一　驼峰概述

Task 1　Hump Overview

模块一　学前准备

Module 1　Preparation before Class

在网上搜集、观看铁路驼峰溜放视频，了解驼峰溜车。

Search videos of railway hump leading on the Internet to understand rolling direction of hump.

课前学习笔记
Study Notes before Class

模块二 课堂学习

知识点一：编组站

1. 什么是编组站

在铁路网中，凡办理数量较大的货物列车解体和编组作业，并为此设有专门调车设备的车站，称为编组站。编组站一般设在几条主要干线的汇合处，也可以设在有大量装卸作业的大城市、港口或大工矿企业附近。编组站的主要作业是大量办理列车的解体和编组，编组站实际上就是一个编组列车的工厂。如图6-1所示。

Module 2 In-class Learning

Key Point 1: Marshaling Station

1. What is Marshaling Station

In railway network, stations with specialized equipment for freight train splitting and marshaling in large quantity are called marshaling stations. Marshaling stations are usually set in the junctions of major trunk lines, big cities, ports or large scale factories of mineral enterprises with large quantity of loading and unloading operation. Major operation in the marshaling station is handling train splitting and marshaling. Marshaling station is in fact the factory of marshaling trains. See Figure 6-1.

图 6-1 铁路车站编组站
Figure 6-1 Railway Station Marshaling Station

2. 编组站分类

编组站按其车场配置方式可分为单向横列式（如图6-2所示）、单向纵列式（如图6-3所示）、单向混合式、双向横列式、双向纵列式（如图6-4所示）和双向混合式等多种类型。

编组站一般都设有比较完善的调车设备，如到达场、驼峰、编组场和出发场等。其作用是解体和编组货物列车。

2. Classification of Marshaling Station

Marshaling stations are divided into unidirectional transversal type (Figure 6-2), unidirectional longitudinal type (Figure 6-3), unidirectional combined type, bidirectional transversal type, bidirectional longitudinal type (Figure 6-4), bidirectional combined type and so on.

There is usually complete dispatching equipment in the marshaling stations, such as arrival yard, hump, marshaling yard, and departure yard for splitting and marshaling freight trains.

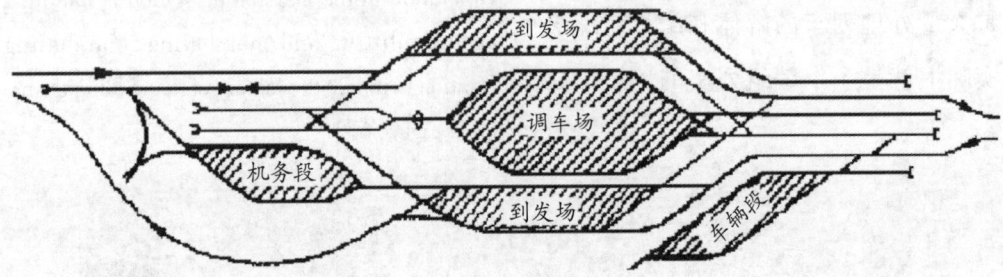

机务段：locomotive depot 到发场：receiving departure yard 调车场：shunting yard
车辆段：train depot

图 6-2 单向横列式配置

Figure 6-2　Unidirectional Transversal Type

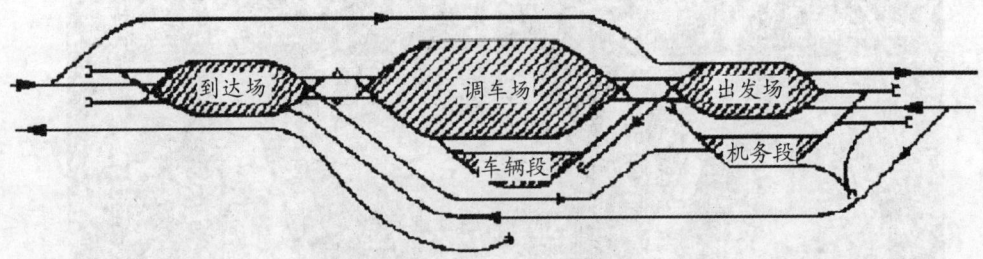

到达场：arrival yard 调车场：shunting yard 出发场：departure yard 车辆段：train depot
机务段：locomotive depot

图 6-3 单向纵列式配置

Figure 6-3　Unidirectional Longitudinal Type

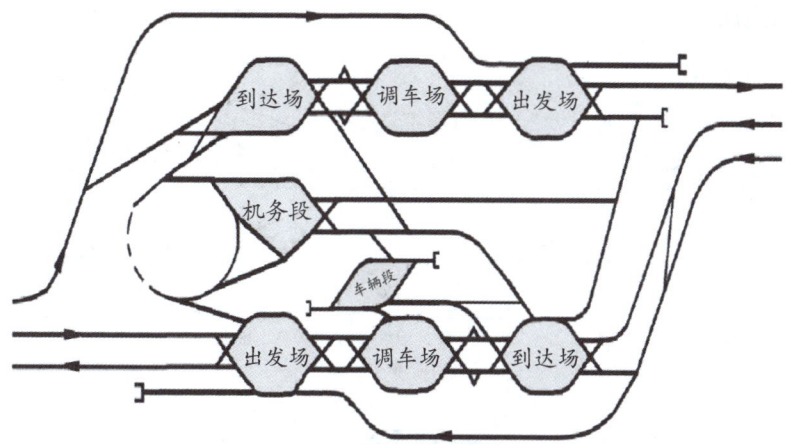

到达场：arrival yard   调车场：shunting yard   出发场：departure yard   机务段：locomotive depot
车辆段：train depot

图 6-4 双向三级六场纵列式编组站
Figure 6-4 Bidirectional Three-grade Six-yard Longitudinal Marshaling Station

知识点二：驼峰

1. 什么是驼峰

所谓驼峰，就是在编组场头部建一个高于调车场平面的土丘，因其断面形状类似于"单峰骆驼"的驼峰，就简称为"驼峰"，如图 6-5 所示。

Key Point 2：Hump

1. What is Hump

Hump is a hummock built on the head of the marshaling yard and higher than the dispatching yard. It is called "hump" as its sectional form is similar to dromedary, as shown in Figure 6-5.

图 6-5 铁路驼峰（图片来源于百度百科）
Figure 6-5 Railway Hump（picture from Baidu Baike）

2. 驼峰组成 / 2. Composition of Hump

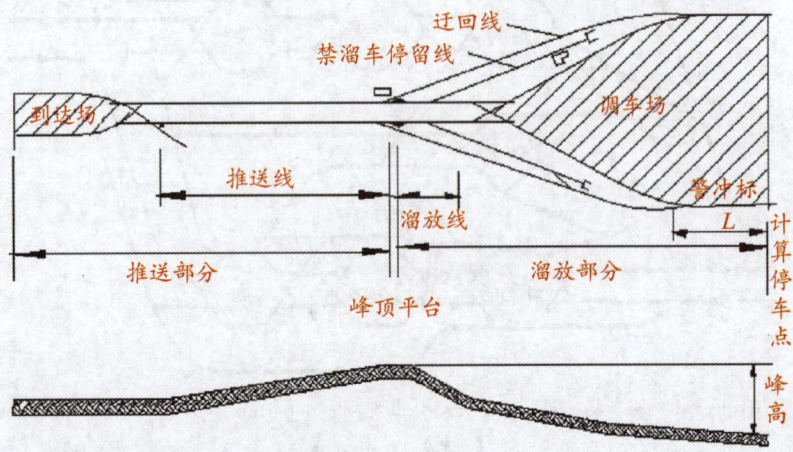

到达场：arrival yard　迂回线：detour line　禁溜车停留线：no slip stop line　推送线：push line
溜放线：setting out　调车场：shunting yard　警冲标：warning mark　推送部分：push part
溜放部分：slip part　峰顶平台：capping platform　计算停车点：calculation of parking points
峰高：peak height

图 6-6　驼峰各组成部分示意图（驼峰平、纵断面）

Figure 6-6　Components of Hump（Plan and Sectional Form of Hump）

如图 6-6 所示。	See Figure 6-6.
（1）推送部分。	（1）Pushing section of hump.
（2）溜放部分。	（2）Rolling section of hump.
（3）峰顶平台。	（3）Platform of hump crest.
（4）计算停车点。	（4）Computed stop point.

3. 驼峰分类（按昼夜解体能力） / 3. Classification of Hump（Based on Night-day Splitting Capacity）

（1）大能力驼峰。　　（1）Large capacity hump.
（2）中能力驼峰。　　（2）Medium capacity hump.
（3）小能力驼峰。　　（3）Small capacity hump.

4. 驼峰调车作业 / 4. Hump Shunting Operation

在进行驼峰调车作业时，先由调车

In hump shunting, shunting locomotive pushes train to the hump. When the trains

机车将车列推向驼峰，当最前面的车组（或车辆）接近峰顶时，（车钩压紧时）提开车钩，过峰顶后就可以利用车辆自身的重力，顺坡自动溜放到编组场的预定线路上，从而可以大大提高调车作业的效率。

驼峰解体车列一般包括连挂车列、推峰、解体、下峰整理等作业过程。

（1）连挂车列。

驼峰调车机车驶往到达场连挂车列。

（2）推峰。

驼峰调车机车将车列推至峰顶或预推至峰前信号机。

（3）解体。

驼峰机车推送车列经过峰顶，使被摘解的车组脱钩后，依靠自身重力溜向调车场内制定线路。

（4）下峰整理。

驼峰机车下峰整理调车场，主要任务包括：消除股道内停留车组之间的空挡（又称"天窗"）、将"堵门车"推至调车场内适当位置以便继续溜放、取送禁溜车等。

(train) in the head approach the peak, (coupler compressed) coupler is elevated. The trains automatically roll to the preset line as a result of gravity after passing the peak, thus, shunting capacity is greatly enhanced.

Operation procedures such as train coupling, peak push, splitting and down peak are included in hump train splitting.

(1) Train set coupling.

Hump shunting locomotive drives to the arrival yard for train set coupling.

(2) Peak push.

Hump shunting locomotive pushes the trains to the peak or in front of the pre-peak signal machine.

(3) Splitting.

Hump locomotive pushes the train set to the peak and enable the decoupled train set roll to the designated lines in the shunting yard by their own gravity.

(4) Down peak arrangement.

Major tasks include eliminating the vacancy (also called light window) among the train sets in the lines, pushing "train stop door" to a proper location in the shunting yard for continuing rolling, taking and sending of no-humping trains.

学习笔记
Study Notes

模块三　课堂练习

结合驼峰解体、编组作业视频，讨论和学习驼峰溜放调车作业特点。

Module 3　In-class Exercises

Discuss and learn features of hump rolling dispatching operation, combining operation videos of hump splitting and marshaling operation.

课堂练习
In-class Exercises

模块四 课后拓展

Module 4　After-class Activity

在全国铁路线路图中标出主要编组站位置及名称。

Mark the location and names of major marshaling stations in china railway map.

After-class Activity

任务二 驼峰基本信号设备认知

Task 2 Understanding Hump Basic Signal Equipment

模块一 学前准备

Module 1 Preparation before Class

复习项目二中信号机、转辙机、轨道电路等联锁设备相关知识。阐述各设备的作用及原理。

Revise knowledge on signal machine, point switch, track circuit and other interlocking equipment in Project 2. State the functions and principles of the equipment.

课前学习笔记
Study Notes before Class

模块二 课堂学习

知识点一：驼峰信号设备

如图 6-7 所示为驼峰调车场信号设备平面布置图，驼峰信号设备包括信号机、转辙机、轨道电路、车辆减速器、电源、动力设备、控制设备等。控制设备因不同类型的驼峰而不同，有手动控制、继电控制和计算机控制。

Module 2 In-class Learning

Key Point 1：Hump Signal Equipment

Figure 6-7 is the signal equipment layout map in hump shunting yard, and hump signal equipment includes signal machine, point switch, track circuit, train decelerator, power source, power equipment, control equipment and so on. Control equipment differs based on different types of humps. The equipment is manually controlled, relay controlled or computer controlled.

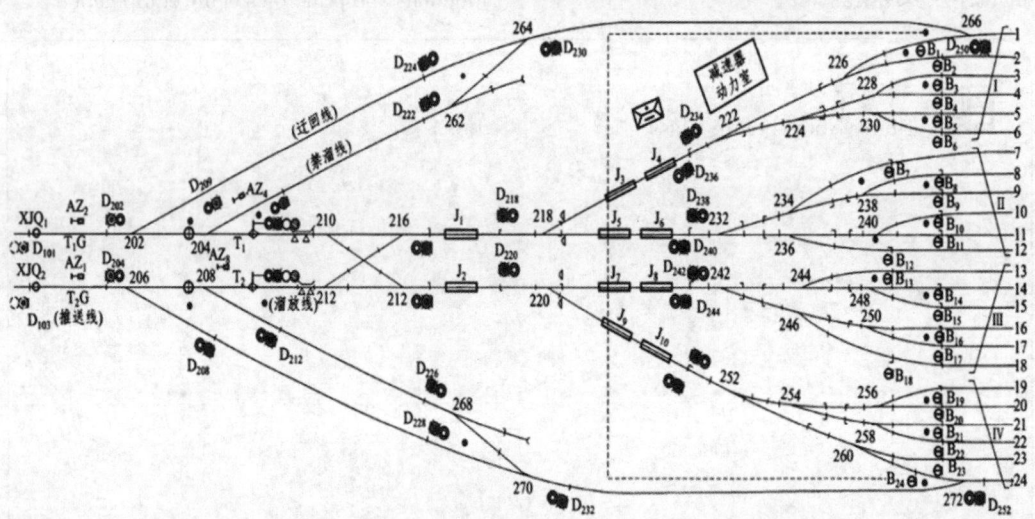

迂回线：detour line　　禁溜线：no slip line　　溜放线：setting out　　减速器动力室：reducer power room

图 6-7　驼峰调车场信号设备平面布置图

Figure 6-7 Signal Equipment Layout Map in Hump Shunting Yard

1. 信号机

（1）驼峰信号机。

① 设置：设在峰顶平台处，每条推送线设一架。

② 作用：指示调车车列能否向峰顶推送，能否越过峰顶向峰下调车场进行

1. Signal Machine

（1）Hump signal machine.

① Setting: on the platform of the peak and one piece for each pushing track.

② Function: indicating if the shunting train set can be pushed to the peak and if rolling can be operated in the down-peak shunting

溜放作业。

如图 6-8 所示为驼峰信号机、驼峰辅助信号机、驼峰复示信号机设置图。

yard passing the peak.

Figure 6-9 is the set-up diagrams of hump signal machine, hump auxiliary signal machine, and hump repeating signal machine.

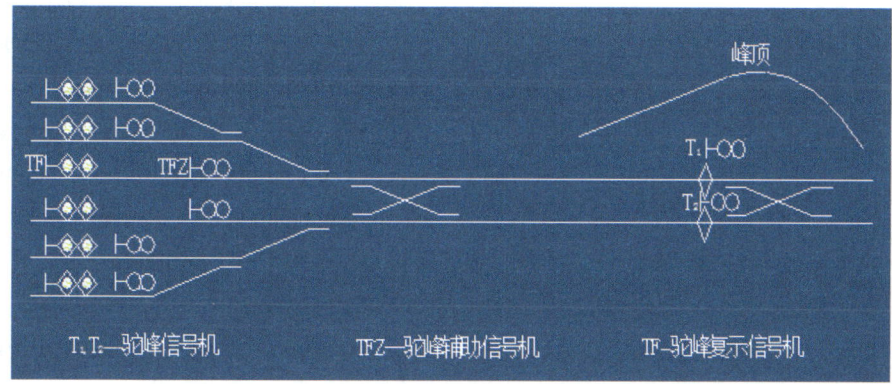

峰顶: peak

图 6-8 驼峰信号机、驼峰辅助信号机、驼峰复示信号机设置图

Figure 6-8　Set-up Diagram of Hump Signal Machine, Hump Auxiliary Signal Machine, Hump Repeating Signal Machine

③ 灯光配列：驼峰信号机为四灯（黄、绿、红、月白）七显示高柱信号机，如图 6-9 所示。

③ Light arrangement: hump signal machine has four-light (yellow, green, red, pale green) and seven-display high pillar signal machine, as shown in Figure 6-9.

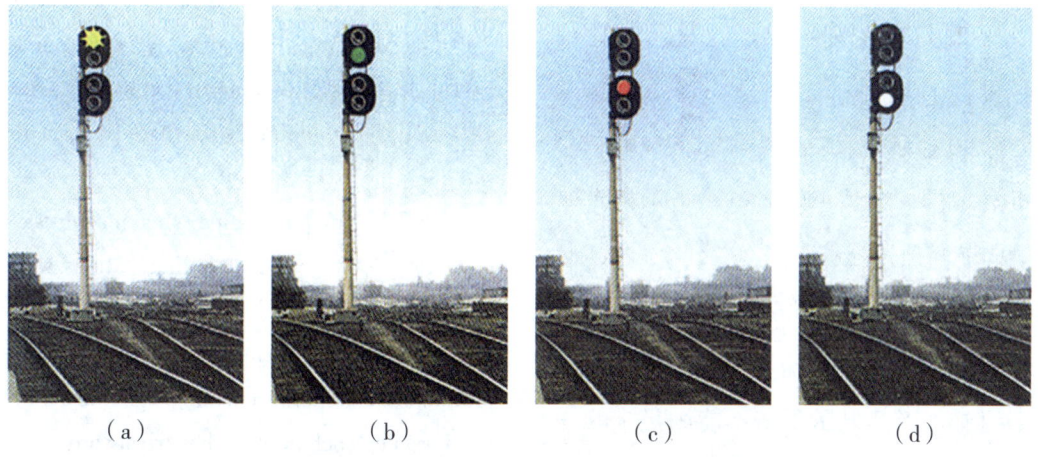

(a)　　　　(b)　　　　(c)　　　　(d)

图 6-9　驼峰信号机灯光配列（黄、绿、红、月白）

Figure 6-9　Hump Signal Machine Light Arrangement (Yellow, Green, Red, Pale green)

④ 显示意义。

一个绿色灯光：准许机车车辆按规定速度向驼峰推进。

一个绿色闪光灯光：指示机车车辆要加速向驼峰推进。

一个黄色闪光灯光：指示机车车辆要减速向驼峰推进。

一个红色灯光：不准机车车辆越过该信号机或指示机车车辆停止作业。

一个红色闪光灯光：指示机车车辆自驼峰退回。

一个月白色灯光：指示机车到峰下。

一个月白色闪光灯光：指示机车车辆去禁溜线。

（2）驼峰辅助信号机。

① 设置：在整个推峰解体过程中，调车机车位于车列尾部，为让机车司机看清驼峰信号显示，在峰前到达场每条到发线靠近驼峰的一端装设驼峰辅助信号机。

② 灯光配列：四灯八显示高柱信号机。

③ 显示意义：灯光显示同驼峰信号机显示，一个黄色灯光——指示机车车辆向驼峰预先推送。

（3）驼峰复示信号机。

① 设置：在设有驼峰辅助信号机的编组站，当其显示距离不能满足推峰作业要求时，根据需要可在到达场每股道上再装设一架驼峰复示信号机。

④ Meanings.

One green light: permitting locomotive pushing to the hump at regulated speed.

One flashing green light: locomotive pushing to the hump at accelerating speed.

One flashing yellow light: locomotive pushing to the hump at decelerating speed.

One red light: forbidding locomotive passing the signal machine or locomotive stopping operation.

One flashing red light: locomotive retreating from hump.

One pale green light: indicating locomotive to peak bottom.

One flashing pale green light: indicating locomotive to no-humping track.

（2）Hump auxiliary signal machine.

① Setting: In the entire process of hump pushing and splitting, shunting locomotive is in the end of the train set for a clear view of hump signal display for drivers. At the end near the hump of each departure and arrival track, hump auxiliary signal machine is set.

② Light arrangement: four-light eight-display high pillar signal machine.

③ Meaning: The display is the same as the hump signal machine display. One yellow light—locomotive is pre-pushed to the hump.

（3）Hump repeating signal machine.

① Setting: In marshaling stations with hump auxiliary signal machine, in case the display distance fails to meet the requirement of humping, a hump repeating signal machine can be set on each track of the arrival yard.

② Meaning of display: using color signal machine with lenticular color light and

② 显示意义：采用透镜式带两个双机柱的色灯信号机，方形背板，如图6-10 所示。

double pillar, square backboard, as shown in Figure 6-10.

图 6-10 驼峰复示信号机机构

Figure 6-10 Hump Repeating Signal Machine Structure

（4）线路表示器。

① 设置：当有两台以上机车在峰下进行作业，或调车线上瞭望线束信号机的显示有困难时，根据需要在各编组线上设置。

② 显示：平时处于灭灯状态，不起信号作用；当线路表示器点亮白灯，指示该线路上的调机上峰作业。

2. 转辙机

峰上道岔采用普通转辙机。峰下分路道岔采用快动转辙机。一般采用 ZD 型电动转辙机（目前较多的是 ZD7 型）和 ZK 型电空转辙机（目前较多的是 ZK3 型）。

（4）Circuit indicator.

① Setting: In case two or more locomotives are operated in down peak, or display of observatory harness signal machine fails to display, it is set on the marshaling track according to the requirement.

② Display: It is usually out without signal function; white light on circuit indicator is on, it indicates shunting up peak on the track.

2. Point Switch

Ordinary point switch is used in up peak turnout. Fast point switch is used in turnouts on branch tracks. Generally, ZD electric point switch (mostly ZD7 type) and ZK electric point switch (mostly ZK3) are used.

·243·

3. 轨道电路

驼峰调车场的轨道电路有峰上轨道电路、峰下分路道岔轨道电路、编组线警冲标区段轨道电路。

4. 按钮柱

按钮柱是为了方便现场作业人员发现危及作业安全时能及时关闭驼峰信号而设置的。一般设置在每架驼峰信号机的前方、其推送线左侧的适当地点。

5. 车辆减速器及限界检查器

车辆减速器的作用是调整溜放车组的速度，如图 6-11 所示。

3. Track Circuit

Track circuits in hump shunting yard are up peak track circuit, down peak branch track turnout circuit and marshaling track warning board section circuit.

4. Button Pillar

Button pillar is set for in-time shutting down of hump signal in case of dangers. It is usually set in proper locations in front of every hump signal machine or on the left of the pushing track.

5. Train Decelerator and Boundary Checker

Function of the decelerator is to adjust the speed of rolling train set, as shown in Figure 6-11.

图 6-11　减速器

Figure 6-11　Decelerator

限界检查器用于检查车辆的底部限界。一般在每条推送线上距峰顶 80~100 米处装设限界检查器，如图 6-12 所示。

Boundary checker is to check the bottom boundary of trains. It is usually set at 80~100 m from hump peak on each pushing track, as shown in Figure 6-12.

图 6-12　限界检查器

Figure 6-12　Boundary Checker

知识点二：驼峰机车信号系统

Key Point 2：Hump Locomotive Signal

1．驼峰机车信号

采用无线传输方式的驼峰无线机车信号，目前被国内外广泛使用。

无线机车信号设备示意图如图 6-13 所示。

1. Hump Locomotive Signal

Hump locomotive signal wireless transmission is widely used worldwide.

Wireless locomotive signal equipment is shown in Figure 6-13.

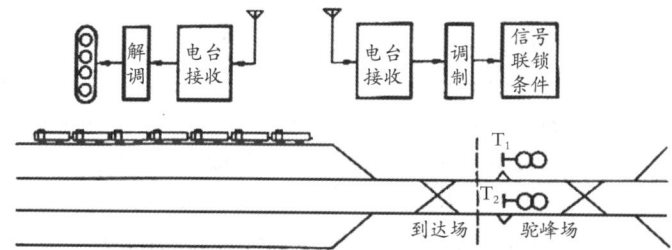

解调：demodulation　电台接收：radio receiving　调制：modulation
信号联锁条件：signal interlocking condition　到达场：arrival yard　驼峰场：hump yard

图 6-13　无线机车信号设备示意图

Figure 6-13　Wireless Locomotive Signal Equipment Diagram

·245·

2. 驼峰机车遥控

驼峰机车遥控设备供驼峰值班员在驼峰信号楼内直接操纵驼峰机车的速度变换、停车、后退等，司机只进行监视；或者由计算机控制变速推送。

（1）驼峰机车无线遥控系统设备组成。

① 控制对象选择设备。

② 控制命令发送及接收设备。

③ 机车速度控制设备。

④ 回执表示。

如图 6-14 所示为驼峰机车推峰无线遥控系统设备框图。

2. Hump Locomotive Remote Control

Hump locomotive remote control equipment is for hump watchman's direct operation of speed change, stop and going back in the signal building. Drivers can only supervise the operation; or speed change is done by computers.

（1） Equipment composition of hump locomotive wireless remote control system.

① Controlled object selection equipment.

② Control order sending and receiving equipment.

③ Locomotive speed control equipment.

④ Receipt display.

Figure 6-14 is hump locomotive pushing wireless remote control system equipment frame.

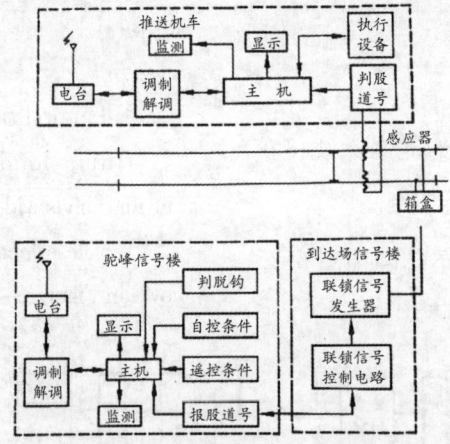

电台：radio　推送机车：push locomotive　监测：surveillance
调制解调：modulation and demodulation　显示：display　主机：host computer
执行设备：execution equipment　判股道号：track number judging　感应器：sensor　箱盒：box
驼峰信号楼：hump signal building　判脱钩：decoupling judge　自控条件：self-control condition
遥控条件：remote control condition　报股道号：track number reporting
到达场信号楼：arrival yard signal building　联锁信号发生器：interlocking signal generator
联锁信号控制电路：interlocking signal controlling circuit

图 6-14　驼峰机车推峰无线遥控系统设备框图

Figure 6-14　Hump Locomotive Pushing Wireless Remote Control System Equipment Frame

（2）该系统可对机车完成下列控制过程。

① 定速度控制。

② 定距离控制。

③ 停车控制。

④ 变速度控制。

⑤ 在推送作业中，司机可随时将遥控变为主动控制。

⑥ 机车接收的控制命令、遥控时实际走行的速度均可直接显示在值班员控制台上，便于值班员掌握推送作业情况。

⑦ 该系统适用于双推送线、多台机车作业的编组站。

⑧ 该系统与地面信号设备及进路具有联锁功能，保证作业安全，值班员控车手续简便。

（2）The system can fulfill the following controlling process over locomotive.

① Regulated speed control.

② Regulated distance control.

③ Stop control.

④ Speed change control.

⑤ In the process of train pushing, divers can change the remote control into active control at any time.

⑥ Control order received by the locomotive and actual remote control speed can display on the control platform of the watchman for commanding of the pushing operation status.

⑦ The system is applicable in marshaling stations with double pushing tracks and multiple locomotive operation.

⑧ The system is interlocked with ground signal equipment and route to ensure safe operation and is convenient for watchman's control.

学习笔记
Study Notes

模块三　课堂练习

根据图 6-7 驼峰调车场信号设备平面布置图，识别驼峰机车信号并说出其主要功能。

Module 3　In-class Exercises

Recognize hump signals and state their functions based on the hump shunting yard signal equipment layout in Figure 6-7.

模块四 课后拓展

Module 4　After-class Activity

参观所在城市铁路驼峰编组场信号设置，画出该驼峰头部平面示意图。

Visit railway hump marshaling yard signal layout in your city and draw its plan diagram.

任务三 驼峰道岔自动集中操纵

Task 3 Hump Turnout Automatic Centralized Control

模块一 学前准备

Module 1 Preparation before Class

在网上搜集驼峰道岔自动集中操纵设备,熟悉其设备组成。

Search hump turnout automatic centralized control equipment on the Internet and get familiar with the equipment components.

课前学习笔记
Study Notes before Class

模块二 课堂学习

知识点一：驼峰道岔自动集中设备

1. 驼峰道岔自动集中控制台

驼峰道岔自动集中控制台如图6-15、6-16所示。驼峰作业员根据调车作业计划，通过控制台操纵或自动控制头部道岔和第一制动位的车辆减速器。

Module 2　In-class Learning

Key Point 1: Hump Turnout Automatic Centralized Equipment

1. Hump Turnout Automatic Centralized Control Platform

The control platform is shown in Figure 6-15 and Figure 6-16. Operator operates head turnout and train decelerator in the first location through control platform or automatically according to shunting plan.

图 6-15　驼峰道岔自动集中控制台

Figure 6-15　Hump Turnout Automatic Centralized Control Platform

2. 驼峰道岔自动集中的操纵按钮

（1）清零按钮。
（2）储存取消按钮。
（3）溜放取消按钮。
（4）增加按钮。
（5）进位检查按钮。
（6）检查按钮和检查停止按钮。

2. Hump Turnout Automatic Centralized Controlling Buttons

（1）Reset button.
（2）Saving cancellation button.
（3）Rolling cancelation button.
（4）Adding button.
（5）Carry check button.
（6）Check button and check stop button.

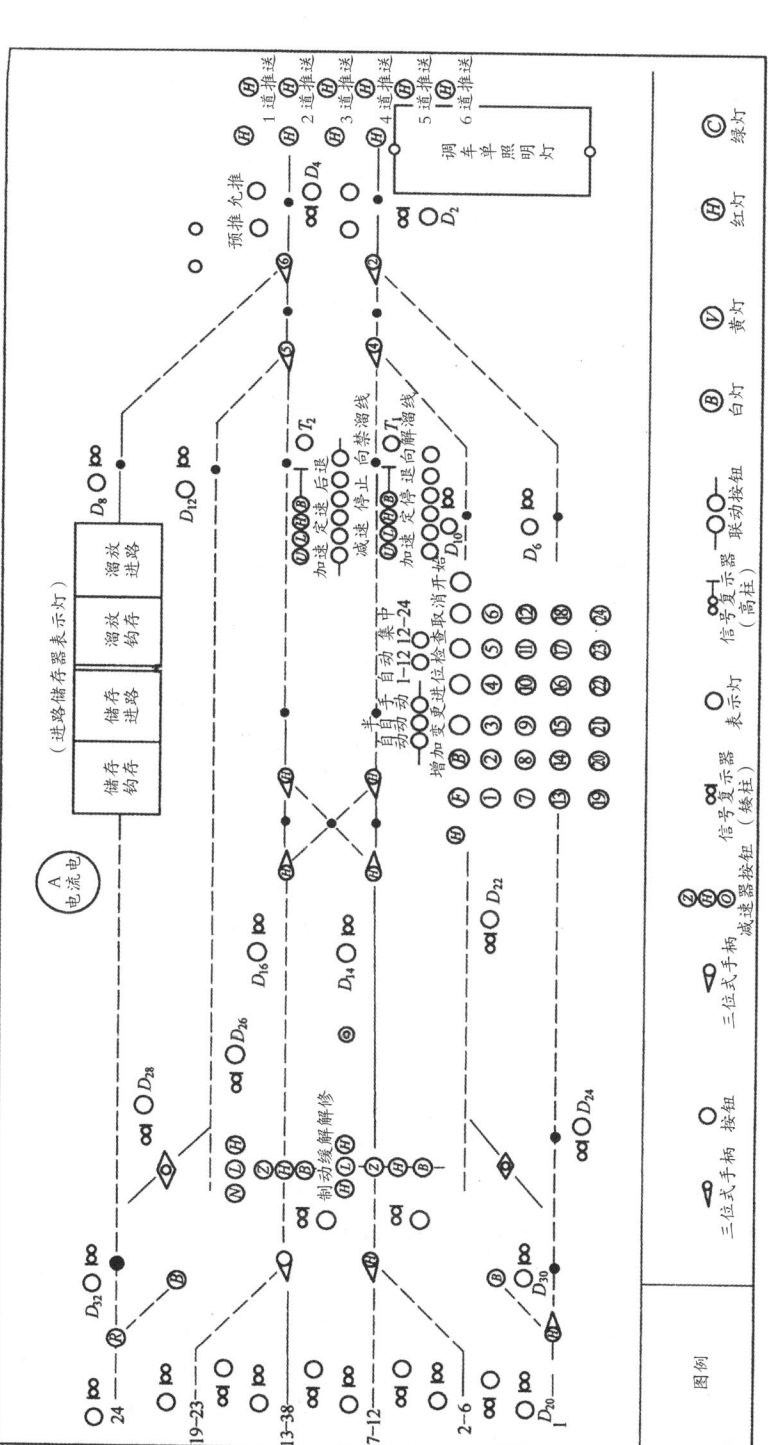

电流电: electric current　进路存储器表示灯: route memory indicator　储存钩存: storage hook storage　储存进路: storage route　溜放钩存: free hook and store
溜放进路: slip route　制动缓解解修: brake release and repair　加速: accelerate　定速: constant speed　后退: back off　减速: slow down　停止: stop it　向
禁溜线: to the no slip line　预推: pre push　允推: allow to push　增加: increase　变更: change　自动: automatic　半自动: semi-automatic　手动: manual　集中: focus　定停: fixed stop
退向解溜线: backward to release line　2 道推送: 2 push　3 道推送: 3 push　4 道推送: 4 push　5 道推送: 5 push　6 道推送: 6 push　进应: carry　检查: inspect　取消: cancel　开始: start　1 道推送: 1 push　2 道推
送: 2 push　三位式手柄: three position handle　按钮: button　减速器按钮: reducer button　信号复示器 (棱柱): signal multiplexer (short column)　调车单照明灯: shunting single lamp　图例: legend　三位式手柄:
three position handle　联动按钮: linkage button
示器 (高柱): signal multiplexer (high column)　白灯: white light　黄灯: yellow light　红灯: red light　表示灯: indicator light　信号复
　　　绿灯: green light

图 6—16　驼峰道岔自动集中控制台

Figure 6—16　Hump Turnout Automatic Centralized Equipment

知识点二：驼峰道岔自动集中的操纵

机械化驼峰采用道岔自动集中设备办理排列溜放进路作业时，对溜放进路的控制可以分为自动、半自动和手动作业三种方式。

1. 储存自动进路

（1）预排进路。

自动道岔手柄置于中间位置；按下"手动"按钮，再按下"自动"按钮，拉出"清零"按钮；根据调车作业通知单所列的钩序和股道号码，逐个按压进路按钮。

（2）检查进路。

按压"检查"按钮，与调车作业计划逐钩核对；发现错误或需要变更进路，按压"取消"按钮，取消该钩进路，再按所需"进路"按钮；检查完毕后，拉出"检查"按钮；必须坚持驼峰调车长与作业员两人核对检查制度，一人读计划和钩序，一人复诵核对。

（3）增加进路。

第一钩车未溜下前，按下"增加"按钮，再按下需增加的"进路"按钮。

（4）取消进路。

① 在储存进路过程中，按下"储存取消"按钮，再按压正确的或需要的"进路"按钮即可。如需全部取消，拉出"清零"按钮即可。

Key Point 2: Hump Turnout Automatic Centralized Control

Arrangement of rolling route of machinery hump with turnout automatic centralized equipment can be controlled automatically, semi-automatically and manually.

1. Saving Automatic Route

（1）Pre-arrangement of route.

Automatic turnout hand bar is set in the middle; press "manual" button and "automatic" button and pull out "reset" button; press route buttons in order according to the coupler order and track number in the shunting operation assignment.

（2）Route check.

Press "check" button and check with shunting assignment one by one; in case of error or need of change, press "cancellation" to cancel the coupling of the route and press the needed "route" button; press "check" button after check completion; stick to the system of check by shunting yard master and operator of reading plan and coupler order by one and repeating reading and check by the other.

（3）Adding route.

Press "adding" before the rolling of the first coupler and then press the "route" button that needs to be added.

（4）Canceling route.

① In the process of route saving, press "saving cancellation" button, and press the correct or required "route" button. If all processes are to be cancelled, pull out "reset" button.

② 在溜放过程中，必须在取消钩溜出之前，关闭驼峰信号停车处理。按下"溜放取消"按钮取消该进路。

2. 储存半自动进路

半自动方式就是储一钩、溜一钩，即随着钩车往下溜放，逐钩控制分路道岔的转换。

采用半自动作业方式前，应将自动集中道岔手柄置于中间位置，自动集中表示灯亮白灯。作业员按压"半自动"按钮，然后根据调车作业计划上第一钩车应进的股道，按压进路按钮。当第一钩车进入第一分路道岔区段后，储存器溜放进路表示灯熄灯，此时，作业员再根据下一钩车需溜入的股道，按压相应的进路按钮，继续溜放第二钩车，直到一个车列溜完为止。

3. 手动办理进路

当设备故障，不能进行自动和半自动作业或驼峰调机进行上、下峰调车作业时，可采用手动作业方式。

采用手动作业方式前，驼峰作业员先按压"手动"按钮。

根据调车作业计划，驼峰作业员用手柄单独操纵道岔的转换。

② In the process of rolling, hump signal is to be shut down before cancellation coupler rolling.

2. Saving Semi-automatic Route

The semi-automatic way is to save one coupler and roll one coupler, namely rolling down with the coupler train and control turnout change in branch tracks by couplers.

Automatic centralized turnout shall be set in the middle before semi-automatic operation and the indicating light is white. Operator presses "semi-automatic", and then presses route button according to the track of the first coupling train on the shunting plan. After the first coupler train enters the turnout section of the first branch track, indicating light in the saver roller is out and the operator presses the corresponding route button according to the next rolling track for the rolling of second rolling train until the rolling completion of the entire train set.

3. Manual Routing

In case equipment fails and automatic and semi-automatic operation, up and down peak shunting in hump shunting are impossible, manual operation is feasible.

Hump operator presses "manual" button before manual operation.

Hump operator switches turnout with handle bar independently.

学习笔记
Study Notes

模块三 课堂练习

根据图 6-16 驼峰道岔自动集中控制台，完成下列作业单：

第一钩 进 3 道
第二钩 进 1 道
第三钩 进 4 道
第四钩 进 2 道

Module 3　In-class Exercises

Finish the following operation assignment according to the hump turnout automatic centralized control platform in Figure 6-16：

first coupler to route 3
second coupler to route 1
third coupler to route 4
fourth coupler to track 2

模块四 课后拓展

利用驼峰道岔自动集中设备模拟预排溜放进路的操纵。

Module 4 After-class Activity

Simulate pre-set rolling route operation with hump automatic turnout automatic centralized equipment.

任务四　自动化驼峰设备认知

Task 4　Understanding Automatic Hump Signal

模块一　学前准备

到图书馆或者上网搜集 TW-2 型驼峰计算机控制系统相关知识，了解其功能。

Module 1　Preparation before Class

Search relevant information on TW-2 hump computer control system in library or on the Internet.

课前学习笔记
Study Notes before Class

模块二　课堂学习

知识点一：自动化驼峰测量设备

驼峰测量设备包括测速设备、测阻设备、测长设备和测重设备。具体的设备主要包括测速雷达、测长器、测重机、车轮传感器、光挡、气象站和车轮存在探测器。

知识点二：驼峰溜放速度自动控制系统

驼峰调速自动化系统的组成如图 6-17 所示。

Module 2　In-class Learning

Key Point 1: Automatic Hump Measuring Equipment

Hump measuring equipment includes speed measurement equipment, rollability measurement equipment, length measurement equipment and weight measurement equipment. The specific equipment is speed measurement radar, length measurement machine, weight measurement machine, wheel sensor, light blocker, meteorologic station and wheel existing detector.

Key Point 2: Hump Rolling Speed Automatic Control System

Composition of hump speed regulation automatic system is as shown in Figure 6-17.

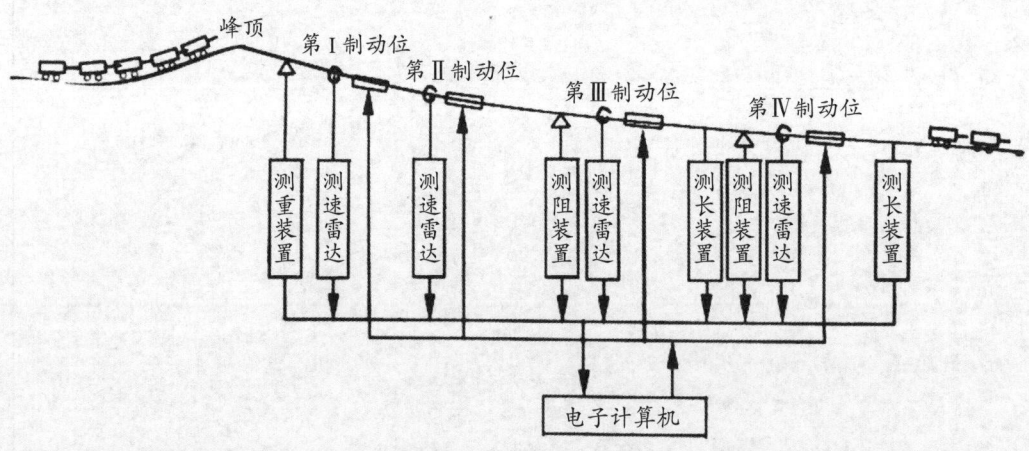

峰顶：summit　第Ⅰ制动位：first brake position　第Ⅱ制动位：2nd brake position
第Ⅲ制动位：third brake position　第Ⅳ制动位：4th brake position　测重装置：weight measuring device
测速雷达：velocity radar　测阻装置：resistance measuring device　测长装置：length measuring device
电子计算机：electronic computer

图 6-17　驼峰调速自动化系统组成示意图
Figure 6-17　Composition of Hump Speed Regulation Automatic System

（1）在驼峰加速坡上，装设有压磁测重器，用以对溜放钩车的重量进行测量，为减速器控制级别提供依据。

（2）在每一制动位前均装设有测速雷达，由轨道电路控制雷达的开机和关机。测速雷达对溜放钩车进入减速器前和经过减速器调整后的速度进行测量，为电子计算机计算钩车走行速度的变化提供依据。

（3）在第Ⅲ、第Ⅳ制动位前均设4个电磁感应器，用以测量钩车溜放阻力，作为调速控制的阻力依据。

（4）音频测长器用于测量股道空闲长度。若测量800 m长的股道空闲长度，可以分为三个测试区段，即第Ⅲ制动位到第Ⅳ制动位间的200 m为第一段，第Ⅳ制动位以后再分为两个区段，每个区段各长300 m。

知识点三：驼峰计算机过程控制系统

1.TW-2系统

驼峰计算机过程控制系统应用最多的是TW-2系统。

TW-2为集散式控制系统，即集中管理、分散控制其硬件结构，如图6-18所示。

（1）Piezomagnetic weight measurement machine is installed on the hump accelerating slope to measure the weight of rolling coupler to provide proof for controlling grades of decelerator.

（2）Speed measurement radar is installed in front of every braking position and controlled by track circuit. Speed measurement radar measures the adjusted speed of rolling coupler before entering decelerator and after passing the decelerator.

（3）4 electromagnetic sensors are set in front of the third and fourth braking position to measure rolling resistance as the resistance basis for speed adjustment control.

（4）Audio length measurement machine to measure track vacancy. To measure the vacant length of 800 m, it can be divided into three testing sections. Namely, 200 m from third braking section to fourth section is the first sections. Area after the fourth braking section is divided into two sections with length of 300 m for each section.

Key Point 3: Hump Computer Process Control System

1. TW-2

The most frequently used is TW-2.

TW-2 is decentralized control system, namely, centralized control and separate control over hardware structure, as shown Figure 6-18.

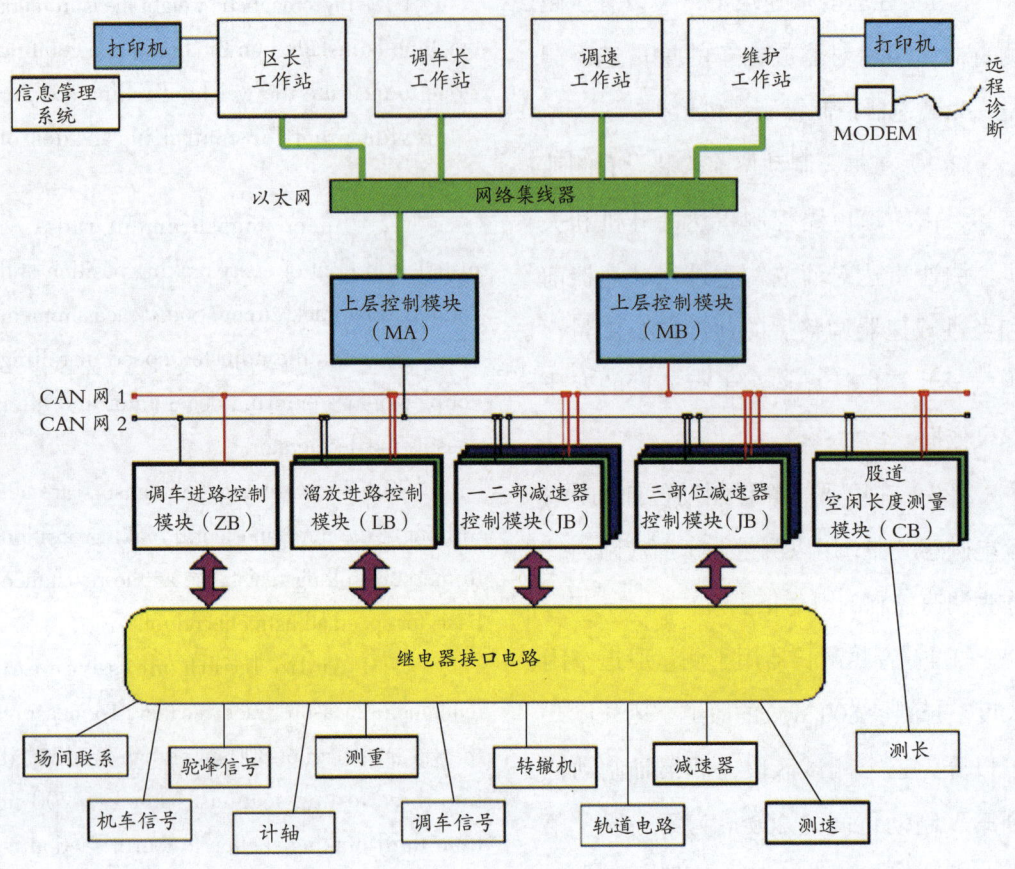

信息管理系统：information management system　打印机：printer　区长工作站：section chief work station
调车长工作站：head of shunting train work station　调速工作站：speed adjustment work station
维护工作站：maintenance work station　远程诊断：remote control　以太网：ethernet
网络集线器：network concentrator　上层控制模块：upper floor control module
调车进路控制模块：shunting route control module　溜放进路控制模块：rolling route control module
一二部减速器控制模块：part one and two decelerator control module
三部位减速器控制模块：part three decelerator control module
股道空闲长度测量模块：track vacancy length measurement module　继电器接口电路：relay port circuit
场间联系：inter-section connection　机车信号：locomotive signal　驼峰信号：hump signal
计轴：axle counting　测重：weight measurement　调车信号：shunting signal　转辙机：point switch
轨道电路：track circuit　减速器：decelerator　测速：speed measurement　测长：length measurement

图 6-18　典型的 TW-2 型组态式控制系统结构示意图
Figure 6-18　Typical TW-2 Configurated Control System Diagram

2. 独特的功能

（1）设计为双推双溜，兼容双推单溜和单推单溜。

（2）采用多媒体操作界面，具有语音报警、核对计划功能。可在扩充站场图形显示的同时，混合图像显示（例如站场摄像信号接入）的功能。

（3）在溜放开始时推送进路自动选路与锁闭，与到达场的场间联系可自动办理。

（4）可自动执行混合型的调车作业计划，除溜放钩外，可按计划逐钩自动执行上下峰遇车进路、禁溜线和迂回线取送车进路，无须操作员介入。

（5）在线束遇车上下峰进路上有死区段及减速器的情况下，实现了调车进路信号自动关闭与进路自动解锁，确保了联锁关系的严密。

（6）采用轨道占用时间屏蔽等独特手段，使系统具有防止轻车跳动的功能，有效地减少了轨道电路分路不良引起的勾车掉道等险性事故，提高了作业安全程度。

（7）支持远程诊断。

（8）系统可以为调车区长设置工作站，并支持运输部门的报警查询及统计报告。

（9）模块插件可带电插拔。

2. Unique Functions

（1）Designed as double push and double rolling, compatible for double push-single rolling and single push and rolling.

（2）Multimedia operation interface with voice alarm and plan check function. Expanding station yard map and simultaneous image display（such as peak coupling）.

（3）Pushing route for automatic route choice and block at the beginning of rolling and connect automatic processing with arrival yard.

（4）Automatic operation of mixed shunting, automatic operation of up peak and down peak train route, train sending route in no-humping track and reroute apart from coupler rolling, no intervention of operator.

（5）In case of dead section and decelerator in harness up peak and down peak, automatic block of route signal and automatic unlocking of route ensure close interlocking connection.

（6）Unique means of track occupancy period shielding prevents light train jumping to reduce the possibility of coupler derail and other dangers as a result of bad track circuit extension.

（7）Supporting remote diagnosis.

（8）Setting work station for shunting chief, supporting transportation section alarm inquiry and statistics report.

（9）Module plug can be plugged and un-plugged with power on.

知识点四：编组站综合集成自动化系统（CIPS）

编组站综合集成自动化系统由管理信息和信号控制集中两部分组成。

1. 系统功能

编组站综合自动化系统包括调度指挥管理、现在车管理、货运管理、统计分析、站内设备集中控制、自动控制、作业过程跟踪、综合信息显示、系统监控与维护等功能。

2. 系统结构

编组站综合集成自动化系统由管理信息系统和信号控制集中系统两部分组成。设置独立的信息网和集中控制网，信息网和集中控制网均应采用双环形自愈网。分别设置信息机房、信号机房。系统结构如图6-19所示。

管理信息系统设备包括数据库服务器、应用服务器、接口服务器、存储设备、终端设备、网络设备、网络安全设备、打印设备、不间断电源设备等；信号控制集中系统设备包括数据库服务器、应用服务器、接口服务器、存储设备、终端设备、网络设备、网络安全设备、打印设备、不间断电源设备等。

编组站综合集成自动化系统可设置值班站长、总站调、车站调度员、车站

Key Point 4: Marshaling Station Comprehensive Integrated Automatic Processing System (CIPS)

CIPS is divided into two parts.

1. System Function

CIPS includes dispatching command management, existing management, freight transportation management, statistics analysis, in-station equipment centralized control, automatic control, operation process track, comprehensive information display, system supervision and maintenance and so on.

2. System Structure

CIPS consists of management information system and signal control centralization system. Independent information network and centralized control network is set with double circular self-healing network. Information room and signal room are set. The system structure diagram is shown in Figure 6-19.

Management information system equipment includes data base server, application server, port server, saving device, terminal equipment, network equipment, network safety equipment, printing equipment, constant power source equipment and so on; signal centralized control system equipment includes database server, application server, port server, saving device, terminal device, network equipment, network safety equipment, printing equipment, instant power source and so on.

Marshaling station comprehensive automatic system can set position terminals such as station

助理调度员、调车区长、货运调度员、车号员、货检值班员、列检值班员、列尾值班员、总值班员、车站值班员、车站助理值班员、货检员、拉风、统计报告员、系统维护员等岗位终端。

chief on duty, chief station dispatch man, station dispatch man, station assisting dispatch man, shunting section chief, train number worker, freight check duty man, train check watch man, train end watch man, chief watch man, station watch man, station assisting watch man, freight checker, windbreak valve puller, statistics reporter, system maintainer and so on.

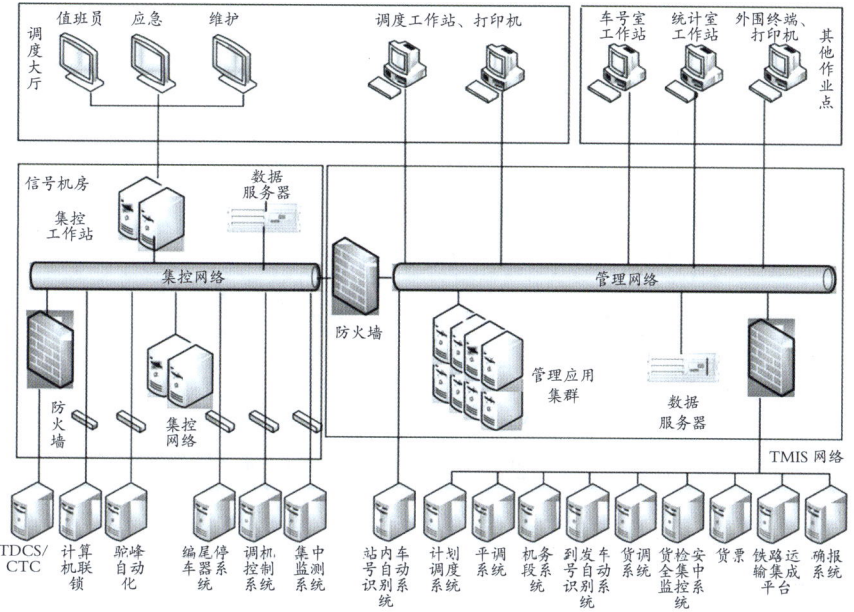

调度大厅：dispatching hall　值班员：watchman　应急：emergency　维护：maintenance
调度工作站：dispatching work station　打印机：printer　车号室工作站：train number work station
统计室工作站：statistics room work station　外围终端：peripheral terminal　其他作业点：other operation locations
信号机房：signal room　集控工作站：centralized control work station　数据服务器：data server
集控网络：centralized control work station　防火墙：firewall　集控网络：centralized control network
计算机联锁：computer interlock　驼峰自动化：hump automation　管理网络：management network
编尾停车器系统：marshaling end stopper system　调机控制系统：shunting locomotive control system
集中监测系统：centralized supervision system　管理应用集群：management application trunk
站内车号自动识别系统：in-station train number automatic recognition system
计划调度系统：plan dispatching system　平调系统：flat regulation system
机务段系统：locomotive depot system　到发车号自动识别系统：arrival and departure train number automatic recognition system　货调系统：freight dispatching system
货检安全集中监控系统：freight safety centralized supervision system　货票：freight bill
铁路运输集成平台：railway transportation centralized platform　确报系统：confirmation system

图 6-19　编组站综合自动化系统结构示意图

Figure 6-19　Marshaling Station Comprehensive Automatic System Structure

学习笔记
Study Notes

模块三　课堂练习

画出 TW-2 型驼峰计算机过程控制系统硬件结构图。

Module 3　In-class Exercises

Draw a structure diagram of TW-2 hump computer remote control system hardware.

模块四　课后拓展

画出驼峰调速自动化系统组成示意图。

Module 4　After-class Activity

Draw a diagram of hump speed adjustment automatic system composition.

项目七　铁路通信设备

Project 7　Railway Communication Equipment

任务一　铁路通信概述

Task 1　Railway Communication Overview

模块一　学前准备　　　　　　　　　Module 1　Preparation before Class

查资料，了解什么是铁路通信。　　　Search information to understand railway communication.

课前学习笔记
Study Notes before Class

模块二　课堂学习

知识点一：铁路通信

铁路通信是利用有线通信、无线通信、光纤通信等技术和设备，传输和交换处理铁路运输生产和建设过程中各种信息的。

铁路通信技术以运输生产为重点，主要功能是实现行车和机车车辆作业的统一调度与指挥。其是确保行车安全，提高运输效率和改进管理水平的重要技术，如图 7-1 所示。

Module 2　In-class Learning

Key Point 1: Railway Communication

Railway communication transmits, exchanges and processes various kinds of information in the process of railway communication and construction, using technologies and equipment of wired communication, wireless communication, optical fibre.

Railway communication technology focuses on transportation with the major function of unified dispatching and command of train operation and locomotive operation to ensure transportation efficiency and improving management level.

图 7-1　铁路通信

Figure 7-1　Railway Communication

知识点二：铁路通信技术发展历程

如图 7-2 所示。

Key Point 2: Development of Railway Communication Technology

See Figure 7-2.

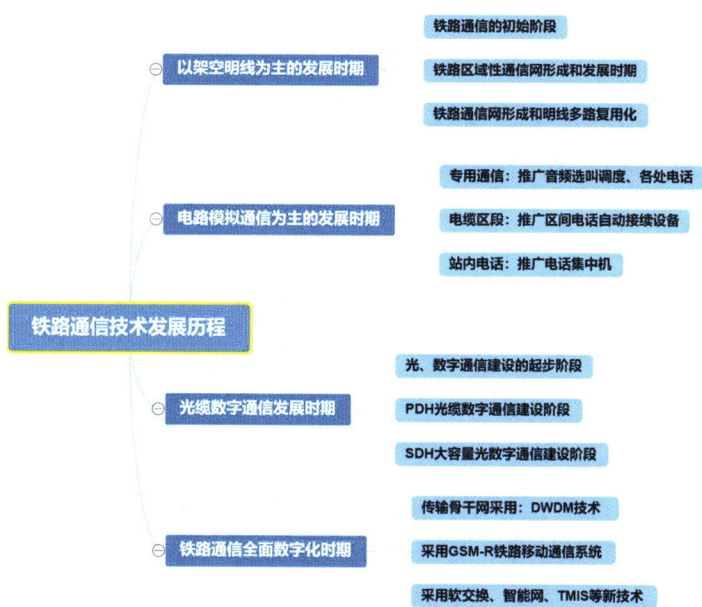

铁路通信技术发展历程：development history of railway communication technology　以架空明线为主的发展时期：development period of overhead open line　电路模拟通信为主的发展时期：the development period of circuit analog communication　光缆数字通信发展时期：the development period of cable digital communication　铁路通信全面数字化时期：the period of comprehensive digitalization of railway communication　铁路通信的初始阶段：the initial stage of railway communication　铁路区域性通信网形成和发展时期：formation and development period of railway regional communication network　铁路通信网形成和明线多路复用化：formation of railway communication network and multiplexing of open lines　专用通信：推广音频选叫调度、各处电话：special communication: promotion of audio selective call dispatching and local telephone　电缆区段：推广区间电话自动接续设备：cable section: promoting automatic connection equipment of section telephone　站内电话：推广电话集中机：station telephone: promotion of centralized telephone　光、数字通信建设的起步阶段：the initial stage of optical and digital communication construction　PDH光缆数字通信建设阶段：PDH optical cable digital communication construction stage　SDH大容量光数字通信建设阶段：SDH large capacity optical digital communication construction stage　传输骨干网采用：DWDM技术：the transmission backbone network adopts DWDM technology　采用GSM-R铁路移动通信系统：using GSM-R railway mobile communication system　采用软交换、智能网、TMIS等新技术：new technologies such as softswitch, intelligent network and TMIS are adopted

图 7-2　铁路通信技术发展历程

Figure 7-2　Railway Communication Technology Development

知识点三：铁路通信分类

Key Point 3：Classification of Railway Communication

1. 按通达地区和范围分

（1）铁路长途通信。

1. Classification by Accessible Areas and Range

（1）Railway long distance communication.

铁路长途通信是经过长途传输设备连接的铁路电话、电报和数据通信，使用人工交换机和长途自动交换机。存储程序控制电子交换机也用于长途交换，如图7-3所示。

（2）铁路地区通信。

铁路地区通信为同一地区的铁路系统用户间的通信，主要是采用电话通信，通过长途交换设备可接长途通信网，设置市话中继线可接入市话系统。地区通信一般使用电缆传输，将广泛采用存储程序控制数字交换机，如图7-4所示。

Railway long distance communication is the communication of railway telephone, telegraph and data communication connected by long distance transmission equipment with manual interchanger and long distance automatic interchanger. Electronic interchanger controlled by saving procedure is also used for long distance interchange.

（2）Railway regional communication.

Railway regional communication is used by railway system users in the same region, and the major means is telephone communication. Long distance communication can be connected with long distance interchange equipment. Local calls system can be connected with local calls relay line. Regional communication uses cable communication and digital interchanger controlled by saving procedures widely, as shown in Figure 7-4.

图7-3 铁路通信基站
Figure 7-3 Railway Communication Base Station

图7-4 铁路通信一体化机房及铁塔
Figure 7-4 Railway Communication Integrated Equipment Room and Iron Tower

（3）铁路区段通信。

铁路区段通信为铁路沿线各部门用于指挥、调度、行车、管理等公务的专用通信系统，包括调度电话、站间行车电话、基层业务电话、区间电话和列车预报确报电报等。

（4）铁路站内通信。

铁路站内通信用于铁路站场各种作业指挥和生产联系，采用站场有线电话、站场无线电话、站内电报和电视，以及站场扩音和信息控制。

2. 按通信的业务性质分

（1）铁路公用。

（2）专用通信。

（3）Railway section communication.

Railway section communication is the specialized communication system for commanding, dispatching, train operation, management by the offices along the railway, and it includes dispatching call, interstation train operation call, basic level operation call, section call and train forecast and confirmation telegraph and so on.

（4）Railway in-station communication.

Railway in-station communication is used in operation command and connection in railway yards with yard wire telephone, yard radio telephone, in-station telegraph and television, yard amplifier and information control.

2. Classification by Operation Feature of Communication

（1）Railway public use.

（2）Specialized communication.

学习笔记
Study Notes

模块三　课堂练习

练习1：同学们都坐过火车吧，请你结合自己的乘车体验，想一想在乘坐火车时你碰到过哪些与铁路通信相关的事宜。

练习2：谈一谈铁路通信的重要性。

Module 3　In-class Exercises

Exercise 1：Everyone has travelled by train, think about the affairs related to railway communication based on your travel experience.

Exercise 2：Talk about the importance of railway communication.

课堂练习
In-class Exercises

模块四　课后拓展

拿起你手中的相机，拍一幅和铁路通信相关的照片并加以说明。

Module 4　After-class Activity

Take a picture about railway communication and explain it.

After-class Activity

任务二　铁路专用通信设备运用

Task 2　Railway Specialized Communication Equipment Application

模块一　学前准备

查资料，了解铁路通信设备有哪些，列举出 1 种至 2 种，并说出设备的功能。

Module 1　Preparation before Class

Search information to learn about railway communication equipment, give one or two examples and illustrate their functions.

课前学习笔记
Study Notes before Class

模块二　课堂学习

知识点一：铁路专用通信设备

铁路专用通信设备一般是指专门用于组织、指挥铁路运输生产的专用通信设备。这些设备专用于某一目的，接通一些指定用户，一般不与公务通信的电报、电话网连接。

知识点二：铁路专用通信分类

根据铁路运输的特点，铁路专用通信又可分为区段专用通信和站场专用通信两大类。

1．区段专用通信

如图7-5、7-6、7-7所示，铁路区段专用通信是为了组织与指挥铁路沿线各作业点的铁路运输协调工作，将铁路沿线划分为若干管理区段，在其中用来进行业务联系的专用通信设备。

Module 2　In-class Learning

Key Point 1：Railway Specialized Communication Equipment

Railway specialized communication equipment is the specialized communication equipment for organizing and commanding railway transportation. The equipment is used for a certain purpose to connect designated users, and is generally not connected with telegraph and telephone network used for business communication.

Key Point 2：Classification of Railway Specialized Communication

Railway specialized communication is divided into section specialized communication and yard specialized communication based on the features of railway transportation.

1. Section Specialized Communication

As shown in figures 7-5, 7-6 and 7-7, railway section specialized communication uses specialized communication equipment to organizing and commanding transportation on railway by dividing the railway into several sections.

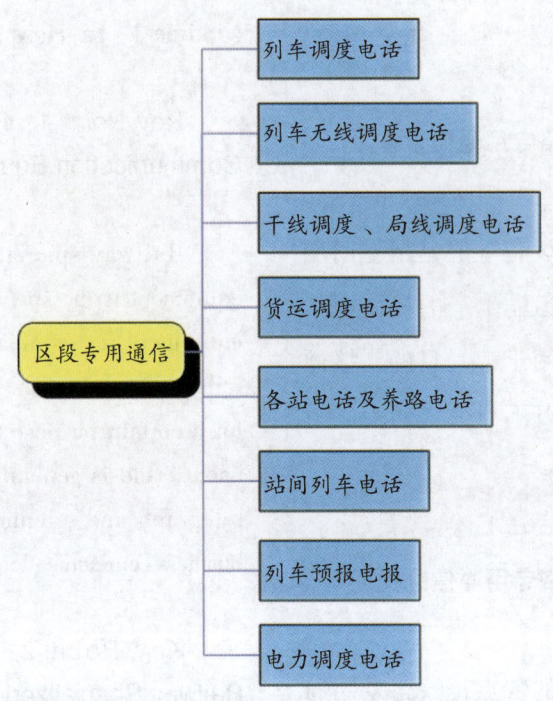

区段专用通信：section specialized communication　列车调度电话：train dispatching telephone
列车无线调度电话：train radio telephone dispatching telephone
干线调度、局线调度电话：trunk line/bureau line dispatching telephone
货运调度电话：freight transportation dispatching telephone
各站电话及养路电话：telephone and railway maintenance telephone of the stations
站间列车电话：interstation telephone　列车预报电报：train forecast telegram
电力调度电话：power source telephone

图 7-5　列车区段专用通信分类图

Figure 7-5　Railway Section Specialized Communication Classification

图 7-6　列车调度电话

Figure 7-6　Railway Dispatching Telephone

图 7-7 列车无线调度电话
Figure 7-7　Train Radio Dispatching Telephone

2. 站场专用通信

站场专用通信是在站内用来指挥站内各部门作业联系用的通信设备，如图7-8、7-9所示。

2. Yard Specialized Communication

Yard specialized communication is the communication equipment used for commanding operation connections in the station, as shown in figures 7-8 and 7-9.

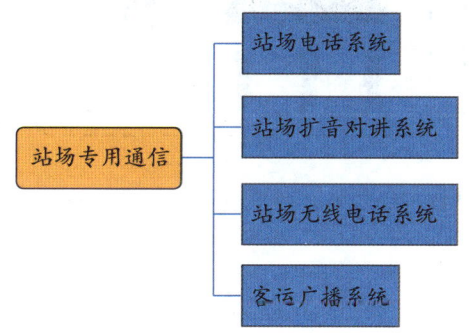

站场专用通信：yard specialized communication　站场电话系统：yard telephone system
站场扩音对讲系统：yard amplification and intercom system
站场无线电话系统：yard radio telephone system　客运广播系统：passenger transportation system

图 7-8　列车站场专用通信
Figure 7-8　Train Yard Specialized Communication

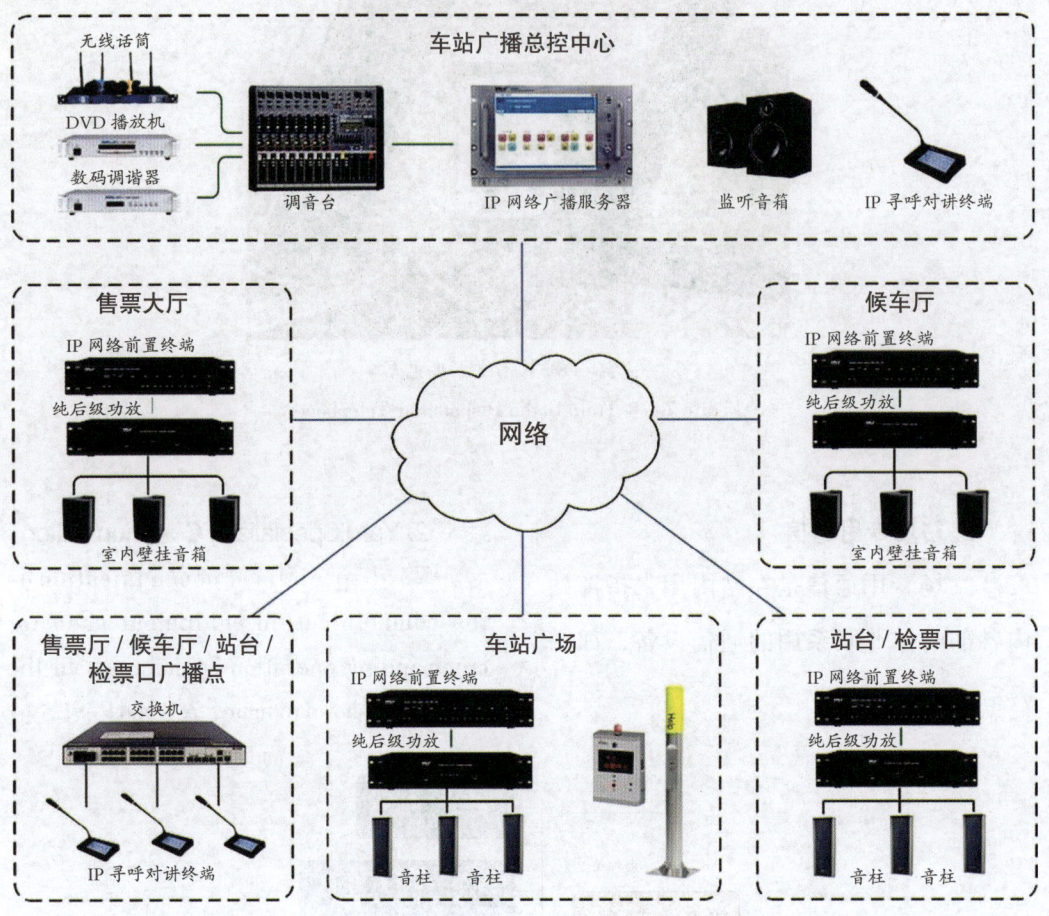

车站智能广播系统拓扑图：station smart broadcast system topological graph
车站广播总控中心：station broadcast general control center　无线话筒：wireless microphone
DVD 播放机：DVD player　数码调谐器：digital tuning unit　调音台：sound console
IP 网络广播服务器：IP network broadcast server　监听音箱：studio monitor
IP 寻呼对讲终端：IP paging intercom terminal　售票大厅：ticket hall
IP 网络前置终端：IP network preposition terminal　纯后级功放：Hi-fi amplifier
室内壁挂音箱：indoor hanging loudspeaker　网络：network　候车厅：waiting hall
售票厅/候车厅/站台/检票口广播点：ticket hall/waiting hall/platform/check-in entrance broadcast station
车站广场：station square　音柱：column loudspeaker　站台/检票口：platform/check-in entrance

图 7-9　列车站场广播系统
Figure 7-9　Train Yard Broadcast System

学习笔记

Study Notes

模块三　课堂练习

练习1：什么叫作列车调度电话，它的作用是什么？

练习2：什么叫作站场电话系统，它的作用是什么？

Module 3　In-class Exercises

Exercise 1: What is train dispatching telephone, what is its function?

Exercise 2: What is yard telephone system, what is its function?

课堂练习
In-class Exercises

模块四 课后拓展

请到学校附近的火车站调查有哪些站场专用通信设备,对设备拍照并进行简单说明。

Module 4 After-class Activity

Go to the nearby train station to learn about yard specialized communication equipment, and briefly explain the equipment pictures.

任务三 铁路综合数字移动通信系统（GSM-R）运用

Task 3　Global System for Mobile Communications-Railway（GSM-R）Application

模块一　学前准备

查资料，了解什么叫作 GSM-R，请把你查到的 GSM-R 相关知识记录在课前学习笔记中。

Module 1　Preparation before Class

Search information to learn about GSM-R and write the relevant knowledge in the form below.

课前学习笔记
Study Notes before Class

模块二 课堂学习

知识点一：GSM-R

GSM-R（Global System for Mobile Communications-Railway）是一项用于铁路通信及应用的国际无线通信标准。采用该标准进行通信时，当列车时速高达500千米/小时（310英里/小时）时，也不会丢失任何通信信号。

铁路专用全球数字移动通信系统是保证行车安全、防止作业事故、提高运输效率、加速机车周转，以及改善服务质量等不可缺少的通信手段，是铁路通信的重要组成部分。

知识点二：GSM-R 网络结构

GSM-R 移动通信网络主要由基站子系统、网络子系统、操作与维护子系统三个主要部分组成，如图 7-10 所示。

基站子系统主要由基站控制器、基站收发信息台组成。

网络子系统一般包括移动交换中心、归属位置寄存器、来访位置寄存器、鉴权中心、设备识别寄存器、组呼寄存器等。

操作与维护子系统可分为对应基站子系统及对应网络子系统的操作与维护中心。

Module 2 In-class Learning

Key Point 1：GSM-R

GSM-R is international wireless communication standard used in railway communication and its applications. There is no loss of any communication signal at the speed of 500 km/h (310 miles/h) in the standard communication.

GSM-R is the indispensable communication method to ensure train operation safety, prevent accident, improve transportation efficiency, speed up locomotive turnover and improve service quality. It is a significant component part of railway communication.

Key Point 2：GSM-R Network Structure

GSM-R consists of base station sub-system, network sub-system, operation and maintenance system, as shown in Figure 7-10.

Base station sub-system consists of base station controller, base station information sending and receiving information desk.

Network sub-system generally consists of mobile exchange center, home location register (HLR), visitor location register (VLR), authentication center, equipment identification register, group call register and so on.

Operation and maintenance sub-system can be divided into operation and maintenance center in corresponding base station sub-system and corresponding network sub-system.

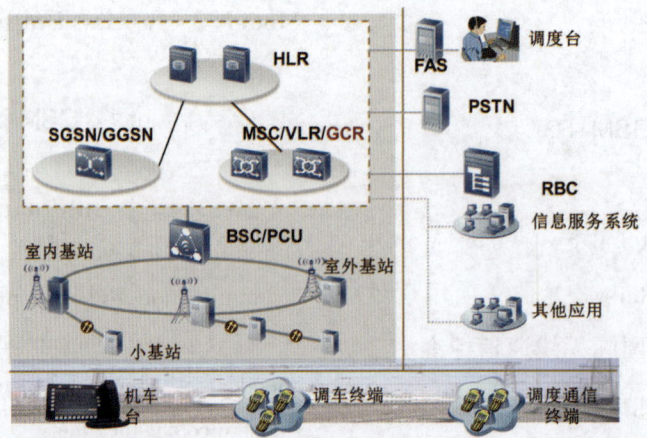

室内基站：indoor base station　　室外基站：outdoor base station　　小基站：small base station
调度台：dispatching platform　　信息服务系统：information service system　　其他应用：other application
机车台：locomotive platform　　调车终端：shunting terminal　　调度通信终端：dispatching communication terminal

图 7-10　GSM-R 系统结构

Figure 7-10　GSM-R System Structure

知识点三：GSM-R 的业务模型

Key Point 3：Business Model of GSM-R

如图 7-11 所示。

See Figure 7-11.

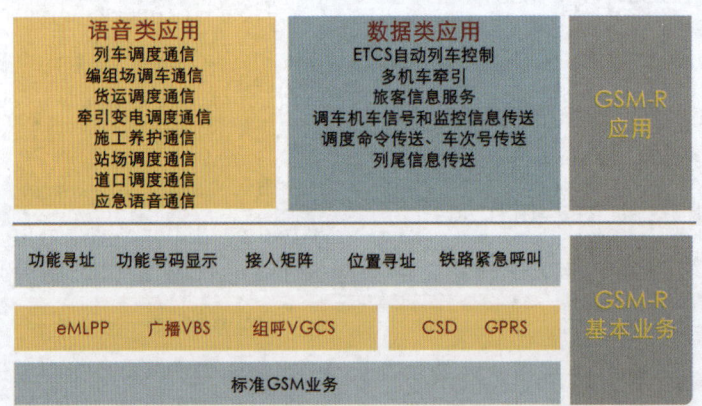

GSM-R 应用：GSM-R application　　语音类应用：voice application
列车调度通信：train dispatching communication　　编组场调车通信：marshaling station shunting communication
货运调度通信：freight transportation communication
牵引变电调度通信：traction transformation dispatching communication
施工养护通信：construction maintenance communication　　站场调度通信：yard dispatching communication
道口调度通信：railroad crossing dispatching communication　　应急语音通信：emergency voice communication
数据类应用：data application　　ETCS 自动列车控制：ETCS automatic train control
多机车牵引：multiple locomotive traction　　旅客信息服务：passenger information service

调车机车信号和监控信息传送：shunting locomotive signal and supervision
调度命令传送、车次号传送：dispatching order sending/train number sending
列尾信息传送：information transmission at the rear of train
GSM-R 基本业务：GSM-R basic business　功能寻址：function addressing
功能号码显示：function number display　接入矩阵：matrix access　位置寻址：location addressing
铁路紧急呼叫：railway emergency call　广播 VBS：broadcastVBS　组呼 VGCS：group call VGCS
标准 GSM 业务：standard GSM business

图 7-11　GSM-R 业务模型

Figure 7-11　GSM-R Business Model

1. 组呼

如图 7-12 所示。

1.VGCS Group Call VGCS

See Figure 7-12.

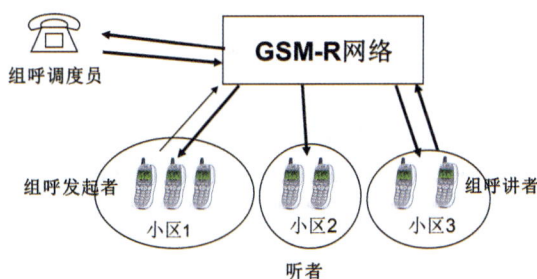

组呼调度员：group call dispatch man　GSM-R 网络：GSM-R network
组呼发起者：group call originator　小区：section　组呼讲者：group call speaker　听者：listener

图 7-12　组呼 VGCS 业务

Figure 7-12　Group Call VGCS Business

2. CSD 电路型数据业务

2. CSD Circuit Data Business

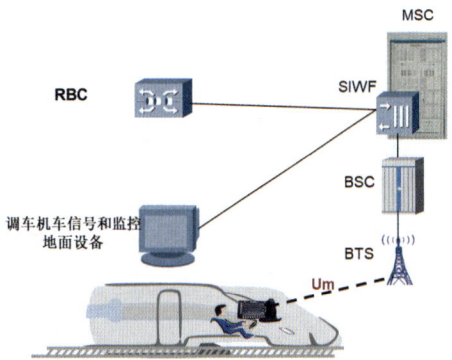

调车机车信号和监控地面设备：shunting locomotive signal and supervision ground equipment

图 7-13　CSD 电路型数据业务

Figure 7-13　CSD Circuit Data Business

·287·

3. GPRS 分组数据业务

如图 7-14 所示。

3.GPRS Group Dividing Data Business

See Figure 7–14.

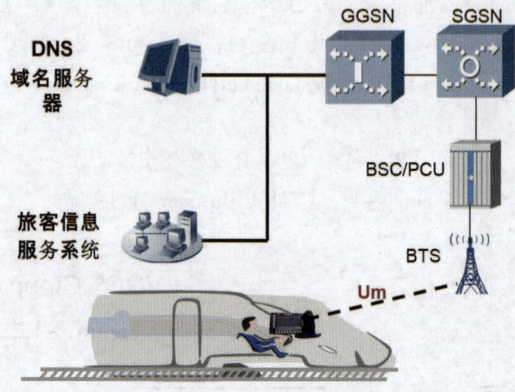

DNS 域名服务器：DNS domain name server　旅客信息服务系统：passenger information service system

图 7-14　GPRS 分组数据业务
Figure 7–14　GPRS Group Dividing Data Business

学习笔记
Study Notes

模块三 课堂练习

Module 3　In-class Exercises

图 7-15 是铁路紧急呼叫业务的示意图。请说明各部分的功能及紧急呼叫信号的传输方式。

Figure 7-15 is railway emergency call business diagram. Explain functions of the parts and transmission method of emergency call signal.

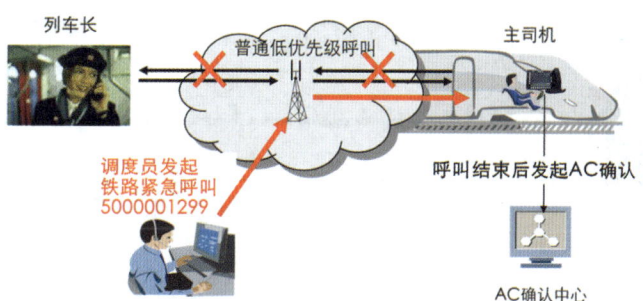

列车长：head of crew　普通低优先级呼叫：ordinary priority call　主司机：major driver
调度员发起铁路紧急呼叫：dispatch man initiates railway emergency call
呼叫结束后发起 AC 确认：initiate AC confirmation after call ends　AC 确认中心：AC confirmation center

图 7-15　铁路紧急呼叫业务

Figure 7-15　Railway Emergency Call Business

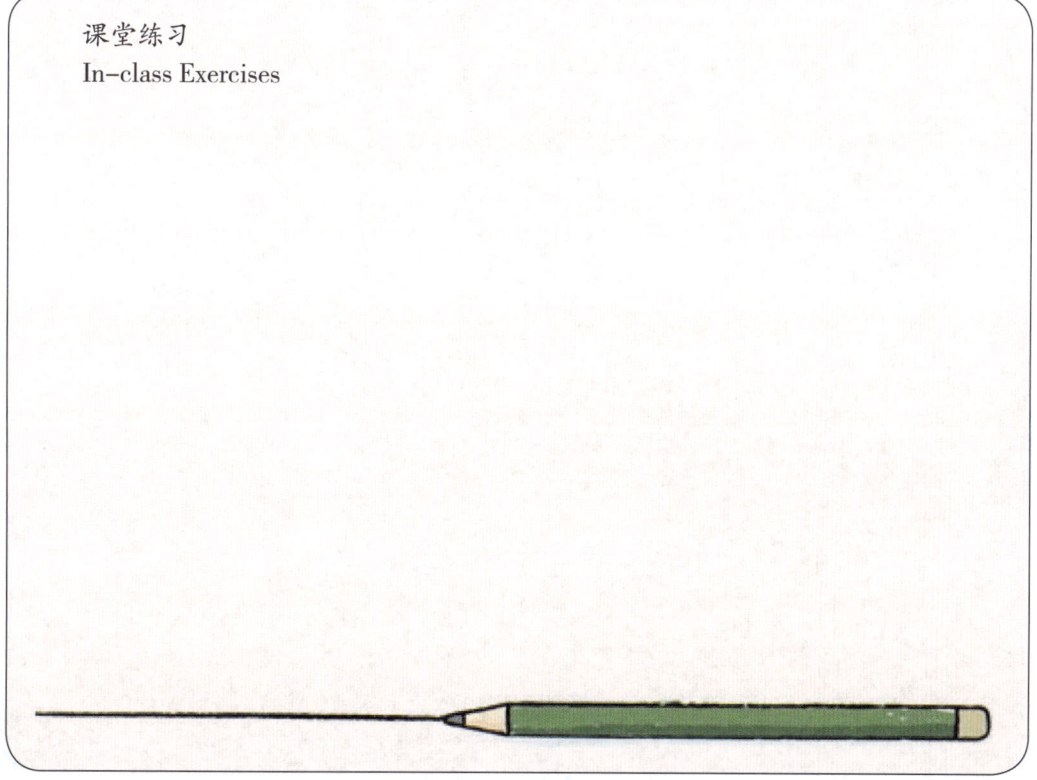

课堂练习
In-class Exercises

模块四　课后拓展

根据所学知识，请你归纳出 GSM-R 的主要业务功能，并对这些业务功能简单说明解释。

Module 4　After-class Activity

Conclude major business functions of GSM-R based on what you have learned and briefly explain the functions.

参考文献

Reference

［1］何文卿.6502电气集中电路［M］.北京：中国铁道出版社，1997.

［2］洪立新等.铁路信号与通信设备运用［M］.成都：西南交通大学出版社，2013.

［3］张唯.铁道运输设备［M］.北京：中国铁道出版社，2002.

［4］林瑜筠.新型移频自动闭塞：第3版［M］.北京：中国铁道出版社，2007.

［5］徐洪泽等.车站信号计算机联锁控制系统：原理及应用［M］.北京：中国铁道出版社，2006.

［6］中华人民共和国铁道部.铁路列车调度指挥系统［M］.北京：中国铁道出版社，2006.

［7］侯启同.调度集中和列车调度指挥系统［M］.北京：中国铁道出版社，2008.

［8］贾毓杰.铁路信号与通信设备：第2版［M］.北京：中国铁道出版社，2017.

［9］李映红.铁路通信信号［M］.成都：西南交通大学出版社，2011.

［1］He Wenqing. 6502 Electrical Circuit Concentration［M］. Beijing: China Railway Publishing House, 1997.

［2］Hong Lixin and others. Railway Signal and Communication Equipment Application［M］. Chengdu: Southwest Jiaotong University Press, 2013.

［3］Zhang Wei. Railway Transportation Equipment［M］. Beijing: China Railway Publishing House, 2002.

［4］Lin Yujun. New Type Frequency Shift Automatic Blocking: 3rd edition［M］. Beijing: China Railway Publishing House, 2007.

［5］Xu Hongze and others. Station Signal Computer Interlocking Control System：Principle and Application［M］. Beijing: China Railway Publishing House, 2006.

［6］Ministry of Railways, the People's Republic of China. Train Operation Dispatching and Command System［M］. Beijing: China Railway Publishing House, 2006.

［7］Hou Qitong. Centralized Command and Train Operation Dispatching and Command System［M］. Beijing: China Railway Publishing House, 2008.

［8］Jia Yujie. Railway Signal and Communication Equipment: 2nd edition［M］. Beijing: China Railway Publishing House, 2017.

［9］Li Yinghong. Railway Communication Signal［M］. Chengdu: Southwest Jiaotong

[10] 李向国. 高速铁路技术：第2版 [M]. 北京：中国铁道出版社，2009.

[11] 魏宇，宫艳芳. 铁路信号与通信设备运用 [M]. 北京：中国财富出版社，2014.

[12] 张曙光. CTCS-3级列控系统总体技术方案 [M]. 北京：中国铁道出版社，2008.

[13] 铁道部运输局. 铁路列车调度指挥系统（TDCS）[M]. 北京：中国铁道出版社，2005.

[14] 刘朝英. 中国铁路分散自律调度集中 [M]. 北京：中国铁道出版社，2009.

[15] 卡斯柯公司. FZk-CTC调度集中操作手册 [Z]. 上海，2012.

[16] 李俊娥. 驼峰信号 [M]. 北京：中国铁道出版社，2008.

[17] 北京通号设计院. TW-2驼峰自动控制系统操作手册 [M]. 北京，2000.

[18] 铁道部科学技术司. 中国列车运行控制系统CTCS技术规范总则（暂行）[M]. 北京：中国铁道出版社，2003.

[19] 铁道部科学技术司. 铁路信号集中监测系统技术条件 [M]. 北京：中国铁道出版社，2010.

[20] 刘建国. 高速铁路信号与通信 [M]. 北京：中国铁道出版社，2016.

University Press, 2011.

[10] Li Xiangguo. High Speed Railway Technology: 2nd edition [M]. Beijing: China Railway Publishing House, 2009.

[11] Wei Yu, Gong Yanfang. Railway Signal and Communication Equipment Application [M]. Beijing: China Wealth, 2014.

[12] Zhang Shuguang. CTCS-3 Train Control System Overall Technical Solutions [M]. Beijing: China Railway Publishing House, 2008.

[13] Transportation Bureau of Ministry of Railway. Train Operation Dispatching and Command System (TDCS) [M]. Beijing: China Railway Publishing House, 2005.

[14] Liu Chaoying. Decentralized Autonomous Dispatching and Command of China Railway [M]. Beijing: China Railway Publishing House, 2009.

[15] CASCO. FZk-CTC Centralized Dispatching Operation Manual [Z]. Shanghai, 2012.

[16] Li Jun'e. Hump Signal [M]. Beijing: China Railway Publishing House, 2008.

[17] Beijing Tonghao Design Institute. TW-2 Hump Automatic Control System Operation Manual [M]. Beijing, 2000.

[18] Division of Science and Technology, Ministry of Railway. CTCS Technical Standard general Rules (provisional) [M]. Beijing: China Railway Publishing House, 2003.

[19] Division of Science and Technology, Ministry of Railway. Railway Signal Centralized Monitoring System Technical Conditions [M]. Beijing: China Railway Publishing House, 2010.

[20] Liu Jianguo. High Speed Railway Signal and Communication [M]. Beijing: China Railway Publishing House, 2016.